# THE
# ENEMY
# WITHIN

# History Workshop Series

*General Editor*
Raphael Samuel, *Ruskin College, Oxford*

*Already published*

**Village Life and Labour**
Edited by Raphael Samuel

**Miners, Quarrymen and
Saltworkers**
(ed.) Raphael Samuel

**Rothschild Buildings**
Life in an East End tenement
block 1887–1920
Jerry White

**East End Underworld**
Chapters in the life of Arthur
Harding
Edited by Raphael Samuel

**People's History and Socialist
Theory**
(ed.) Raphael Samuel

**Culture, Ideology and Politics**
(eds) Raphael Samuel and Gareth
Stedman Jones

**Sex and Class in Women's History**
Judith L Newton and Mary
P Ryan

**Living the Fishing**
Paul Thompson, Tony Wailey and
Trevor Lummis

**Fenwomen**
A portrait of women in an English
village
Mary Chamberlain

**Late Marx and the Russian Road**
Edited by Teodor Shanin

**Poor Labouring Men**
Rural radicalism in Norfolk
1870-1923
Alun Howkins

**Theatres of the Left 1880-1935**
Workers' Theatre Movements in
Britain and America
Raphael Samuel, Ewan MacColl
and Stuart Cosgrove

**Making Cars**
A history of car making in Cowley
Television History Workshop

**Language, Gender and Childhood**
(eds) Carolyn Steedman, Cathy
Urwin and Valerie Walkerdine

**The Worst Street in North London**
Campbell Bunk, Islington,
between the Wars
Jerry White

**Independent Spirits**
Spiritualism and English Plebeians
1850-1910
Logie Barrow

Routledge & Kegan Paul
London and New York

# THE ENEMY WITHIN

Pit villages and the miners' strike of 1984-5

Edited by
RAPHAEL SAMUEL
BARBARA BLOOMFIELD
GUY BOANAS

**To the Durham Mechanics, most ancient of the mining trade unions** (c.f. W.S. Hall, *A Historical Survey of the Durham Colliery Mechanics Association, 1879-1929*) and now leaders of the 'Justice for Miners' campaign.

*First published in 1986 by*
*Routledge & Kegan Paul Ltd*
*11 New Fetter Lane, London EC4P 4EE*

*Published in the USA by*
*Routledge & Kegan Paul Inc.*
*in association with Methuen Inc.*
*29 West 35th Street, New York, NY 10001*

*Set in 10/11pt Times*
*by Columns of Reading*
*and printed in Great Britain*
*by T.J. Press (Padstow) Ltd*
*Padstow, Cornwall*

*Library of Congress Cataloging in Publication Data*

*The Enemy within.*
*(History workshop series)*
*Includes index.*
*1. Coal Strike, Great Britain, 1984-1985.*
*I. Samuel, Raphael.   II. Bloomfield, Barbara.*
*III. Boanas, Guy.   IV. Series.*
*HD5365.M6152 1984.E54 1986        86-12192*
*                331.89'2822334'0941*

*British Library CIP Data also available*

*ISBN 0-7102-0888-X*

# CONTENTS

**PREFACE**
*Raphael Samuel*                                                    ix

**ACKNOWLEDGMENTS**                                                 xix

**GLOSSARY**                                                        xxi

**INTRODUCTION**
*Raphael Samuel*                                                     1

**1  PRELUDES**                                                     40
Best suit, the Afan Valley in 1969
*Barbara Walters*                                                   40
Horden Colliery, Co. Durham
*Huw Beynon, Ray Hudson and Dave Sadler*                           43
The Doncaster Panel, 1969-84
*Dave Douglass*                                                     51

**2  RUMOURS**                                                      55
Interviews, South Wales miners at Porthcawl, July 1983             55

**3  START OF THE STRIKE**                                          67
Ruskin tapes: How the strike began at Cortonwood                   67
Ruskin tapes: How the strike began at Hatfield Main               69
Interview: How the strike began at Armthorpe                       70
Interview: How the strike failed at Bentinck
   Colliery, Notts
*Barbara Bloomfield*                                                72
Memoir: North Staffs, a tale of two pits
*Dave Cliff*                                                        86
Agit-prop: Delegate's speech at Hatfield Main
*Dave Douglass*                                                     92

**4  A STRIKE DIARY**                                              100
Brookhouse, South Yorkshire
*Iris Preston*                                                     100

**5  RIOTS**                                                       118
Mansfield, May 1984
*Bobby Girvan*                                                     118

Grimethorpe, October 1984
*Harold Hancock* 119

**6 SELF-HELP** 122
Upton, the Infants' Support Group
*Iris Knight* 122
Hatfield Main Welfare Organisation
*Bob Hume* 128

**7 LETTERS FROM THE COALFIELD** 139
Letters from Frickley and South London
*Allan Lowe and Keith Proverbs* 139

**8 WOMɪ !'S GROUPS** 154
Women's support group at Maerdy
*Barbara Bloomfield* 154

**9 PROFILES** 166
Interviews at Armthorpe, December 1984
*Mike Brogden* 166
Interviews at Grimethorpe, June 1985
*Guy Boanas* 202

**10 PRISON** 216
Letters
*Ray Patton* 216
Diary
*Steve Lowe* 218

**11 THE RETURN TO WORK** 224
Pit delegate's report at Hatfield Main, March 1985
*Dave Douglass* 224
Lost rights at Hatfield Main, November 1985
*Dave Douglass* 231
A resignation at Bentinck Colliery, Notts
*Todd Clark* 232
Letters from South Wales, April, October 1985
*Barbara Walters* 233

**12 AFTERTHOUGHTS** 236
Letter from Yorkshire, March 1986
*Dave Douglass* 236
Interview with Iris Preston, April 1986 240

**NAME INDEX** 251

**SUBJECT INDEX** 256

# ILLUSTRATIONS

1 Barbara Walters, Glyncorrwg    40
2 Dave Douglass, Hatfield Main    51
3 Pro-strike leaflet put out by South Wales NUM
   which circulated throughout the coalfields    57
4 Women on the picket line at Bevercotes
   Colliery, Nottinghamshire (Brenda Prince)    71
5 Pro-UDM and pro-NUM stickers, Nottinghamshire    73
6 At the end of February 1984, Colin Bottomore,
   the NUM Branch Secretary, was urging men
   at Bentinck to support the strike. Later he
   changed his mind    74
7 'Don't Let A Tory Win The Glory', slogan on
   banner at an NUM mass picket at Babbington Colliery,
   Notts, 9 April 1984 (John Sturrock, *Network*)    75
8 Pro-UDM leaflet for the 'breakaway ballot'
   of October 1985    78
9 The Berry Hill Working Miners' Demonstration
   against Scargill and the NUM on 1 May 1984
   (*Nottingham Evening Post*)    81
10 Iris Preston on her motorbike    100
11 The role of the police: black miner expresses
   his opinion    105
12 NACODS won't support the NUM strike.
   Pickets at Bentley Colliery, South Yorks break
   the news to Maureen Page and Jill Fox
   (Raissa Page)    119
13 The group's badge for the Infants Support Group    123
14 Self-help: different groups find their own ways to
   raise funds (with thanks to Kevin Machin)    127
15 Saturday night out and social clubs: Barnsley
   and South Wales (Raissa Page, Val Wilmer)    135
16 An unusual fundraiser: pavement artists for
   striking miners, Nottingham City Centre
   (Brenda Prince)    137
17 Great correspondents: London dustman Allan
   Lowe and Frickley miner Keith Proverbs    140–1

18 Agit-prop in Frickley                                          146–7
19 Megan Webster and Jean Bromage from Maerdy
   Pit Wives Group                                                 155
20 Members of Windhill and Woolley soup kitchens,
   South Yorks (Raissa Page) and Ann Burrell
   of Rhodesia Women's Action Group at home
   with sons Richard and Ross, Rhodesia, Notts
   (Raissa Page)                                                   171
21 Confrontations between miners and police on the
   streets of Armthorpe, 21 and 22 August 1984                     195
22 Elsie Walker – whose father, husband (now dead)
   and sons were all miners – outside Grimethorpe
   Colliery (Raissa Page)                                          205
23 6.30am picket duty, Tilbury Power Station.
   Bill Martin from Betteshanger Colliery, Kent
   (Jenny Matthews)                                                219

# PREFACE

Raphael Samuel

When we started work on this book, in February 1985, convening a 'History Workshop' on the strike, and inviting miners and their families to a working weekend at Ruskin College, Oxford, we argued – in the words of the invitation – that the meaning of the strike would

> not be determined by the terms of the settlement – if there is a settlement – or even by the events of the past year but by the way in which it is assimilated in popular memory, by . . . *retrospective* understanding both in the pit villages themselves and in the country at large.

We launched our project at a time of hope, when a belated but powerful case against pit closures was being mounted by independent accountants, economists and historians (the strangely neglected *Aberystwyth Report on Coal* was perhaps the most noteworthy); when the secondary issues which had monopolised attention, on either side, during the first nine months of the dispute (e.g. the clashes between pickets and police) were giving way to the substantive matter at the heart of it: the fate of the coal communities; and when there seemed to be a gravitational movement of public opinion in favour of the miners' cause. As one of us wrote at the time:

> The miners' strike, almost in spite of itself, offered some of the elements of a new Labour politics, one which linked the protection of living conditions with the defence of local rights, the assertion of women's power with the maintenance of family integrity, the preservation of jobs with the re-unification of work and home. . . . It was a 'special case' which yet provided a symbolic focus for the fight-back against unemployment and regional impoverishment. Like the defence of the GLC it was one of those rare public issues in which Labour found itself linked to a genuinely popular cause, albeit one which, until the very end of the strike, commanded only a minority support in the country. Equally rare, it managed to consolidate, or at any rate speak directly to, a majority of Labour's electoral support. Uniquely it contrived to unite Party opinion of all stripes.

None of these hopes has been realised. Within a week of the end of the strike, town hall socialists in London – a mainstay of the miners' outside support – were coming to blows with each other, on the very day that they were acting as hosts to a South Wales miners' crusade. In the localities it seems, from angry correspondence sent to us, some of the support groups came under immediate strain. The Labour leadership made sympathetic noises, and indeed the Deputy Leader, in the *Sunday Times*, wrote a fierce vindication of the strikers, but within a month the Party was launching its 'Jobs and Industry' campaign without so much as a word about those who had risked livelihoods and homes, during twelve long months, for that cause. The Communist Party, preoccupied, even obsessed, by its struggle against the 'hardline' supporters of its errant daily newspaper, the *Morning Star*, hailed the end of the strike as a defeat for 'Hard Left' politics, and launched a public post-mortem on where the miners had gone wrong. ('Our struggle,' as an aggrieved NUM supporter put it, 'became a Punch-and-Judy baby for the battle in the CP.')

At the time of writing (August 1986), the sacked miners stay sacked, though at the end of the strike there was a large majority of public opinion in favour of reinstating them. The programme of pit closures continues at an accelerated pace (in South Wales, ten of the district's twenty-eight pits have been closed since March 1985); and Mr MacGregor is able to serve out his time at Hobart House, notwithstanding public rebukes from the Energy Minister, and the appointment of a notably more corporatist successor. In July 1986 he was knighted, and in the most recent account of the strike he is beginning to take shape as an iconoclastic hero.

In retrospect it can be seen that support for the strike, though fervently expressed, was also precarious; that it was predicated on the miners' weakness rather than their strength; and that it owed more to a humanitarian spirit of Good Works than, in any classical trade union sense, solidarity, and it is perhaps indicative of this that the local organisation of aid took the form of Miners' Support Groups rather than, as in 1926 – an analogy fruitlessly invoked – Councils of Action. The support was heartfelt and generous, but, with the important exception of the seamen, the railwaymen and the Fleet Street printers, it did not involve stoppages of work, nor even workplace demonstrations. It was not affinity which drew sympathy and support for the miners, but in the first place difference – the uniqueness of the pit villages in the landscape of contemporary life – and it is clear that some of it was given in spite of the NUM's voiced demands rather than because of them. The Left – the political Left if not the trade union movement – was apparently simmering with doubts, and some of the venom which has been directed at the NUM in the aftermath of the strike seems to have to do with the fact that in the course of the dispute itself they were half suppressed. It is interesting, in this respect, that some of the most heartfelt pleas for the miners came from paternalist, old-fashioned High Tories and, if in more muted tones, from liberal Conservative dissidents. One thinks of the bell-like clarity of the aged Earl of Stockton's outburst, and his reminder of what this country owes to its miners; of Sir Anthony Meyer, the outspoken MP for Clwyd, who at New Year 1985 saluted the unselfishness of the strikers ('wrong as they are, maybe they have something to teach us all about solidarity'); of the Carmarthen farmer who remarked at the end of the strike that the President of the NUM had behaved like a 'true' general ('he never deserted his soldiers'); or of John Gorst, the very right-wing MP for Hendon North, who led the parliamentary pleas for the reinstatement of victimised miners.

It is interesting that the attacks on the NUM have come from the Left rather than the Right. In the aftermath of the strike Tories have been anxious to appear, if not magnanimous at least not vindictive: even Mrs Thatcher has publicly rebuked Mr MacGregor, and she seems to have shrunk from his maximal programme of pit closures. Right-wing trade union leaders have, by and large, refrained from public criticism of the NUM (even Mr Hammond's 'lions led by donkeys' speech at the TUC was touched by a kind of grudging respect for the strikers). The TUC itself has taken some part in the campaign to reinstate the sacked miners, while Stan Orme, from the Labour front bench – a notably warm supporter of the miners – has been working with the three coalfield unions to produce a *Plan for Coal*. On the Left, however, especially among the metropolitan intelligentsia, hostility to the miners' union has grown increasingly implacable. Already during the strike itself there was a simmering rage, it seems, at having to support a cause which many only half believed in, and in the immediate aftermath of the strike, the front-running was taken by St John Street, the young Turks around *Marxism Today* and their fellow-travellers on the *New Statesman* and the *Financial Times*. Coming with the impeccably left-wing credentials of the Communist Party, it served to legitimate a whole line of self-questioning, and to immobilise the miners' support.

Another feature of the criticism is that it has grown progressively more hostile as memory of the strike recedes. This is particularly clear in the case of the industrial correspondents, 'friends' and even confidantes of the miners' leaders during the strike, sympathetic if critical in the aftermath and now unqualified in hostility. Adeney and Lloyd's book (*The Miners' Strike 1984-5*,

Routledge & Kegan Paul, 1986) is by far the most implacable, and quite apart from its own strengths – it is a brilliant melodrama, extremely well written and very well informed – is likely, in the present climate of opinion, to carry all before it. It not only endorses but amplifies the government's case against the miners, playing up divisions within the NUM – some of them, a close reading of the text suggests, of the authors' own making – playing down those in the NCB. It endorses the Buckingham Palace view that, as the Queen put it, in a rare excursus into historical causality, it was 'all down to one man': it is Arthur Scargill, in their account, who single-handedly masterminds the strike and precipitates it, and he does so with the intention not only of bringing down the government but of overthrowing the British state. Scargill, in short, was a megalomaniac, and the strike, in embryo at least, a revolutionary threat to civilisation as we know it. Adeney and Lloyd have provided Mrs Thatcher with a script with which her Party could yet win the next election.

In the light of the above, it seems worth recalling – as we hope the documents and texts in our book will do – the essentially *defensive* nature of the miners' action, and the essential *modesty* of their claims – to defend a settled way of life, not to embark on the struggle for power.

Journalists, even it seems higher journalists, such as the editor of the *New Statesman* (joint author with Martin Adeney of *The Miners' Strike*, and in 1984-5 Labour Correspondent of the *Financial Times*), exist to sensationalise (or dramatise) events. They personalise issues to give their narrative shape. They are professionally obliged to discover novelty. Historians, by their trade, are more sceptical, and confronted by the claim that this was 'Scargill's Strike' they are likely to be on guard. They will know that leaders are not *causes* but *effects*. They may remember, if they are readers of Tolstoy, or students of the First World War, that in a battle nobody is less in command than the generals. And they will be familiar, from labour history, with the demonisation of strike leaders. Both A.J. Cook, the miners' leader in 1926, and Jim Larkin were widely regarded as mad: Dickens' venomous portrait of Slackbridge in *Hard Times* (allegedly based on a real-life original) is a literary prototype. (For further examples, the reader is referred to 'Moral Panic' on pp. 1-6 of this book.)

In the 1984-5 strike, we argue in this book, all of the crucial initiatives came from below, and, as our documents and testimonies suggest, this was also the source of its peculiar energy. The real nerve-centre was not the National Union of Mineworkers headquarters in Sheffield (in a *federal* union, it has no directive force of its own), but the Miners' Welfare in the villages, curiously unvisited, or at any rate uncommented on, by the industrial correspondents, for all their year-long attention to the strike, and their sleuth-like eye for detail. *Opposition* to the strike was no less local, the Nottinghamshire men refusing to go on strike in defiance of the area leadership and often (as in the case of Bentinck colliery discussed on pp. 72-7 of this book) the lodge secretary.

Melodramatic caricatures of the President of the NUM – an English Lenin, a Yorkshire Stalin, a union dictator, a dangerous revolutionary according to scaremongering taste – seem, if anything, even wider from the mark. Historians are likely to take a different view from polemicists or journalists. To Kenneth Morgan (*New Society*, 21 February 1985) as to the present writers, Arthur Scargill appears rather as a chip off the old block, a rather old-fashioned miners' leader, centrally concerned with the protection of his members and determined, like miners' leaders in the past, not to be separated physically or emotionally from them. For a union 'dictator' he seems singularly isolated within the NUM, showing none of that flare for factionalism which characterises the present Euro-Communist Party even more than its less respectable predecessor, nor yet of that ability to create a 'machine' which, since the days of Ernie Bevin, has so often characterised the successful right-wing union leader. (It is worth recalling that the basic doctrine of the strike – 'We will not be constitutionalised out of existence' – was formulated by the Communist Vice-President of the NUM, and that the form of the return to work was decided by pressure from below.) As a would-be 'Lenin' he has shown singularly little interest in political parties, either the Communist Party, in which he served his political apprenticeship, or the Labour Party in which he has worked for the past twenty years, and a singular aversion to the metropolis (removing the union headquarters from London to Sheffield) hardly seems a prelude to some revolutionary seizure of power. He also seems very far from being what Adeney and Lloyd call 'revolutionary syndicalist', being deeply attached both to the corporatist structure of the industry (critics of nationalisation might pause on the fact that the miners have been saying this is 'their industry'), and to existing union structures. It is not Mr Scargill but – as a stream of resignations from Hobart House testifies – the NCB which, under its present rulership, has been trying to break up or to escape from the industry's machinery for conciliation and consultation, and it was indeed one of their efforts in this direction – the proclamation of pit closures in March 1984 – which precipitated the year-long strike.

Long ago, in 1931, Vera Brittain remarked on the phenomenon of socialists 'who didn't like the smell of the proletariat'. Their number seems to have increased mightily in recent years, though on grounds of 'mindless militancy' or decorum rather than, as in that recurrent phobia of the 1930s, 'germs'. In the case of the SDP, whose leader, Dr Owen, turned out, in the 1984-5 strike, to be the most implacable of the miners' enemies (in August 1984 he was urging Mrs Thatcher to stand firm at the one time when her resolution temporarily wavered), one is confronted by a collective narcissism in which the working class is constructed as a kind of reverse image of their idealised selves – tribal rather than thinking in its loyalties, loud-mouthed and beer-swilling, narrow-minded and prejudiced. In the case of the New Left – or perhaps one should say the ex-New Left class of '68, among whom the terms 'workerist' and 'populist' are banded about as unargued-for pejoratives – there is rather a dialectic of disenchantment at work on which the miners serve as the displaced object of the Left's discomfort with itself, of a Communist Party which is no longer certain what it exists for, and of a Labour Party which is no longer sure what it believes in. Scargill, the symbolic object of their hostility, is, on this reading, hated because he has failed to be the leader of their dreams, just as the working class, since it is failing to fulfil its historically appointed mission, can no longer do anything right. When he appears on television he speaks to and for his members rather than attempting to appeal to – or to charm – a wider audience. The miners comport themselves as angry human beings rather than as the symbolic victims of injustice, and they show what, to the non-trade unionist, is an incomprehensible hatred for 'scabs'.

The miners' strike, by its intransigence – the limited but un-negotiable character of its demands – threatened to expose the hidden doubts which gnaw at the Socialist project, and the absence of any clear left-wing or even Keynesian alternative to the economic policies of the present government. It highlighted the ideological collapse of both social democracy and Communism when faced, on the one hand, with the renewed vitality of capitalism as a world system and, on the other, with the apparently staunchless loss of jobs. Instead of the fate of mining demonstrating the 'anarchy' of the market (as it would have done to our 1930s forebears), it shows rather – unless one is a maverick High Tory, a Conservative dissident, or a regionalist Liberal – the inexorable working out of forces over which no government can claim control. Faced with streamlining and super-pits, or with the energetically promoted nuclear-powered alternative, there is nothing for the coalfields to do but fade away. In short, the disarray of the Left in face of the miners' strike is, in one aspect, part of a larger discomfort both about the alternative to Thatcherism, and of the very possibility of a socialism which is in any sense representative of popular desire and will. The Left seems quite amnesiac about its own part in the miners' tragedy, or the fate of the unemployed. A 'People's March' for jobs every three or four years, or now a Labour Party sponsored ride, is hardly a substitute for sustained agitation, or for that kind of high-level lobbying and pressure group which, in the 1930s, put planning on the agenda of national politics.

The proper job of a historian, if intervening in a matter of public debate, is explanation, not adding to the chorus of recrimination and blame nor treating the actors as sovereign agents, but showing, or attempting to show, the ways in which history is made behind our backs, in spite of our best intentions rather than because of them. Where others see events, the historian looks for process, in which a thousand different circumstances conspire. Where others see high-level decisions, the historian will look for the unspoken premises of any action, the hidden determinations which it obeys, the unforeseen consequences which result from it. Where others offer images far clearer than any reality could be, the historian disrupts the narrative, and asks what is happening off-stage.

When asked for his opinion on the results of the French Revolution of 1789, Mao Tse Tung is reported to have replied that it was 'too early' to judge yet. The story – told by the French journalist who claimed to be his interlocutor – is possibly apocryphal, but it may serve as a reminder of the provisional and contingent nature of historical interpretation. Whatever its ostensible subject, history always tells us as much or more about the present than it does about the past. It is conditioned by the state of contemporary opinion, and this is inescapably the case when, as with the miners' strike, or some very recent event, there are lessons to be learnt, balance sheets to be drawn up, blame and praise to be allocated which are also the common currency of political discourse. In compiling this book, we have tried to take account of, or at any rate to recognise, these limitations by presenting the strike as it was rather than as its supporters would have liked it to be; and by giving a privileged place to actuality – i.e. to documents produced in the heat of the moment and free of subsequent refinement. Hence, to us, the importance of 'Rumours at the Miners' Fortnight', recordings made some nine months before the outbreak of the strike in which some of its explosive divisions are prefigured. Hence, too, the importance to us of the Armthorpe recordings, taken in the ninth month of the strike, and offering a broad spectrum of village opinion, that of the doubting or hostile schoolmistress and shopkeeper as well as the activists of the lodge and the women's group. Hence, too, the importance to us of strike diaries – such as Iris Preston's – which urgently need to be retrieved and copied before they disappear in family papers.

The strike of 1984–5 cannot be written about as though it were a single event. The issues as stake changed from one phase of the strike to the next, so did public perception of them, and the miners' own experience. The drama was played out, simultaneously, on an astonishing variety of different stages, not only those which figure in this book – the food kitchens, the picket lines, the parlour – but also the penthouse suite at Claridge's where Mr David Hart – amanuensis to Mr MacGregor and go-between for Mrs Thatcher – directed his strike-breaking activities; the country retreats where Conservative lawyers and working miners drew up their injunctions against the NUM, the Irish banks and Luxembourg clearing houses which secreted the miners' funds. The *dramatis personae* would have to include not only the principal protagonists but also a host of characters who enjoyed walk-on parts: Robert Maxwell, the newspaper proprietor, who briefly emerged in the persona of honest broker; Ken Foulsom, the working miner who took the NUM to the law courts and set in train the process which led to the sequestration of the union funds – a Yorkshire burglar (as he later turned out to be) briefly cast in the role of Robin Goodfellow; the Doncaster shopkeeper, whose ill-fated initiative embroiled the NUM with Colonel Gadafy.

The strike of 1984–5 cannot be treated in any simple sense as a gladiatorial contest of wills. The government, the principal enemy of the NUM, acted from start to finish by proxy, maintaining an elaborate pretence of not being party to the dispute, so that any negotiation in which the NUM engaged was apt to turn out triangular. So far as coercion was concerned, each of the departments of state seems to have acted on its own account: the Department of Health and Social Security taking on welfare benefits; the Home Secretary the deployment of the police; the Law Officers the orchestration of court cases. There were not two protagonists in the strike but any number: not only the NUM and the NCB but also the Central Electricity Generating Board, which did so much to create the space for Mr MacGregor's initiatives, by winning (as early as 1979) the right to import foreign coal, and by pressing for the nuclear option; British Rail, which settled its own labour troubles for fear of sympathy action spreading; the dockers who spectacularly failed to come to the aid of the miners; the TUC which was embarrassed by them; the two Labour Parties (the one in the country which gave the miners such heartfelt support, the one at Westminster which distanced itself); the local and public services which allowed the miners to pile up debts; the building societies and the banks which postponed monthly repayments; the metropolitan and county constabularies, the magistrates, the education authorities, local government. None of these bodies was unified. Regional differences within the NCB, for instance, were almost as pronounced as those among the miners; in the localities numbers of colliery managers conspicuously failed to act in the spirit of Hobart House; and it was in fact a division on management's side – the threatened strike of the deputies and overmen in September – which seems to have come closest to bringing the government to its knees.

There are as many different histories of the miners' strike to be written as there are particular experiences. Even within a single family they will be radically different. Iris Preston's son Lance, a 'flier' from Day One of the strike, would have a very different story to tell than Iris herself, a freelance welfare officer and agitator, motorbiking to Nottinghamshire for the early morning picket and getting back in time for her job as an usher in a Sheffield court. Her second son Tarrance would have a different story again, that of one who was 'solid' behind the strike, but hated the pit, was 'appalled at the arrests, the riot gear and the horses' and stayed away from the rallies. The day the strike was over, he renounced the industry for ever. Subsequent experiences diverge even more radically. Iris's story is one of continuing agitation and self-discovery: her son Lance, transferred to a better paying pit, reports that, so far as his new workmates are concerned, the strike might never have happened:

> They don't show that much interest. If they have to strike, they'll strike. Majority of them, all they think about is going to work and going home. They're not interested in aught else. If the money's wrong they'll strike all right. If their mate gets sacked or summat they'll strike over that. But apart from that you can't get them interested in aught. They're also-rans the majority of them.

This book is not a history of the coal strike but a reminder of some of the voices it ought to give a hearing to. Its focus is on individual experience and imaginative perception rather than on the nature of collective acts. It is about moments rather than movements. Its principal strengths are the first-hand quality of its testimonies – letters, diaries, addresses made in the thick of the struggle, testimonies collected at the time, for the most part. They have the immediacy of what is loosely termed 'oral' history, but they do not suffer from the displacements which memory and retrospection imposes.

The books produced by the miners' support groups (at the time of writing there are already a dozen or more of them) are *celebratory*, reaffirming the justice of the miners' cause and pride in the sacrifices made. The faces in the photographs are strong, determined, joyous. These books correspond to what supporters of the strike would have liked it to be – a new page in a heroic history. They take no account of the sombre stories which come from the pit villages; of the mysterious dissensions which have rent the support groups; of sacked miners who feel abandoned; of the divisions within the NUM itself; of the seeming fatality about loss of jobs. In this book we have tried to take account of some of these uncomfortable realities, by the testimonies from Nottinghamshire, and by those in the concluding section of our book. We have also tried to focus attention on some of those features of the strike which radically differentiate it from the past: the absence, for instance, even in the villages most active in support of the strike, of political ferment (both the prison letters and the Maerdy report are instructive in this respect); the much greater salience of the home, which may help to explain both the importance of the Women's Action groups, and the ways in which the strike was dignified by reference to the future of 'the children'; the new forms of solidarity arising when older ones fray. Those who read the magnificent prose with which we open the book (Barbara Walters, 'Best Suit'), or the electrifying speech of Dave Douglass, may nevertheless see how, even when the threads with the past are broken they are constantly, as in the strike of 1984–5, being remade.

A longer and more polemic version of this preface appears in the October 1986 issue of *New Socialist*

# ACKNOWLEDGMENTS

This book, though coming out in the name of the three editors, is the work of many different hands. The project was launched with the aid of Ruskin College, Oxford, and helped by the personal support of John Hughes, the Principal, David Horsfield the librarian, Russell Read and Sue Hearne of the administrative staff, and Michael the Ruskin cook who, drawing on his Scottish mining childhood, put on a feast for our Yorkshire and other visitors. Francis Rifkin of 'Banner Theatre', Birmingham, taped the Ruskin weekend, and it was financed by personal donations from Bridget and Christopher Hill, John and Mary Walsh, Teodor Shanin, Jeff Weeks, Alex Potts and Shula Marks. Joanna Innes of Somerville College, Oxford, acted as convenor of the organising group, Iris Thorpe, Brian Roberts, Sandra Legate – Ruskin worker-students – as hosts. Joy Copley of *Labour Weekly*, a former Ruskin student and a miner's daughter from Rossington, helped us to launch the national appeal for documents; Peter Thomas of Rotherham and Mick Mulligan of Stainforth gave us strike diaries; Hughie Griffith of Leamington Spa Miners' Support Group, Haydn Thomas of Westbury Constituency Labour Party, Vera Darlington of Hemel Hempstead, Robin Bevis of South Hams Constituency Labour Party were among those who responded to it. We are sorry not to have been able to use their material in this book but it is being deposited, along with other documents collected in the course of this work, in the Ruskin College labour history archive.

Peggy Seeger gave us Iris Preston's strike diary, from which a small selection appears in this volume. Television History Workshop gave us the transcripts of *Rumours at the Miners' Fortnight* and Sally Alexander of *History Workshop Journal* edited them. Hugh Stephenson of the *New Statesman*, Paul Barker of *New Society*, Richard Gott of the *Guardian* and Stuart Weir of *New Socialist* gave the hospitality of their columns to rehearse the themes on which the introduction to this book is based. Guy Boanas would like to thank Margaret Keneally and her family, and Gail and Keith Hancock for hospitality at Grimethorpe, and Lyndal Roper for help in transcribing the

Grimethorpe tapes. Barbara Bloomfield and Raphael Samuel would like to thank Drs Julian and Mary Tudor-Hart for hospitality and help at Glyncorrwg. Barbara Bloomfield would like to thank 'all the generous people of Maerdy and Merthyr Vale' who helped her with her work, also Derek Smith from Upton and Ben Gatt for his help in proofreading the manuscript. Raphael Samuel would like to thank Hywel Francis of the South Wales Miners' Library, Karel Williams of Aberystwyth University, Merfyn Jones of *Llafur*, Frank Cave, area agent NUM Doncaster, Maureen Douglass, Tony and Lynn Clegg of Dunscroft, Ray Palmer of Bates NUM, Northumberland, Raymond Challenor of Newcastle, Hilary Wainwright of the Miners' National Christmas Appeal, Jean McCrindle of the National Women's Support Groups, Anna Davin and Gareth Stedman Jones of *History Workshop Journal* and Mike Brodgen of Liverpool provided us with the splendid tapes from Armthorpe which are a centrepiece of this book.

# GLOSSARY

**NUM** National Union of Mineworkers.

**NACODS** National Association of Colliery Overseers, Deputies and Shotfirers who, after a ballot, decided not to strike in support of the NUM.

**Deputies, firemen** Terms for members of NACODS.

**NCB** National Coal Board.

**UDM** Union of Democratic Mineworkers. A breakaway union from the NUM which formed in Nottinghamshire after a ballot of all Notts miners in October 1985.

**Flying pickets, going flying, fliers, Arthur's fliers** Bands of striking miners who travelled to other pits to try to 'picket them out', i.e., to persuade non-strikers to join the dispute.

**Twinned pits** Pits joined by underground tunnels which may be several miles long. If one pit closes the other can remain open, working the same seams with a reduced workforce. Miners may be transferred to the 'twin' pit in another village.

## MIDLANDS COALFIELD

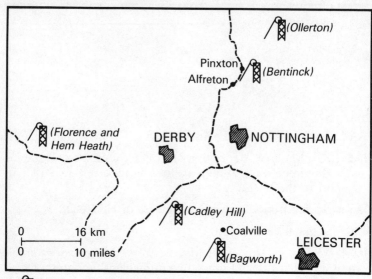

 Pits mentioned in this book

## SOUTH WALES COALFIELD

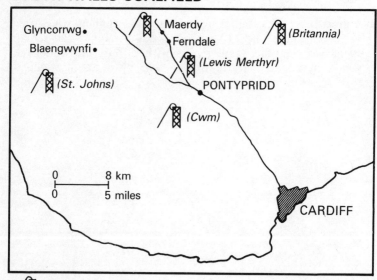

 Pits mentioned in this book

# SOUTH YORKSHIRE COALFIELD

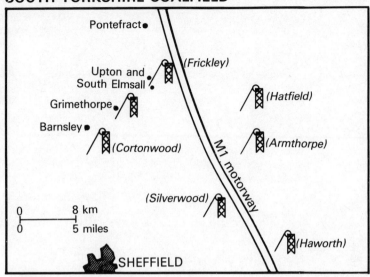

Pontefract●

*(Frickley)*

Upton and
South Elmsall

Grimethorpe●

Barnsley●

*(Cortonwood)*

*(Hatfield)*

*(Armthorpe)*

M1 motorway

*(Silverwood)*

*(Haworth)*

0 — 8 km
0 — 5 miles

SHEFFIELD

Pits mentioned in this book

# INTRODUCTION

Raphael Samuel

## I  Moral panic

A miners' strike, with all its symbolical associations, as a revolt
from the lower depths, generates anxieties out of all proportion
to its economic or industrial effects. If it arouses sympathy in
some, it moves others to hysteria, while authority typically meets
it by coercive shows of strength. Even a quite local dispute, if it is
at all protracted, can produce a moral panic, the case with the
Grimethorpe strike of 1947 which, according to the more alarmist
ministerial statements of the time, was putting post-war recovery
at risk.

The Betteshanger dispute of 1942 was treated as a kind of
treason: the strikers were accused of sabotaging the war effort;
the ringleaders were jailed. The Cambrian Combine strike of
1910, when General Macready rode his cavalry up and down the
Rhondda, and the whole district was under military occupation,
is an earlier example. As a sceptical historian comments (George
Dangerfield, *The Strange Death of Liberal England*): 'There was
terror in the air, which never appears quite to have taken shape.
Rumours flew up and down. The strikers were armed with
revolvers, they had looted quantities of high explosives, they
planned to blow up the manager's house at Gilfach Goch. . . .' In
the nineteenth century it was normal for the coalfields to be
treated as 'disturbed areas' whenever there was a district strike.
Troops would be stationed at sensitive points; the Yeomanry
enlisted; special constables sworn in; while the local magistrates,
frantic with anxiety, bombarded the Home Secretary with
alarmist reports. Tremanheere, the government inspector of
Mines, writing of the Lanarkshire coalfields in his Report for
1855–6, proposed a permanent, coercive presence:

> The habitual presence of a few mounted police in those districts
> where the large villages, filled almost entirely with colliers and
> miners, are found at every two or three miles apart, would have at all
> times a good effect in support of order, and in ensuring the capture
> of persons amenable to justice; but they would be particularly useful

on the recurrence of a strike. Living in, or patrolling the villages, they would soon become acquainted with the faces of their inhabitants. If, during a strike, the practice which baffled the authorities and the employers on the last occasion was repeated, and large bodies of men belonging to one village assembled and marched to another some miles off, for the purposes of intimidation, the mounted police would be able to give early intelligence of their movements in the proper quarter; would afford time for an adequate civil or, if necessary, military force to be brought to the spot, ready to support the well-disposed in their desire to proceed to their work, or would follow and be ready at the right moment to identify the intimidators and thus lead to their apprehension and punishment.

Report, 'State of the Mining Population', p. 51

It is a tribute to Mrs Thatcher's powers of persuasion that the public believes there is something qualitatively different about the strikes of recent years; that indulgence was typically extended to them in the past; and that it is only now that they have been brought under the long arm of the law. In fact, strikes have normally been treated as a threat to public order, and locally or nationally, they have often been the occasion of moral panic. In the years from 1945 to 1958, when almost every strike was 'unofficial', strikes were invariably stigmatised as Communist conspiracies; the rank-and-file movements of the 1960s were put down to the work of 'wreckers' – Alan Thornett, the sacked shop steward at British Leyland, Cowley being a representative example. National strikes, ever since they made their appearance at the beginning of this century, have typically been represented as holding the country to ransom – the charge laid most famously against the miners in 1926, during their six-month strike against wage cuts. The railwaymen's action of 1919 was treated by the government as a revolutionary threat (troops were stationed in Hyde Park as a precautionary measure); that of 1911 – a two-day national strike – as an invitation to anarchy and chaos. The miners' strike of 1926, according to the normally phlegmatic Mr Baldwin, raised the spectre of 'civil war' (outside agitators were banned from holding meetings in the disaffected districts; battleships – and even a submarine– were despatched to Cardiff). The seamen in 1966 were accused of plotting against the state, the miners in 1974 of putting the constitutional order into question (the claim that the miners 'brought down' the Heath government, though often repeated, is a myth: to the contrary, Mr Heath, enthusiastically backed by his party, tried to capitalise on the unpopularity of the strike by forcing an election on the issue and stumping the country under the slogan 'Who Governs?').
Strike leaders have often, even, one is tempted to suggest,

normally, been represented as folk devils, figures of darkness plotting evil deeds, emissaries of Satan bent on a mission of destruction. Mick McGahey, then as now Vice-President of the NUM, was stigmatised in this way during the miners' strike of 1974: a Communist plotting the overthrow of a democratically-elected government. 'Give me the chance to go and pick up Mr McGahey and if it turns out to be my last assignment in the army I should die happy', said an army commander at the time. Earlier, during the power workers' dispute of 1970, one could point to the immensely sinister influence attributed to the rank-and-file leader, Bert Slack. Strike leaders have quite often been thought of as mad – like Jim Larkin, the leader of the Dublin general strike of 1913 – and they have been habitually depicted as 'wreckers'. This was a favourite newspaper epithet for Mr Scargill during the recent miners' strike, and a leitmotif of caricature: a *Sun* cartoon on the day the strike ended had him bestriding the ruins of the coalfields, and crushing a skull with his feet, saying 'Just wait till the next time!'. Readers of *Hard Times* will recall Dickens' venomous portrait of Slackbridge, the leader of the cotton operatives at Coketown, 'ranting at the top of his voice . . . clenching his fists, knitting his brows, setting his teeth . . . pounding with his arms', as he whipped up his audience to frenzy, and it is salutary to remember that, though one of Dickens' nightmare figures, he was allegedly based on a real-life original (Dickens spent time in Preston during the great strike of 1853-4, collecting copy for the book). It has also been common for strike leaders to be credited with a mesmeric hold on their followers, both as the instigators of a strike and as its moving spirit. Thus 'paid agitators' were held responsible – at least by Tories – for the 'revolt of the field' (the farm labourers' strikes of the 1870s), 'desperate demagogues' and 'itinerant orators' – exploiting grievances 'to further their own revolutionary views' – for the Lancashire weavers' strikes of 1816 and 1818, 'secret agents' for the strikes of the Tyneside keelmen.

Strikes have normally been treated in the courts of law, when the issue has come before them, as intimidatory; indeed, as late as 1872, when ten London gas stokers were imprisoned on this charge, the mere threat of a strike was deemed actionable. 'You cannot' said Lord Justice Lindley in 1896, 'make a strike effective without doing more than is lawful.'

The idea of the 'enemy within' – Mrs Thatcher's description of the miners during the strike of 1984-5 – is, if anything, even more venerable. It is to be found at the very dawn of modern Conservatism, in the 1790s, when every manifestation of civil disaffection was treated as seditious. Here, for instance, is the judgement of Lord Chief Justice Kenyon on a trial of three Essex farm labourers, indicted in 1800 for insurrection and conspiracy. They had organised a strike to compel the farmers of Dengie Hundred to raise their wages and supply them with cheaper provisions. Kenyon expressed horror at such behaviour and described it as:

> Little short of raising troops and levying war against King and government of the country . . . many thousands of lives had been sacrificed in riots and insurrections which had beginnings as small and leaders as insignificant as the present. The promoters and ringleaders of this conspiracy were not persons in distress and suffering particularly by the hardships of the times, but clearly they were people of unquiet and ill disposed minds. . . . Not want but wickedness and discontent prompted them to this insurrection. They were actually in the habit of earning from 18s to 20s per week, in work of hoeing beans. . . . Their cry of scarcity was with them only an ostensible, and not a real cause . . . but they were sufficiently artful . . . to know it to be a popular cry. . . . If they had been suffered to proceed, scarcity and famine would have marked their footsteps and the country would have been a prey to devastation.
>
> (*The Times*, 9 August 1800)

A strike, in the Conservative imagination, is second cousin to chaos. It is a manifestation of insubordination, the symptom of a restless spirit. It is a threat to law and order. It endangers private property. It disturbs the public peace. A strike is also, by definition, against the 'national interest'. It cuts at the roots of commercial prosperity; it strangles economic initiatives; it undermines the security of the state. A strike, in the Conservative imagination, is an *unnatural* act, at best the result of delusion, at worst the work of subversives. Whatever its ostensible justification, it is the result of some sort of conspiracy. Workers do not go on strike of their own free will. They are *corrupted* into it, either duped by troublemakers (the 'Red Moles' of the motor-car factories are a recent example, the rank-and-file leaders of the London docks an older one), or else compelled to leave work through intimidation: the case, Mrs Thatcher insisted, with the miners, throughout the twelve long months of the strike. Strikes, to the Conservative, are always in the final analysis coercive, an abridgement of the liberties of the subject, as well as a rupture in workplace amity.

The 1984-5 strike stirred primal Tory fears – fear of the mob, fear of chaos, fear of the 'enemy within'. The miners, as so often in the past, were 'a lawless and misguided set of men'; their leader was destructive – a Yorkshire Hitler, according to the one much-publicised photograph of him. To stand on a picket line was threatening behaviour, even if, like those at Orgreave, one was dressed in T-shirt and trainers: to charge it with horses or batons was to maintain the rule of law. The strikebreakers, like their deferential nineteenth-century forbears, were 'men of steady habits and good character', 'sensible', 'honest', 'the peaceable and well-disposed'; though ferried to and fro in armoured cars, they were the free-born Englishman *redivivus*. In the grip of moral panic – if one credits them, as one should, with their own passionately held beliefs – the Conservatives completely misrecognised the character of the strike, preferring to the evidence before their eyes, the timeless figure of myth. The miners, though making modest and even conservative demands – 'wanting to do what they've always done' in the words of Michael Eaton, the NCB conciliator – were nevertheless pictured as destructives, and their rather traditional leader – a man of precedent and the rule book – as a dangerous revolutionary. Nor were they able to recognise or acknowledge, except in a punitive way, the remarkable demonstration which the strike afforded of community self-help. The miners, in fact, though stigmatised as the 'enemy within' were defending precisely those 'old-fashioned' values – 'Victorian values' – which, in other spheres, the Prime Minister has made it her platform to defend: the dignity of work, the sanctity of the family, 'roots'.

On the miners' side, too, archetypal images came into play, remembered traumas of the bad old days, sleeping images which sprang to life under the impress of crisis, figures of speech which conjured up lost unities, notions of collective honour which pre-empted personal choice. Siege imagery was frequent in the later stages of the strike, more particularly in the villages subject to police invasion; at Cortonwood, where the picketers' hut was named the 'Alamo', the notion of a Last Stand seems to have been anticipated from the start. In a more familiar idiom, there was a whole range of images which domesticated the struggle and brought it within the ambit of local loyalties. Jobs were defended as a patrimony, a kind of family trust which passed from father to son. Housing estates were talked of as though they were villages, places of hereditary settlements where generations of miners had lived. The Union, too, was conceptualised parentally, as something which looked after miners when there was no one else who cared. It was the miners' protection in time of trouble, their welfare in time of need, their security in face of change.

In the miners' strike of 1984-5, the concrete and immediate issues were continually being overlain with the symbolic reverberations of the past, both the historical past of remembered struggles, and the timeless past of 'tradition'. Memories of earlier conflicts structured the strategy and tactics of the strike, and its progress was measured by analogy. In the opening months, when the miners seemed to be on the offensive, the reference was to earlier triumphs. The siege of Orgreave, in June 1984, was on either side a re-run of the Battle of Saltley, a high point of the 1972 strike, when a picket of 20,000 forced a Birmingham coke-works to shut its gates. The sombre example of 1926 came more to the fore as winter drew in and hope receded. The strike took on the character of a Passion Play, a drama whose outcome was hardly in doubt but redeemed, it might be, by the very magnitude of the sacrifice. In the New Year, when hope finally departed, the memories of industrial conflict were overlain by a more cosmic sense of suffering – what a coalfield leader of the nineteenth century, Edward Rymer, called 'The Martyrdom of the Mine'. Another whole theatre of memories opened up with the 'organised' return to work. The pageantry, and even the humours, of the miners' gala were enlisted to demonstrate defiance; the banners of the departed were called upon to give the miners an imaginary strength. As an exercise in resurrection, it mobilised the old world to redress the balance of the new. As catharsis it enabled the miners to celebrate in ceremonial form, and on a very public stage, the victory which in real life had cruelly been denied them. Historical analogies were no less evident on the Conservative side: the *Daily Telegraph* compared the defeat suffered by the National Union of Mineworkers to the fall of King Ludd, and likened the government's position to that of Wellington after Waterloo ('the next greatest misfortune to losing a battle is to win one'). In one aspect the strike was a war of ghosts, in which the living actors were dwarfed by the shadows they had conjured up.

## II The discovery of 'community'

The starting point for any discussion of the strike ought to be a sense of wonder that it took place at all, and reflection on why, in spite of the way it was called, it commanded such enduring support (the great majority of those who came out on strike in March 1984 were still on strike a year later). The strike went beyond any conceivable utilitarian calculations of self-interest: the sacrifices were out of all proportion to any conceivable financial gain, even if money had been an issue in the strike, which it was not. Men in middle-age scorned generous offers of redundancy pay to stand out with their fellows. Young single men, subsisting on a strike allowance of £1 a day, gave up serious drinking and abandoned the heavy metal clubs and the discos to take their place on the picket lines. Families used up their savings, cashed insurance policies and entered into quite terrifying debt – unpaid gas and electricity bills, deferred mortgages, catalogue bills 'a mile high'. Old people, living on retirement pensions, supported their married children until (as we were told at the Ruskin weekend) 'they had nowt left to give'. Yet miners are not a peculiar species-being. They are not less attached to material comforts than the rest of us, and they don't take more easily to being poor. They run cars; they spend freely in the clubs; they like to have food in the freezer, and enough winter fuel for the fire. Husbands and wives quarrel over money matters; they save up for their holidays; they worry about their children and like to buy them treats. Like many British people, they have a deep-rooted aversion to receiving charity, and indeed 'false pride' held some back from using the food kitchens.

One partial explanation for the resilience of the strike might be its unexpectedness. Though lasting fully twelve months its outcome seemed uncertain from one week to the next. For all its sombre setting, and the elemental issues at stake, it was more like a suspense story than an epic. In the first three months there was the euphoria of newly-discovered unity. With the strike solid everywhere except in Nottinghamshire, the miners seemed to be carrying all before them. 'Another few weeks and it will be over.' In July there was the negotiation between the union and the NCB, and then the government's panic over the dock strikes, a first sign, it seemed, of solidarity on the scale of 1972. In September there was the NACODs ballot and the threat that the deputies and overmen would join the strike, the one occasion, according to Mr MacGregor's subsequent account, when the Prime Minister's confidence wavered. With the advent of winter there was the hope that the coal stocks might finally be exhausted, a receding hope, but one which had kept the miners going ever since the imposition of the overtime ban some three months before the outbreak of the strike. 'Maybe there'll be a storm in the Channel,' Dave Douglass remembers thinking about November, 'Maybe the snow will come down that thick it would stop the lorries from moving.' Finally there was the belief – owing more perhaps to religion and morality than to an undertanding of Mrs Thatcher's government – that suffering and self-denial must bring their own reward. 'If we can get through Christmas, we've won.'

The exceptional character of the strike might also be partly explained by reference to pre-existing, everyday realities. The miners' deep attachment and unconditional loyalty to the Union, one of the great sustaining forces of the strike, could usefully be related to its function as both a real and symbolic security against the hazards of underground life. It is conceived of not so much as a representative body, but rather as an all-purpose protector, a collective insurance against disaster. A pit delegate, in Dave

Douglass's description of his work, fulfils a pastoral role: 'the first person in the line to help out – it's 24-hour day'. In addition to his basic union duties, representing members at conferences and tribunals, dealing with family benefit, invalidity benefit, concessionary coal allowances, appeals to the DHSS and in industrial injury cases, there are also a mass of personal problems for which he may be the first call: 'You're a citizen's advice bureau . . . you're a marriage bureau. . . . If the coal's not on time for the pensioners you deal with it, if there are repairs to a pensioner's house. . . . If a man wants a proper letter written, or help for his children with "O" levels . . . or unemployment benefit for a son. . . .' By the same token the comradeship of the picket line and the readiness to stand up to police charges might more usefully be related to a working environment which privileges physical courage and endurance and makes reciprocity and trust a very condition of survival. Similarly, the verbal violence against scabs, freely likened in the newspaper press to that of the football terraces, might be better understood as a version of 'pillicking', the verbal duelling which is the common idiom of underground life. (There is an extended description of it in Dave Douglass, 'Pit Talk in County Durham' in *A Miner's Life*.) More speculatively, the willingness of the miners to risk their all in the strike, and of the union to stake its very existence on it, might be thought to have some ultimate origin, however mediated, with the peculiarities of an industry on which the face worker is engaged, in the last analysis, in a daily wager with death. (As the testimony on p. 246 reminds us, hatred for the pit, delight in escaping from it, and quite often a determination never to go back is as much a feature of a miners' strike as the claim to dignity and respect.)

Demography might help to explain some of the peculiar energies of the strike. The age of the mining labour force has been dropping ever since the introduction of the Redundancy Payments Act of 1967, designed to encourage men over 55 to leave their jobs: in 1984, according to the NCB, the industry had the youngest age force since the advent of nationalisation. In many places the lion's share of the picketing was done by single young men, and there were strong material inducements for them to do so: since the DHSS denied them any welfare benefits at all, the picketing allowance was the only money which came their way. They were also the earliest enthusiasts for the strike, less troubled than their elders at the divisions of opinion on the coalfield. They were the first off the mark as flying pickets – 'Arthur's fliers' as they were known in South Yorkshire; they imported a warrior ethic into the conduct of the strike and it is symptomatic of their part in it that 'Here We Go' – the song which they adopted from the football terraces – became the picketers' anthem.

Kinship might also help to account for the resilience of the strike, i.e. the practice of those 'old-fashioned' family values which it is allegedly Mrs Thatcher's mission to restore. Attention might be given particularly to inter-generational solidarity and exchange. It was improvised in the private rather than the public sphere, and so received none of the attention given to the soup kitchens and the village action committees. But in many cases, to judge by individual accounts, it was Mums and Dads and in-laws who kept a family afloat, who provided treats and presents for grandchildren and brought food to the family table, and fuel to the boiler and the fire (one reason why the NCB cut down on old people's fuel allowances seems to have been because so much of it was getting back to strikers' families). Here is an account from a young mother at Armthorpe:

'We haven't found it too difficult to manage, because we have such a lot of help from me neighbours and my parents. . . . They've sort of got us through. The neighbours are not miners, they pass food over, even money. I felt a bit degraded when they first offered to help. . . . My husband's Mum also helps, she's divorced, but she sends us what she can, a cabbage or a cauli, any little bit that she can she'll send and she gives the children 10p for sweets at night. We have been lucky. We go to my Mum's every Sunday and have a good Sunday dinner and some days in week as well, that saves our electricity as well, so we don't do too bad. The thing that gets me most is sitting without a fire, now it's winter. I mean over the months we've got used to going without luxuries, not going out, not buying clothes, but it's mainly the cold now that gets you down. We can sit wrapped up but we have to put Leanne in our bed. She's only 18 months and it's too cold to put her on her own. And getting baths, we've got an immersion heater but we try not to use it to save electricity so we have to get bathed at Mum's.'

'Community', a term which constantly appears in strike rhetoric, as also in subsequent explanations of its strength, is much less self-evident than kinship as a moving force in the strike. In Maerdy, as Barbara Bloomfield explains in her account of the women's support group there, it was a community of spirit rather than place, a social rather than a physical nexus, drawing together women who had previously been strangers. At Armthorpe, a village where the strike was particularly solid, and where mining is the principal source of livelihood, the constant reference, in the testimonies reproduced on pp. 166-202, is of the strike, not so much as an expression of community as a *discovery* of it, and the dominant note one of gratitude for the restoration of a world that had apparently been lost.

> 'When we were children, this was a small close-knit village. As years passed – I suppose this happened all over – people got a bit better off, bought their own houses and community spirit was disappearing. But this has brought it all back. It's like it was years ago. People banding together, helping one another, sharing and shopping. . . The electric shop . . . where I got my video has been good. I went to school with him. I went to take it back. He said "Keep it". I said, "I can't pay". He said, "Pay me when you go back".
>
> Community's a lot closer. Before the strike everybody had money in their purse and went about their own business. Now we stop and talk for hours in the street. Community's back together like it were years ago. Money is not important any more, friendship . . . is.
>
> Those who are working buy us drinks and maybe send us some food over. It's very good, it's getting back to an old community, where you can go next door and borrow a cup of sugar or tea from a neighbour, it's great, it's made us really close . . . whereas at one time you wouldn't talk to one another.'

The Miners' Welfare was at the heart of this communal bonding. It was the nerve centre of the strike operations, and open, for that purpose, 24 hours a day. It combined the functions of a union office with that of a warehouse for jumble and a distribution point for food parcels. It was the daily port-of-call for the more active supporters of the strike (at Bates Colliery, Northumberland, some 400 or 500 men out of a work-force of 2,000), and an early morning starting point for the pickets. At lunch-time it was a gigantic communal restaurant. In the evenings, the venue of benefits, parties and 'dos'. Hardship cases were monitored there, strike relief paid out, emergency services maintained (at Hatfield Main, a very militant pit, there was a special 'Arrest Officer' charged with seeing men through the courts). At the same time the Miners' Welfare functioned as a more or less continuous social club. It was also a mothers' creche, for those who worked in the food kitchens, and an adventure playground for children on their way to or from school. Mike Brogden's description of the Armthorpe Welfare – 'a cross between a church hall, a snooker club, and a private officer' – conveys very well the day-to-day interplay of self-help and sociability, hardship and play which marked the conduct of the strike in the villages:

> Early morning, 2 or 3 am, the travelling pickets arrive ready for departure to a destination known only to the local organiser. . . . Tea is churned out, last night's sandwiches chewed. A queue forms at

the pay-out desk, as pickets collect their £1 a day allowance. . . . A range of battered vehicles, veterans of many a Nottingham hedgerow, ditch, and unmetalled road, pull out into the gloom of South Yorkshire. An hour later, most return – more tea for some, the snooker table or the floor as a bed for others, waiting for the Markham turn-out at 7 am. As dawn rises, more older men and women make their way to the pit gates, ready for the ritual push-and-shove. More women and some children roll up at the Welfare as younger men drift home to a makeshift breakfast and to bed. Tables are shifted, buns donated by the nearby baker collected and sliced into a thousand sandwiches. The Calcutta hole of a kitchen, dominated by a deep-fat fryer and oversized extractor fan, takes on the day's occupancy. Outside, towards ten o'clock, a remarkable daily scene unfolds. From all over the village, the wheelbarrows emerge. A trickle at first, then a stream, and then a deluge as miners head for the wood-yard behind the Welfare. Acres of woodland, ravaged by Dutch elm disease, have been donated to the local NUM by the District Council. Ten o'clock is log-time – the daily sack of logs from the wood-pile, occupying a corner of the Armthorpe Football Club, felled and sawn by the miners' lumber team. . . . In the Welfare, cooking, cleaning and sandwich-making now dominate time and space. Food parcels, with numbers and contents based on supply rather than on demand, are packed as on a conveyor belt. The proverbial can of beans, packet of margarine and ten potatoes . . . are bundled into makeshift containers ready for collection by locals for delivery to some of the many Markham miners who live outside the village. Potatoes are peeled for the expected 600, and tables laid by a handful of women while a solitary older miner sweeps the floor and chivvies all who walk on it. Meanwhile, this being Christmas there are donations to distribute. Part of the hall is like a gigantic jumble sale, full of gear ranging from . . . yesterday's Paris fashion to grandmother's throw-outs. . . . Meals are rapidly cleared away, ready for a pensioners' party, an afternoon measured in sups is still a long afternoon. The entirely-young male grouping, after a 2 pm sortie to the pit gates, had divided into two over cards and snooker before being eventually evicted by a club manager who is evidently enjoying the strike the least.

For all its hardship and suffering, the strike for many was a time of *enjoyment*, and this was surely one of the secrets of its strength. 'Best year of my life from beginning to end' is how one young Nottinghamshire miner remembers it, 'I felt freer – capable of doing things I'd never done before'. For those who were sent away fund-raising, or were stationed at distant points, like the Maerdy and Merthyr Vale men at Oxford, it was a release from the care of home. 'Married men, with a lot of responsibility lifted from their shoulders, it was like a second childhood.' For the flying pickets evading the police road blocks, it was a time of travel and adventure. 'Hide and seek matches with the police . . . walking three or four miles across fields and woodland to get to colliery . . . quite amusing unless they caught you and beat you up.' The round-the-clock pickets, such as that at the port of Lancaster, where men from Bates colliery, Northumberland, were stationed for weeks at a time, also had their humours: 'Brewing tea up in a bucket . . . cooking 600 sausages on a gas-ring. . . . Blokes of 40 or 50 puffing and blowing – they wouldn't have played football since they were kids at school.' Stay-at-home miners had their own quieter pleasures. At Blyth, Northumberland, 'a lot went to collect sea-coal' in the harbour; some went fishing; and in the summer and autumn months they spent day after day on the allotments. 'There were some good leeks turned out – that were an exceptional year at the Leek Shows.' It is the early months of the strike, when there was sunshine in the air, and when the miners still had money in their pockets, or family savings to fall back on – the spring and summer months when miners seemed to be on the offensive – that are remembered as being particularly 'brilliant'. But the pleasure principle did not disappear even in the harshness of winter, when the money had run out for picketing, and the miners were holed up in their own villages: by far the most sustained collective effort of the entire strike went into the provision of children's Christmas parties. A description of the more improvised pleasures of the strike comes from Harold Hancock at Grimethorpe, writing in October 1984, when the village was under police occupation.

> On the lighter side, the art of making wine for 20p a pint and beer and lager for 10p a pint has reached professional standards. Jumble sales of nearly new clothing, footwear, baby napkins and food are held regularly. Pea and pie suppers with free lager and beer thrown in – all you can eat and drink for a pound – happen nearly every week. They help to keep morale high and to swell the funds of the women's support group parcels fund which, every week, distributes a hundred or more food parcels to the needy.

## III  Obstacles to the strike

The outbreak of the strike, in March 1984, is generally ascribed to a deliberate act of will. According to the NUM and its supporters it was the outcome of a deep-laid Conservative plan, whose basis was being laid as early as 1977. According to the government's supporters, the strike was Mr Scargill's doing, the inevitable result of his determination to seek a showdown with the NCB. A historian is naturally resistant to such conspiracy theory and might find it more illuminating to discuss the obstacles to the calling of the strike rather than tracing its precipitating 'causes'. As in the great lock-outs of the 1870s – and in the general strike of 1926 – the miners were acting counter-cyclically. They were standing out against market forces, with no natural bargaining counters on their side. There was nothing in the society at large to encourage the calling of a strike, or to suggest that if called it would be successful. In the trade union movement 'new realism' was the order of the day. Workers in other occupations, both manual and professional, when faced with job-cutting, had succumbed to the lure of redundancy pay and early retirement. Union attempts to make a stand, whether at national or local level, had been powerless against the members' will: 'a gadarene rush' was how an aggrieved shop steward spoke of the situation at Swan Hunter's, the Tyneside shipyard, when a projected work-in collapsed.

There was no reason to suppose that miners would be an exception. Early retirement was already a well-developed practice on the coalfields, and the announcement of the pit closure programme, in March 1984, was coupled with the offer of generous terms which older miners might have been expected to take up: £1,000 a year for every year of service. Younger miners, it was thought – 'this new materialistic miner who had the big mortgage and the new car and video' – would be in no position to strike, even if they were tempted to do so. Militancy in the coalfield, as in other sectors of British industry, was evidently in decline, despite, and even perhaps because of, the leadership's commitment to it: three national ballots on strike action had been lost in the space of two years, despite energetic campaigning in its favour. At the start of the strike the NCB seems to have thought it could repeat the success of Mr Edwardes at British Leyland, appealing over the head of the union to the members, a strategy which was to be pursued throughout the strike – by the offer of cash bribes and windfalls to those who would return to work, by threatening letters, by advertisements in the local press, finally – in the big push which began in November 1984, by telephone calls from the colliery managers, and a systematic canvass of waverers.

In the NUM it was the conventional wisdom that pit closures, though the most emotive of issues, were also the most divisive, and that resistance, however locally fierce, was apt to peter out at area or national level. Arthur Scargill, primed with inside information about the NCB's hit-lists, had been attempting to make them a focal point of action ever since 1981, and in the months before the strike he and the NUM Secretary had been addressing lodges throughout the coalfield to warn of the coming threat. The most they could win agreement to was an overtime ban. In 1983 the movement to save Lewis Merthyr – the last but one pit in the Rhondda – failed to win support in other regions, even militant ones like South Yorkshire, and petered out amidst angry charges of 'betrayal'. When the NUM put the issue to the ballot, coupling it with the allegedly more unifying one of wages, strike action was voted down with only 9 per cent of the Nottinghamshire miners supporting the Executive's call.

The March 1984 closures were announced in as provocative a way as possible, bypassing the industry's machinery for joint consultation, and the government – as soon appeared – had made contingency plans for a strike. But even if the NCB was bent on a showdown with the NUM (it had been treating Union representatives with increasing contempt during the previous six months), there was no reason to suppose that resistance to pit closure would be any more sustained than in the past. Indeed, at Cortonwood, the original flashpoint of the strike, it seemed that there would be no resistance at all. The first response of the miners, when the closure was announced, was to *celebrate*, as can be seen from the testimony on p. 67. 'The men were really happy about it, singing and dancing. They couldn't wait. . . . "Let us get the bloody pit closed, let us get a better pit".' It was only on the Sunday, three days after the initial announcement, that opinion hardened in favour of action. In Yorkshire, too, the real heartland of the strike, the initial response of the Area Executive Council to follow the first-hand account given by Dave Douglass on p. 70 was hesitant, members fearing that if they endorsed picketing out they would create a coalfield split.

A measure of these uncertainties – and of the depth of the coalfield division – can be seen in the recordings made by Television History Workshop reprinted on pp. 55-66 of this volume. They were taken in July 1983, some months before the outbreak of the strike, and presciently titled 'Rumours at the Miners' Fortnight'. Here, on the caravan sites of Porthcawl, during the holiday fortnight of the South Wales miners, all the major issues of the strike were already being debated and rehearsed – the division between 'economic' and 'uneconomic' pits, between militant and non-militant coalfields, between direct action or putting the matter to a majority vote. From pit after pit there comes the report of faces mysteriously closed, of plant run down, of jobs disappearing. A whole industry, it seems, was to be rationalised into oblivion, if not in England certainly in South Wales. Everybody seemed to be expecting a showdown, with the newly appointed Mr MacGregor as the butcher of the industry, and the newly re-elected Prime Minister to back him up. But even among those most committed to making a fight of it, there was no confidence that concerted action would be possible. The miners' unity, according to these testimonies, had gone; the bonus system had divided them into rival camps. The peripheral pits could hardly hope to have the support of the high production ones. 'What do you think the union strategy will be?', Roy Walters, a miner from Tower Colliery, was asked:

> 'That is a very difficult question to answer. I hope that they will try and resist pit closures that are going to come when MacGregor takes over. But whether they go about it in the right way or not is a different thing. If they are going to start holding ballots again, then I'm afraid we're going to close. The only way, the only strategy is a strike. Forget about your ballot, forget all the talking, the only strategy if the pit is nearing to close . . . is to come out on strike and get the rest of the coalfields and start picketing the pits out . . . the one comradeship that we have got left is that a miner won't cross a picket line.'

The miners entered the fight quite unprepared for the ordeal they were to face. Despite ritual appeals to solidarity and the expectation that, as in the strike of 1972, picket lines would be respected, the miners seem to have believed, at least in the early months of the strike, they could go it alone, as they had done in 1981, when the mere threat of a national strike had been sufficient to make the government withdraw its programme of pit closures; as in 1981, too – the most misleading, perhaps, of those historical analogies which figured so largely in the strike – 'picketing out' was thought sufficient to spread the message of the strike, not only in the coalfields but also in the power stations and the steelworks. Not until the September TUC was there a concerted attempt to enlist trade union support, and by then it was too late for even token solidarities. It seems clear, too, not only from Arthur Scargill's speeches – on which the press directed its exclusive attention – but also from those at local level, that the miners greatly overestimated the effects of the overtime ban in throttling supplies to the power stations, and took no account at all of the government's readiness, through expensive imports of oil and coal, to buy itself out of trouble. In one hopeful scenario, reproduced on p. 93 – the speech which launched the strike at Hatfield Main – the NCB had only provoked the strike to escape from a threatening fuel famine. In the battle for public opinion, the NUM had only one official press officer compared with eighty at the NCB, and no detailed statement of the miners' cause, such as that which had prepared the ground in the 1972 strike. Whatever it lacked in compassion, the Coal

Board seemed to have economic rationality on its side.

Above all, for understandable reasons, the miners were quite unprepared for the scale and ferocity of the police assault. Village cunning (e.g. scrawled notices telling pickets to keep their destination secret) had to compete with sophisticated national operation which – heavily backed by the courts – effected no fewer than 10,000 arrests. Straggling lines of miners found themselves confronted with a well-drilled paramilitary force. Villages were subject to police invasion; county borders were closely patrolled; sensitive districts occupied. Peter Thomas, a 59-year-old Rotherham miner, registers some of the effects of this in his diary. 'Thatcher is becoming more and more authoritarian and Soviet in her approach to problems of Working People' he writes on 14 March 1984, after a spell of picketing in Nottinghamshire. And a week later, 'Police set up East European type road blocks all over the country. It is now easier to get out of East Berlin than it is to get out of South Yorkshire.' 'Unbelievable' was the refrain of those at the Ruskin weekend who described the experience of Orgreave. 'It was like a medieval battlefield – and you were the peasants.' A similar note of bewilderment comes from Bobby Girvan's account of the police attack which followed a miners' demonstration at Mansfield:

> We went walking up the road towards the bus and the bus had gone and we were sitting on a grass verge and then I seen something . . . I couldn't believe it . . . it was like watching one of these science fiction movies, like a dark cloud coming out of the streets . . . you hadn't seen a policeman all day . . . on horseback, they were just getting anybody.
>
> I never felt so fightened or so angry in my life. . . . I could see . . . three or four . . . policeman kicking hell out of a youth. . . . He managed to stagger to his feet and his face was covered in blood . . . and one of them . . . it was like one of these African executions, he got his stick out about a yard long and whacked him across the face with it and the ambulance man was angry and was effing and blinding to the police and they had to put that young lad on an oxygen tank for about 20 minutes before they moved him. . . . I've never seen a sight like it. And I never thought I would pick up a brick in anger, but that day I did.

## IV    Charismatic leadership

The first thing which the historian confronts, if writing close up to the event, is the personalisation of the issues and the extraordinary powers attributed to the President of the NUM. It seems to be the conventional wisdom on the Left – or at any rate among armchair strategists and know-alls – that the miners' strike could have been won if it had been better, more adroitly, led. Some point to July as the month when the NUM should have agreed to a compromise settlement; some to October; all concur that the decision to launch the strike without a ballot was a disaster. The President of the NUM is held responsible for these decisions and much the same account was given during the strike by the popular press. A *Daily Mirror* front page lead which appeared towards the end of the strike is representative.

> Arthur Scargill has lost the miners' strike. . . .. He had led the crack guards of the union to disaster. No one else is to blame. Not the men. Not the miners who struck. Not those who stayed at work. Not those forced by poverty to go back. He lets himself down. Every move he made was wrong. Had he balloted the men to begin with he would have had a solid strike. A solid strike wouldn't have needed intimidatory picketing or police. Without them there would have been no violence. And without violence, the strike might have been won. Mr Scargill stabbed himself in the back. No one did it to him.

Historians may be better inoculated against such forms of explanation than others. They will know that leaders – especially charismatic leaders, who give voice to the collective unconscious – are not so much causes as effects, and that the salience attributed to them is an optical illusion. They will know that decision-making is not an event but a process in which a thousand different circumstances conspire. And they may remember – if they are readers of Tolstoy, or students of the First World War – that in a battle nobody is less in command than the generals.

The very idea of executive power is problematical when applied to an industrial dispute. A strike is not a controllable process, but a huge wave of happenings, in which emergency succeeds upon emergency, and instructions and directives are constantly being overtaken by events. Priorities compete for attention. Strategies emerge from the necessities of the moment. Decisions are made by default. Arguments flare over relatively trivial issues, differences are envenomed by personalities. Area and national leaderships pull in different directions – a constant sub-theme in the miners' strike. Local leaders defend their fiefs as though they were miniature empires. Ad hoc committees bring together unlikely partners and are then scythed by jealousies and factions – the fate of some of the miners' outside support groups in the immediate aftermath of the strike, and of some of the women's support groups during it, 'Everything in this dispute was at short notice.'

Even when a strike appears to be directed from above, its

energies come from below. A good example of this would be the emergence of 'twinning' as a major source of welfare and relief, i.e. the 'adoption' of individual villages by outside support groups and trade union branches. It produced jealousies between neighbouring villages, and for reasons of equity, as well as to maintain executive control, it was opposed by area leaderships, while the NUM nationally tried to channel funds through union headquarters. But local Labour parties, in their fumbling, untheoretic way, stumbled on it as a symbolic focus for mobilising support; trade union branches adopted it with alacrity; and as a method of fund-raising it was a brilliant success: the miners' support group in Oxford, for instance, raised almost half as much for Maerdy and Merthyr Vale – the villages which it adopted at an early stage of the strike – as did the Miners' National Christmas Appeal.

The pit villages themselves, increasingly resourceless as the strike continued, took their own initiatives in spite of national and area policies, sending out collectors to distant points, getting themselves adopted, reciprocating gifts with hospitality. 'Twinning' was an emotional and imaginative as well as financial success, corresponding on either side to heartfelt passionate need. It made the plight of the mining villages meaningful to outsiders. It produced a vigorous two-way traffic, with a whole host of ceremonies to mark the passage of gifts and creating links which have been maintained with unabated vigour – if the case of Oxford is anything to go by – in the year since the strike ended. 'Twinning' was a completely extempore form of bonding. It was never officially recognised by the miners' union, yet by the later stages of the strike it was both a major means of material support and an almost solitary point of growth.

Nobody acts in a strike of their own free will. Leaders have the power to betray a strike, and they have the duty to negotiate or attempt to negotiate a settlement, but as the pressure for unity grows, the scope for manoeuvre is narrowed, and this is especially the case on the coalfields, where the leaders are peculiarly close to the members – often living in the same villages – and where to break ranks in any form is to invite accusations of 'scabbing'. At the start of the strike there were deep divisions of opinion and genuine strategy options, and it is indicative of this that the delegate conference which sanctioned a national strike – in April 1984, more than a month after the action had begun – did so by quite a small majority. The unexpected strength of the strike – and the ferocity of the police attack on it – transformed opinion, while inter-regional picketing (with the crucial exception of Nottinghamshire) produced a community spirit. In July, when the first major negotiations with the Coal Board took place, the miners were convinced that they were going to win. The initially hesitant Welsh district was making guerrilla raids on the steelworks; Durham, which had voted in favour of a national ballot, was solid. There was a national dock strike in the offing. The 'common sense' of the strike – the psychology of the picket line – imposed itself: the negotiators could accept nothing less than a government surrender. By the time of the next crucial round of negotiations, in October, the miners had sacrificed too much for anything less than 'victory' as a reward, while with the beginning of the drift back to work, the government progressively upped its demands, until by the end of the strike it was offering ultimatum only. The longer the strike went on, the less room there was for manoeuvre. Negotiations, like everything else in the strike, became a test of loyalty and strength, and leaders were more concerned to demonstrate integrity – to keep faith with their members – than to exploit divisions in the enemy ranks. Hereditary enmities seem to have prevented joint action with NACODS – deputies were still 'gaffers men', even though a majority of them refused to cross picket lines and in September were threatening a strike of their own. By the end of the strike, when the honour and even the continued existence of the union was at stake, the NUM executive achieved a rare unanimity in rejecting the last offer they were made.

Scargill, the ostensible leader of the strike, was to a peculiar degree its creature, a rather isolated figure depending entirely on his special relationship with the members, as the voice of the more active spirits. He was not a member of a vanguard group which, like the Communist Party of old, might have ordered or persuaded him to bear a strategic retreat; nor – since the move of the NUM national headquarters to Sheffield – did he have metropolitan trade union officialdom as a peer group. He was not in command of his executive, nor of the area leadership, least of all in his native Yorkshire. He was viewed with some suspicion in the Welsh and Scottish coalfields, which had their own local heroes and their own distinctive version of militancy – more 'educated', more Communist, more statesmanlike than those characteristic of the Barnsley and Doncaster coalfields. The one area of the strike in which he enjoyed unchallenged command was that of public statement. His power – if so medium-like a quality can be called a power – was that of an evangelist, one who, like A.J. Cook, the 'leader' of the miners in 1926, spoke, at public meetings and rallies, not *to* the miners but (as Arthur Horner once put it) *for* them. As for A.J. Cook and Herbert Smith in 1926, the rhetoric became the reality: the miners had to win because, given the scale of the sacrifice, any other outcome was unthinkable.

If one wanted to personalise the issues of the strike, it is perhaps to others one should look. The man who brought the miners out on strike, if one wanted to assign individual responsibility, was not Mr Scargill but Mr MacGregor. He was notoriously the axeman of British steel, presiding over a reduction in that industry's labour force from 220,000 to 70,000. It was his appointment to the Coal Board in July 1983 which produced an emergency sense and it is indicative of the feeling against him that, only a month before the outbreak of the strike, he was physically attacked when he visited a pit in Northumberland. Space should be given, too, to Mrs Thatcher, universally referred to as 'She' in the coalfields – long before the strike broke out she had been identified as the miners' enemy. As Television History Workshop was told in July by one of the South Wales miners: 'She's not . . . closing the colliery down, she's closing the environment down.'

## V  Village radicalism

The strike of 1984-5, though national in form, was regional in character, and it was shaped at every crucial point, not only on the miners' side, but arguably even on that of the NCB and the government, by local initiatives. This is most obviously the case in the outbreak of the strike, which was precipitated by the action of the men at Cortonwood, and then spread from district to district and region to region before it became a national strike. It can also be seen in one of the decisive early acts of the strike, the choice of 'picketing out' as a means of spreading the strike, and the rejection of a national ballot (the ways in which picketing out was started in advance of, and even in defiance of, the area leadership in Yorkshire is described by the testimonies on pp. 69-70 of this volume). The *failure* of the strike in Nottinghamshire, like its initial success elsewhere, seems likewise to have been the result of local initiative, the miners there refusing to follow either the area leadership or their own delegate conference. In many pits they also ignored, as Barbara Bloomfield describes in the case of the Bentinck Colliery (see pp. 72-85), the recommendation of their lodge officials. There was no national coordination of picketing, no national office to direct the conduct of the strike, or even, in the opening months, much area control: tactics were devised and activities coordinated in local subdistricts, in ways described on pp. 67-71 of this volume. At one crucial moment – the battle of Orgreave in June 1984 – there seems to have been a decisive split between 'Arthur's fliers' and the village pits of South Yorkshire, on the one side, and, on the other, the Yorkshire Executive alarmed at the scale of confrontation (there was a similar division at the start of the strike over the Yorkshire pickets in Notts).

An even more spontaneous expression of local initiative, dating from the earliest days of the strike (Iris Preston's diary on pp. 100-21 of this volume describes some of the initial processes) was the formation, in the pit villages, of the women's support groups, which transformed the strike from an industrial stoppage into a communal act, while at the same time creating an alternative centre of power in the villages (there seems to have been considerable friction between the lodge committees and the women's support groups over the control of funds). All of the dynamism in welfare relief, from the starting of the kitchens – in some places as early as week one of the strike – to the bilateral relationships involved in 'twinning', came from below. Finally, at the close of the strike, the decision to return to work, and the ceremonial form of it, was first agitated in the localities – South Wales in particular – and then imposed on a reluctant national leadership.

On the other side of the divide, though in the absence of documentation the proposition is necessarily speculative, it seems that the most successful strategies of the NCB arose from local or regional initiatives. The whole propaganda of the government and the NCB was predicated on the existence of the 'working miner', an originally half mythical figure who, under the efforts of NCB area directors, began to make a real-life appearance. Within a few months of the strike pocket Napoleons began to appear on the coalfields, with strike-breaking strategies of their own, high-profile area managers, in the first place, like Albert Whelan, the bull-headed Scottish area director, who was to sustain his reputation for toughness and his claims to national promotion when the strike was over by insisting that all his sacked miners stay sacked, or Ken Moses, the Derbyshire area director, who appeared almost nightly on Yorkshire TV – a small man with cropped hair, 'like an army general', with a map on the wall and flags to indicate the number of return-to-works – who devised his own scheme of wire-meshed convoys to ferry strike-breakers to and from the pits. By November, when the NCB's big push began, the idea of a decisive breach with the union seems to have caught on with numbers of colliery managers. It took the form not only of intensive canvassing of potential waverers and the issue of black propaganda, but also of the withdrawal of coal deliveries, the policing of coal tips and prosecutions for coal-picking, a handle for pressure on the victim (in numbers of places, coal-pickers were offered an amnesty on condition that they returned to work), as well as a symbolic break with the whole system of informal co-partnership which for forty years had marked the local relationship of the NUM and the NCB.

Local initiatives are no doubt a feature of any national strike, and so are regional differences. What gives them special purchase in the coalfields is the molecular character of mining trade unionism as reflected in the federal make-up of the NUM's national executive, the financial independence of the regions, and the relative autonomy of the miners' lodge. As the history of the strike and the subsequent fight over breakaway suggest, centripetal influences have survived forty years of amalgamation (the NUM was established as a supposedly unitary body in 1945) almost untouched: whatever the constitutionalities of the matter, miners are accustomed to acting on their own. The women's support groups followed suit. Though coming together for national rallies – the 10,000 Barnsley demonstration of 12 May 1984 marked their arrival as a national presence – they seem to have been no less resistant than the lodges to coordination from above.

To the historian, the strike of 1984-5, especially in Yorkshire, exhibits affinities to the village radicalism of nineteenth-century England. One sees the same preference for direct action, not least – despite NUM tradition to the contrary – in the impatience with the idea of the ballot ('We're not letting other people vote us out of the pits'). One finds the same attachment to customary rights, the same territorial sense of place. The police intervention was experienced – as it was in comparable cases in the nineteenth century – as an *invasion*, a violation of an almost private space – the colliery and the village which the miners and their families regarded as their own ('our pit', 'our village'). The disciplines of the strike, like its organisation, were highly local. There was no Sheffield or Barnsley Kremlin to coordinate picketing or to mastermind community self-help. Even locally the disciplines were extempore and ad hoc, a matter not of giving or taking orders, but of people 'slotting in', of taking up whatever needed doing, of volunteering to make up a squad that was short-handed, or undertaking a particular task. 'Nobody told them what to do. They just did it.' 'We were all in charge. We discussed what had to be done.'

## VI Radical conservatism

The animating spirit of the 1984-5 strike – its 'common sense' or implicit ideology – was that of *radical conservatism*. As very often in popular movements of the past, it was a defence of the known against the unknown, the familiar against the alien, the local and the human against the anonymous and the gigantesque. The miners were fighting against *losing* something, 'defending what little we've got left', as a miner put it in February 1985, speaking for a squad of men who had been reduced to picketing their own pit. Or, as a Maerdy woman put it to Barbara Bloomfield, 'we just want to keep what we've got!' Beneath the rhetoric of 'victory' – the 'death or glory' perorations at the public rallies – they were engaged in a desperate battle for survival, and bewildered that a cause so obviously just and demands so essentially modest should bring down on them the organised might of the state. Job security, personal dignity were, on the miners' side, the issues at stake in the strike; family, hearth and home among the most potent of its mobilising appeals; 'old-fashioned' values its continual point of reference.

One of the many remarkable features of the strike was the assertion of the hereditary principle, in relation to the union, in relation to the village, and above all in relation to the miner's job. The NUM appears again and again in platform oratory as 'the union your fathers and grandfathers built'; to stand out on the picket lines – and to stand up to the police – was an act of filial loyalty, a loyalty which extended from real-life fathers to a more indeterminate ancestry of struggle and sacrifice. The trade union was both the trustee of the miner's future, and the custodian of his past. 'We only borrow the Union,' a branch president at Ferrymoor Ridings, a pit near Barnsley, told his members, 'It belongs to our fathers and sons.' At NUM rallies historical time was measured in family life-cycles – genealogically, as in the Old Testament, rather than by reference to political events – while the union itself was conceptualised in terms of father-to-son succession rather than (or as well as) in the more conventional trade union language of brotherhood. 'They're not taking your money, or my money,' Jack Taylor, the Yorkshire miners' president, told a Barnsley rally, reporting on the legal seques-tration of NUM funds, 'But our father's and grandfather's money – the people who formed this union' (the Yorkshire union dates from the 1860s, so the statement has the force of a metaphorical rather than literal truth). Reference to the martyred dead – the generations of miners whose lives were sacrificed to the greed of the coal-owners – were also apt to be put in ancestral terms: the NCB was turning the clock back 'to the conditions your fathers and grandfathers had to contend with'. The miners had a debt to repay to the past, as well as an obligation to the future: they were bound by the sacrifices of their ancestors.

The hereditary principle was no less apparent in the central issue of the state – so far as the miners were concerned – the defence of pits and jobs. The right to work was legitimated and objectified by reference to the generations to come. It was by definition inalienable. As Arthur Scargill put it, in one of his most effective rhetorical tropes, the miner's job was not his to give away because it belonged to the miner's posterity.

The hereditary principle can also be seen in the miner's attachment to place, both as a physical setting and as a social nexus. The strike revealed a simmering resentment at the 'gipsy-like' existence which the NCB's pit closures had brought about and the ever-extending phenomenon of 'bussing' which followed it; and a growing sense, too, that with nowhere else to go, the only security was staying put. The fact that the miners' 'villages' are in many cases post-war estates, and that their own settlement is in many cases quite recent, does not undermine, but may actually enhance, the strength of attachment to place. The 'villages' are conceived of as places of family settlement, even if, as in the case of Armthorpe or the very militant pits of the Kent coalfield, they were peopled in the 1920s by strangers. Calling for a strike vote from his lodge at Hatfield Main, Dave Douglass argued (see the speech reproduced on pp. 92-6) that the closing of Cortonwood put the whole of the Doncaster coalfield at risk. As an ex-Tyneside miner, he could see nowhere else to go. 'When our pits were closed up yon, we came to Yorkshire. Where is Yorkshire going to be? There is no place left to run. Us backs are to the wall!'

More shadowy but not less potent fears surfaced in the course of the strike itself. A spectre which Arthur Scargill conjured up, speaking in the Yorkshire villages, was that of the urban disaster, the 'helplessness' and the 'hopelessness' of youth in the big city – Liverpool in particular – in which the reality of life 'becomes . . . something to escape from on the end of a hypodermic syringe'. Others pointed to 'ghost towns' such as Shotton, or to the blighted industrial hinterland, such as those around Sheffield, where factories had been put to the bulldozer. Not least, even for those with a prospect of transfer, there was the threat of being swallowed up in the NCB's new super-pits, tearing up roots and selling up homes to become a mere appendage of micro-electronically operated technologies. Change, in whatever guise it presented itself, was threatening. Jobs were a security, an insurance against the future, 'the right to choose where you live', a refusal to be disturbed, a sense of both real and imaginary roots.

One important element in this territorial sentiment was the spread of home ownership -- a novel phenomenon in the Yorkshire coalfield though a long-established one in South Wales. So far from weakening the miners' resolve by burdening them with mortgage payments – as had been commonly believed before the strike, by moderates and militants alike – it seems actually to have stiffened the will to resist. The property-owning democracy became an unexpected ally of the strike. Home-ownership may have given the new purchasers a 'stake in the country' as Conservatives had always believed, but it was one which pit closures threatened as much as they did the miner's job. 'No way could we sell the houses we had bought.' The building societies and the local banks seem to have had some appreciation of this: as the testimonies in this volume confirm, they were extremely accommodating to the home-owner, relieving them, for the duration of the dispute, of the burden of weekly or monthly payments.

Another conservative sentiment which the strike mobilised was 'Loyalty'. It figures constantly in the language of the strike, usually in relation to the Union, but by metaphorical extension embracing all those who made sacrifices for the miners' cause – the wives who were 'solid' behind their husbands; the local shopkeepers (such as those who donated to the food kitchens) who were 'brilliant'; the old people whose help to their married children was 'unbelievable'. The imaginative appeal of 'Loyalty' was inconceivably greater than such politicised terms as 'solidarity' or 'unity', and it is indicative of this that the commemorative parties, held all over the villages of South Yorkshire in the immediate aftermath of the return to work, were known as 'Loyalty' parties (they had originally been designated 'Victory' parties, and were eagerly anticipated in the last long months of the strike: but in the sombre circumstances the name was changed to 'Loyalty' instead). The commemorative badges – a characteristic cultural expression of the strike, and of the fiercely local sense of pride – testify to similar sentiments: 'Loyal and Undefeated' (Kiveton Park NUM); 'Heads High We Fought to the End' (Brookhouse NUM); 'Lest We Forget' (Welbeck NUM); 'Unbroken Allegiance' (Yorkshire NUM). At Hem Heath, Staffs, where as Dave Cliff recounts (see, 'A Tale of Two Pits', pp. 86-92), the work-force was split, the first of the strikers' badges carried a miner's lamp and the simple words 'Hem Heath – Loyalty'; the second, a commemorative badge struck in the aftermath of the strike had the words 'Loyalty to the Last'.

Loyalty was a matter of trust rather than duty and obligation. It drew on the disciplines of working together at the coal face, and reproduced its categorical imperative: 'Stick together no matter what.' At Hem Heath, a pit with no very strong Union tradition, it meant in the first place loyalty to workmates: 'A lot came out who didn't understand what it was about when they saw their friends at the gate. We had to explain it to them.' In some cases, where a village was reputed to be solid as with those in the Doncaster coalfield, it was associated with local pride: preeminently the case with Maerdy, the last pit in the Rhondda, and the 'Little Moscow' of the 1920s, where at the end of twelve months not a single man had returned to work. 'Faith in the union', too, could be seen as an expression – albeit a displaced one – of the miners' faith in themselves. It was a way of being true to each other, a transferred form of allegiance, an extended expression of trust. Loyalty in any of these cases – like mutuality at the coalface – was unconditional. In the villages it meant 'rallying round' those in trouble, irrespective of its causes. In the conduct of the strike it meant basic trade unionism, not crossing picket lines, even if one had been reluctant to join the strike; following the union, even if one disagreed with its tactics: having 'trust' in the leadership not so much for what they did as for who they were.

Loyalty and trust were reciprocated by the miners' leaders. So far from disowning the pickets, as they were constantly being invited to do by politicians and the popular press, they were visibly moved by the intensity of the support, and there is an unmistakable accent of family pride in the way in which NUM officials spoke of the youngsters who had come to the forefront in the strike – a new generation who, by their dedication, had proved themselves worthy of their forefathers: 'the finest young trade unionists this country has ever seen'. In negotiation, the leaders seem to have been more concerned with proving their integrity and keeping faith with their members than with seizing new openings, or exploiting divisions within management's ranks. The miners' leaders also showed a remarkable loyalty to each other: faced with an unprecedented campaign of vilification by the government and the national press, not a single one ran for cover, or attempted to distance himself, in however small a degree, from the symbolic object of national execration, Arthur Scargill.

Closely related to 'Loyalty', in the ruling passions of the strike, one might refer to the almost feudal sense of honour. A strike is always about more than the sum of its causes. It entails not only a division over material interests, but also a struggle for symbolic precedence. The demands are treated, on either side, as totemic. Issues emerge which may have formed no part of the original strike agenda. Interests are subsumed in categorical moral imperatives. Union recognition is always in some sort at stake, even if the dispute is nominally about pay and conditions. So, too, is the power of the employer, or in the language of the 1984-5 strike, 'management's right to manage'. Hence the enormous importance attached to the *form* of negotiation, and to those 'talks about talks' which, in the modern system of industrial relations, often prove far more intractable than the terms of an eventual settlement. The strike of 1984-5 was as much about *how* things happen as about what happens.

A miners' strike – more so, perhaps, than those of any other group of workers – is an implicit claim to respect. It is the eruption of an underground life into the public and political sphere. It demands, quite often – as in the strike of 1972, or that of 1926 – a public acknowledgment that mining is a special case, not only on account of the dangers of the work but also of the primacy of coal. It pits the miners' sense of special worth against the imperatives of market forces. Pride was arguably the central issue at stake in the strike of 1984-5, when the very survival of the industry was in question. The miners were defending their work not only as a source of livelihood but also as a dignity and a resource, a title to collective identity. They were also asking for a recognition of coal as an irreplaceable national asset. Hence the talismanic importance attached to the 1974 *Plan for Coal*, as a declaration of faith in the industry's future. Hence, too, the simmering rage at the NCB's run-down of investment and plant, and the refusal even to countenance the notion of 'uneconomic' pits. Notions of honour and shame were also pivotal in the conduct of the strike itself. To resist the blandishments of the Coal Board (in November 1984, it was offering tax-free earnings to those who returned to work before Christmas), was an act of self-respect; to stand up to the police was a test of physical courage, even a proof of manhood. Union men were steadfast. Weaklings and cowards were scabs. The issue of collective honour was never more important than in the closing stages of the strike, when it was thought better to return to work without a settlement than to compromise the stand of the Union, or to be seen to bow the knee. When every hope had faded, the miners' sense of dignity supported an ultimate in defiance.

Finally, one might refer to the paternalist (or maternalist) idiom which the miners adopted, whether in conceptualising the strike as an act on behalf of others – a kind of *noblesse oblige* – or in looking after their own. In the villages solidarity resolved itself into 'taking care' of those in greatest need, the 'slightly better placed' helping the more vulnerable to survive. Thus, in the distribution of winter fuel, priority was given to families with young children; in the allocation of food parcels to 'single lads living away from home' (i.e. those to whom the DHSS was denying any benefits at all). The NUM lodges, throughout the strike, kept up the pensioners' supply of coal: washing it at the pit face (even, at Cortonwood, mining it underground) was a regular strike duty to which squads of men were assigned. The women's action groups – or 'support group ladies' as they were referred to by the more old-fashioned Union officials – as well as maintaining the food kitchens, engaged in every species of rescue work, monitoring cases of hardship – 'the woman who was poorly', 'the wife whose husband was in jail', 'the miner with a large family' – and taking emergency action at moments of crisis. 'Anyone in desperate trouble with bills, somehow the money would be found.' The spirit of charity – 'people had a *need* to give, they *wanted* to be useful' – merged imperceptibly with strike strategy, and indeed no distinction was made between the two. With necessity as the NCB's Fifth Column in the push for a return to work, the solidity of the strike, in any given village, depended on the strength of the survival networks. In domestic life, as on the picket line and at the coal face, there could be no weak links in the chain.

The function of the Union, too, was seen as protective, as much, perhaps, for what it stood for as for what it did. It was the only safeguard for the miners' welfare, the only security for their conditions of work. In the rhetoric of the strike it appears as a kind of 'philanthropic Hercules', to adopt a phrase from the early days of British trade unionism, a purveyor of 'friendly benefits' as much as a pillar of strength. It represented a higher principle of unity than those to be found in the localities. It incarnated a wider sense of belonging. In the words of an old trade union song, it was 'The Miners' Lifeguard'. The attack on the union was thus experienced as a personal threat, jeopardising securities of all kinds. As miners put it, when reaffirming support for the strike, both echoing platform rhetoric and anticipating it, 'Without the union, we would be lost'.

The most innovative aspects of the strike – the emergence of the women's movement in the pit villages – was also, it could be argued (at the risk of giving offence), umbilically linked to its conservative character. It produced, indeed, a new equality in many families, and in some villages, for the duration of the strike, a kind of dual power. The women of the village action committees were among the most intransigent of the strike's supporters, and the strongest opponents of the return to work. Yet, as they said themselves, the women were 'standing' by their men – husbands, sons, brothers, fathers who were out on strike. The strike, as they also often said, had 'drawn' families closer together. The subjective experience of liberation and power was not at all the same as the appearance of separatism, and the record of the women's support groups since the strike – and of the NUM's wary relationship to them (by a small majority, the annual conference in July 1985 *rejected* the admission of women as associate members of the union) – does not support the belief in a new social-sexual dispensation. The feminism of the 1984-5 strike was real enough, as can be seen from the writings in this book, but it is not one which can be easily aligned to metropolitan versions of it, and it took place within an exceptionally strong system of family and kin solidarities.

## VII   The religion of the coal strike

The strike was experienced by its supporters as a great awakening, an emancipation from anxiety and fear. It released hidden energies. It discovered secret strengths. It called into question conventional roles. Debt lost its terrors when there was no money to pay the bills ('stuff 'em'); 'false pride' didn't seem to matter any more when everyone was in the same boat. Personal troubles were subsumed in the urgencies and excitement of the moment; fears were allayed by collective demonstrations of strength. For the faceworker, exchanging the drudgeries of underground life for the freedom of the open air, the strike was some sort of holiday, albeit one with little or no money to spend, and as so often during a miners' strike there were numbers who declared – like Iris Preston's son Lance (see p. 247) – that they would never go back down the pit. (Since the strike many active and restless spirits seem in fact to have left the industry, quite apart from those victimised by the NCB.) For the women of the support groups – there were some 10,000 of them at the Barnsley demonstration of April 1984 – the strike offered, momentarily at least, an escape from the routines of everyday life, a renunciation of subaltern status. The more active spoke of it with all the intensity of a conversion experience, as something which had opened their eyes to new realities, and transfigured their view of the world: no theme is more insistent in their testimonies than the claim that the strike had 'changed' them, and that when it was over, nothing would be the same.

The strike opened up a whole new theatre of self-expression. Lodge secretaries, editing strike bulletins, tried their hand at journalism. Writers came out of their closet, sending poems and letters to the miners' press. Comics and singers competed for turns at the 'dos' and benefits. Shopkeepers and publicans turned philanthropist, suspending business principles for the duration of the strike. Graffiti artists discovered a talent as cartoonists, picketers as storytellers or strategists. For the women of the village action groups the strike was a huge learning process, a chance to exercise new skills, an introduction to public life. Wives and mothers stepped out of the kitchen to become organisers and entrepreneurs, almoners and welfare officers, clothiers and catering managers. The strike was a school of writing, a training in administration, an apprenticeship in political skills. It initiated them into the mysteries of committee work; it gave them the confidence to speak on public platforms; it opened up a whole range of male preserves. There were long-distance negotiations to be conducted for food supplies and the provision of children's treats. There was the competition with the miners' lodge over the distribution of relief funds. There were accounts to be kept, logs and rosters to be entered and, for the secretary of the women's group, there was a vast amount of correspondence to be answered – the occasion, as the letters which have come to us in the course of compiling this book show, not only for the courtesies of acknowledgment but also for propaganda, persuasion and reaffirmations of faith.

As in the religious revivals which swept the coalfields in the past, the strike served sensibly to diminish the divisions between age-sets. For young, single men it marked a coming of age, drawing them from the peripheries of the village to the centre, transferring their energies from the heavy metal pubs and the discos to the picket line and the Miners' Welfare. It offered them both an education in adult life and the joys of a new belonging. The strike, as older miners put it approvingly, was a time when 'lads became men', learning, in the harsh experience of the picket line – and on a strike allowance of no more than £1 a day – 'what it meant to be a miner'. At the other end of the age scale old people – retired miners and their wives, widows and widowers – from being a burden to the community ('pensioners') emerged as pillars of strength. Not only were they a chief material support for married children, they were also invested with a 'born-again' authority as the survivors of earlier hardship, the protagonists of earlier strikes.

The difference between the miners and the outside world was in certain respects a difference between believers and agnostics. For the miners the strike was an act of faith in their leaders, faith in the union, faith in themselves. The women's support groups were bewildered that a cause so obviously just had failed to win universal support; they could not understand why their own determination was unmatched by that of others. The poetry of the strike, one of its characteristic expressions, rehearses religious themes – redemption through suffering, words as covenants, union as a sacred trust. The public rallies served in some sort as acts of communion, collective reaffirmations of faith which banished darkness and fear. Too many sacrifices had been made for the miners to contemplate surrender, Arthur Scargill told the Labour Party conference in September 1984: 'the strike had been consecrated in the miners' blood'. The belief in 'total victory' – one of the great credibility barriers between miners and the outside world – might also be interpreted in a religious sense. It was as though unseen powers were working in the miners' favour, promising a glorious termination of the dispute even though the entire might of the state was arrayed as against them. The miners were bound to win, because their cause was just. The miners were in some sort 'pledged' to win; they half believed in a benevolent providence.

Closely wedded to the religious spirit was the historical one. Miners have a profound sense of kinship with the past and (it could be argued) a mystic belief in oneness over time. To strike was to prove themselves worthy of their ancestors. It was to defend the rights which their forefathers had fought for. It was to show that miners had not changed. The strike itself was designated from the first as 'historic' and it drew its authority from the past. 'To go back to work was not just letting yourself down, it was your fathers and grandfathers too.' The strike was also 'historic' in its own right, the miners were certain that what they were doing was momentous. They were proud of what they had achieved. They were writing a glorious new chapter in their history, setting an example to the generations to come. The high degree of ceremony which accompanied the strike – not least, the return to work 'a year to the day' from its outbreak – testifies to the historic sense. So too do the commemorative badges which serve as a kind of livery for the flying pickets. The dramatic episodes of the strike acquired a legendary character: locations – such as those where there had been battles with the police – acquired the aura of historical sites; and, most expressively indicative of the historical passion, the strike threw up a host of village re-membrancers – diarists, letter-writers, photographers, book-keepers – concerned to keep a faithful record of events.

The public language of the strike was one of hope, encourage-ment and reassurance. People said what needed to be said. They refused to give voice to doubt, or to admit to signs of weakening. They refused to think the unthinkable – the possibility that the strike might be lost. Words – buoyant, aggressive, strident, in one register, in another, full of moral uplift – served as a prophylactic against anxiety, a refuge from the vertigo of change. The language of 'total victory' served to still incipient doubt. The insistence on the 'historic' nature of the strike could be interpreted in a similar sense. It was not only an act of homage towards the past, but also an insurance against the future, positioning the strike within a continuum. It was a way of asserting the *permanence* of the coal communities, even of claiming *immortality* for the miners' union, as a partnership of the living, the dead and the still unborn. The strike had to be historic if it was to have any meaning at all.

These themes – as can be seen from the many examples in this book – were reproduced in personal testimony and private correspondence. The letters from the coalfield to outside supporters are full of moral uplift. They express pride in the miners' achievement, the sense of honour at rising to a great occasion, the weight of responsibility at being an active participant in a great event. They drew freely on Christian forms of address. Gifts, as can be seen from the exchange of letters between Frickley and Wandsworth in this volume, were not merely acknowledged, they were *solemnised*, as a living proof that the miners had not been abandoned, as a token of sacred bonds. Personal testimonies, too, such as those collected at Armthorpe in December 1984 and reproduced in this volume, are full of the joys of a new belonging. While precise about hardship and economies, they soar into generalities when celebrating the return of a sense of oneness to their world.

One of the distinctive features of the miners' strike, as of any event which is experienced as a spiritual rebirth, was the huge outpouring of words. People felt that what they said really mattered, that their words would be listened to, that what they wrote down was really important. Words served in some sort as a surrogate for power, allowing meanings to be fixed where in fact they were fluid and contested, and establishing imaginary control over events which in real life were intractable. People who had never lifted a pen since leaving school found themselves engaged in a range of clerical tasks, mastering accounts, writing reports. They also learned to speak and to write in a public voice. The rhetoric of the strike was one of its concrete realities, a material force at every stage in the strike's progress, and at the same time an expression of its aim. To put things down in writing was to give them permanence. Like the machineries of village self-help, or the philanthropies of the Miners' Welfare, it was an act of collective security.

The religious spirit is, if anything, even more apparent in the miners' outside support groups, even though they were formed, in many cases, by long-time political or trade union activists. For Allan Lowe, the Wandsworth dustman whose letters we publish in this volume, the activity of support was as intense as that of the mining villages and, as can be seen by the correspondence, it was maintained at a very high pitch of emotionality. It was also a learning experience involving many of those skills demanded of the first-time activists in the pit villages. For a movement living on a depleted moral capital – the case with the Labour and trade union movement generally, as also of those extra-parliamentary Left groups who briefly sank their differences to organise miners' aid – the strike was a stunning example of all those qualities which, in the Socialist ideal, working people are supposed to incarnate: solidarity, unselfishness, the subordination of the individual to the common good. It is difficult to mistake the note of *gratitude* for the strike which sounds in the statements and printed material – there was a great mass of it – issued by the outside support groups.

Outside support for the miners, organised by Labour parties and trade union branches, often with a large contribution from the extra-parliamentary Left, was undertaken in the name of 'solidarity'. But it owed more to Christian notions of charity, or to a Christian-originated notion of 'good works' than to class-consciousness as classically conceived. It is perhaps indicative of this that its high point was the miners' Christmas appeal, when people gave not necessarily to support the strike, but to give the miners' children a decent and (as it turned out) a memorable Christmas. 'Solidarity', with important exceptions – the Blyth seamen, the Coalville railwaymen, the Fleet Street printers – took the form not of industrial action, but of aid. This aid fed on difference rather than affinity, a sense of miners' otherness: it was a measure of regional inequalities of wealth as much as, or as well as, social or political identification. In the case of the trade unions, it had resemblances to conscience money – the generous financial support given by the transport workers union did not stop the dockers unloading coal at the ports, nor the lorry drivers crossing picket lines; trades councils and union branches gave the miners in many cases a heartfelt support, but they were powerless to move their members, and it is expressive of the philanthropic character of their activity that they called themselves Miners' Support Groups rather than, as in 1926, Councils of Action. The great bulk of the donation to the miners' Christmas appeal came from London and the prosperous south-east, and – though often calling upon family associations with the miners or with mining districts – it seems to have been cross-class in character, more akin to the 1920s adoption of pit villages in the Rhondda by places like Bournemouth and Hampstead, than to solidarity. Here is an account which was sent to us of the experience of door-to-door collecting for the miners in Leamington Spa:

'The response was the first surprise. One in five houses gave (where people were in). They gave money, food or clothes or combinations of these three things – seldom just one. Frequently collectors reported that after a run of frustrating blank calls – empty houses or refusals – Hey Presto! Someone would be waiting in their porch with either food, clothes and/or money in surprisingly good/large amounts, e.g. a plastic bag full of clothes plus a £10 note, or a hamper full of tin food plus a £5 note. . . . It was soon realised that Council House areas were . . . not the best, pretty pointless to canvass in fact. Semi-detached suburban owner-occupiers gave generously – these were the one in five donators. However the £50,000-plus detached houses still turned up trumps, i.e. the typical Tory voter. Less people gave it's true but when they did they made up for the rest and would add such encouraging comments as "The miners must not be defeated", or "Maggie (that woman) must be defeated", or "I come from a mining area/family – Good luck".'

## VIII The imaginary and the real

In politics, as in any other sphere, reality is in the eye of the beholder. Events loom large or small according to the imaginative perceptions brought to bear on them and the lineage to which they can be assigned. This was preeminently true of the miners' strike, where the issues were defined by remembered traumas and every engagement was in some sort a re-enactment of ancient struggles. The general public had to cope with a tide of disinformation. For those who took their cues from the newspapers, the strike was on the point of crumbling almost before it started: every Monday, to follow the screaming headlines about 'record' returns to work, was 'Scargill's Blackest', and it required a strong will not to lose sight of one of the central facts of the strike: namely, that the great majority of those who came out on strike in March 1984 were still on strike twelve months later. For the television viewer, bombarded with nightly pictures of picket-line violence, it was difficult not to conclude that it was the miners who were the aggressors, and that it was only intimidation which prevented a return to work. The theatre of the strike – the relatively short-lived and often highly ritualised confrontations between pickets and police – monopolised attention, while the quieter drama taking place in the pit villages – the subject of this book – was, almost to the end of the strike, hidden from public view.

On the miners' side, too, the imaginary was continually at war with the real. Though engaged in a desperate struggle for survival, they adopted a rhetoric of 'total victory', and in the early months of the strike seemed to have been 'really confident' that they were going to win. The exuberant mass picketing reflected this; so did the willingness to take on the police, despite the manifest inequality of the contestants. The rhetoric of 'victory' corresponded to passionate conviction – the belief, in the early months of the strike, that victory was on the horizon; the determination, later on, not to admit the possibility of defeat. But it confused intentionality with effect as though the miners were bound to win, irrespective of the forces arrayed against them, by sheer act of collective will. It set up a barrier of credibility between the miners and their outside supporters. Most damaging of all, it blocked the reservoirs of public sympathy for the miners' cause, and the historically-derived perception of the miners as the victims of injustice. It was not the strength of the miners which won a hearing for their cause, but self-denial, suffering and the power of endurance. So that by the end of the strike what had seemed at the outset an 'impossibilist' demand – the claim that there were no such things as 'uneconomic pits' – was at the close, for that half of public opinion which had swung round to supporting the strike, a negotiable proposition. The strike thus found itself impaled on a cruel dialectic. In the coalfields it mobilised support by demonstrations of strength; in the country at large it won sympathy only to the degree to which the miners appeared defenceless, and could move to commanding a majority support of public opinion, only in the shadow of defeat.

The conduct of the strike commanded inconceivably more attention, on either side of the dispute, than the causes. For the miners 'scabs' became an even more emotive issue than pit closures, and one moreover that seemed more immediately suspectible to collective action. So did police harassment. On the side of the government and the NCB, the marginal economies the pit closure programme was supposed to effect became entirely secondary to 'management's right to manage' and the defeat of the NUM. So far as the general public were concerned, pickets and police were – until the very closing phases – *the* great issue of the strike. It is unfortunately not possible to blame the media for this, however slanted and sensationalist their treatment of strike incidents. The strike aims, whether conceptualised in terms of retaining 'uneconomic pits' or restoring the *Plan for Coal*, were scarcely developed by the NUM, and to the outside they remained for a long time obscure. Imaginative attention was transfixed by the picket lines. As a result, the emotive but secondary issue of policing enabled the government and the NCB, for the first nine months, to avoid the substantive issues at stake. It was only when, by force of necessity, the picketing died away – the result of both court orders and financial stringency – that the extreme modesty of the miners' demands became apparent.

At the start of the strike, it seems as though reason was on one side, compassion on the other. The NCB entered the conflict with a very well-prepared case, which it had lengthily rehearsed before the Monopolies and Mergers Commission (1982) and very largely endorsed by its report. It also had a vision, or perhaps one might better say, a fantasy, of streamlining coal production and confining future operations to a limited number of super-pits, controlled by robotic technology. The NUM had no such detailed brief, no 'Special Case', the research basis for the strike movement in 1972. Nor yet, at a more general level, an alternative vision to that of the NCB. It was not until six months into the strike that the Coal Board's accountancy procedures were seriously questioned; not until February 1985 that the precariousness of its long-term planning was exposed, in both cases as a result of independent initiatives by outside researchers.

In their critique of the Coal Board's procedures (Report on Coal, February 1985), the Aberystwyth economic historians argued that the 'uneconomic' pits which the Board proposed to close were not, in any conventional sense, loss-makers, but those which were peripheral, both geographically and organisationally, to the NCB's strategy of streamlined, centralised production. The savings on pit closure are marginal compared with the enormous sums assigned to super-pits. But since 'uneconomic' pits are labour-intensive, rather than capital-intensive, they are the only savings which the board can make if it is to meet the government target of self-sufficiency: the easiest thing to economise on is always workers' pay.

The NCB closure programme is based on very short-term calculations of profit and loss, even though the pit closures are irreversible, a permanent depreciation of national assets. It takes no account of fluctuations in international trade. Above all, it takes no account of political arithmetic. If coal becomes obsolete, it is not because it has priced itself out of the market, but because the government – without consulting parliament or the public – has chosen the nuclear option, and because the Central Electricity Generating Board, which at present takes some 70 per cent of British coal, has – since 1979 – called the tune.

The coal strike has helped to focus attention on some of the hidden injuries of social change, which a cost-benefit analysis ought to take into account, even if they are difficult to quantify. The Oxford economist, Andrew Glyn, in his study, *The Economic Case against Pit Closures*, has attempted to make projections for some of them – for example, the retirement pensions which the NCB will have to continue to pay, even when the pit on which it was a charge has disappeared; or the cost to the state of unemployment benefit. He argues it would be cheaper to keep miners working than support them on the dole.

To this one could add the ripple effect on mine-related industries in the coalfield areas; the knock-on job losses; the depreciation of property values (home ownership, interestingly, seems to have been one of the elements *stiffening* the miners' collective will to resist rather than, as had been anticipated, undermining it); the small shopkeepers forced into liquidation; the decay of public transport; the withering-away of public services. Conversely, a cost-benefit analysis might make projections for the infrastructure of the proposed new centres of mining settlement – the schools, medical services, drainage and water supply – or, with government pursuing the nuclear option, the environmental hazard of toxic waste.

Less tangible – though, of course, it has been a central issue at stake in the strike – would be the waste of human resources, the undermining of cultural autonomy. Contraction in the mining industry involves the destruction of a whole heritage of non-transferable skills: the sudden and total loss of control of a working environment which, notwithstanding mechanisation of the coal face, has remained to a very large degree in the hands of the self-regulating work group.

Pit closure involves a destruction of those systems of care to which Mrs Thatcher, in another area of discourse, gestures when she speaks of restoring 'old-fashioned' family values. In what are still, to a remarkable extent, hereditary occupational communities, a change in job location, when younger people move away, destroys the inter-generational solidarity, and two-way system of family care, whose strength (as an alternative welfare state) the strike tested and proved to be the secret of the miners' resilience. A cost-benefit analysis of this might make projections of the likely expense of the probation officers and social workers needed for families 'in trouble' when they are forced to move to the urban disaster of the big city estate.

The closure of 'uneconomic' pits creates 'uneconomic' communities. The pit villages do not disappear but enter into a period of decline whose consequences take a long time to disclose their worst effects. At Glyncorrwg, in the Upper Afan Valley, where the pits closed in the 1960s, it is only now that the full impact is being felt. A 10 per cent sample survey of his patients by Julian Tudor-Hart, a local doctor, shows 48 per cent of men aged between 16 and 64 are without jobs; it is 60 per cent in the 16-24 age group.

What Dr Tudor-Hart calls the 'inverse care law' comes into operation. The greater the need for help, the less it is available. The post office where you can draw your benefit closes. There is no chemist for taking prescriptions. Bus services are cut. There is no longer an earnings level sufficient to support small businesses.

There is no doubt that the miners have been saying, as very often in the past, that they are a 'special case'. They argue that pit closures are irreversible; coal is a primary national resource, the one indigenous source of energy which can be safely developed, and its short-term market weakness is something which the nation should bear for the sake of its future. Implicitly they argue for their jobs as *hereditary* – a birthright which they demand the power to bequeath to their posterity. They are arguing for the right to stay put, and to keep work and home together, in an epoch when a large part of the working population, manual as well as professional, has accepted commuting and mobility (what the miners call a 'gypsy-like' life) as normal existence.

The miners have been demanding privileges and rights which others have abandoned or do not claim. Yet the issues raised by the strike are not sectional issues. They have to do with energy policy, job location, industrial democracy, governmental account-ability, the value attached to continuity and belonging, the work ethic, regional impoverishment, youth unemployment, local rights – and the double standards which run through our public life. They will remain with us, given a new poignancy and urgency by the strike.

Coal is no more obsolete than cotton was when Lancashire went under the hammer, or iron shipbuilding when Palmer's yard at Jarrow closed, or bricklaying in the days (happily now past) when systems building and tower blocks were the rage. Anything involving heat or energy can be an efficient coal burner. Technology may yet revolutionise coal transport, and allow liquefied coal to be pumped through the pipelines like oil. The profitability of pits is not a fixed quantity, but is determined by investment and even more by government energy policy. The coal strike took place in the context of a relentless modernisation and restructuring of industry and employment. But it may be that the bitterness and tenacity of the miners' resistance may alert us not only to the hidden injuries of social change, but also to the alternative ways in which modernisation can be carried out. The strategies of the NCB – centralisation of decision-making, concentration of production, streamlining and rationalisation – are, in certain respects, a throwback to the Wilsonian modernis-ations of the 1960s. They run counter to one of the main tendencies of high-tech industry which makes possible more adaptable technologies, and a dispersal rather than a concentration of work.

In recent years, even big corporations have been forced to acknowledge that the work-place cannot be divorced from the hinterland of related dependencies, the living environment as a whole. The company is responsible not only for those it employs directly, but also for those indirectly affected by its activity. Yet at a time of mass unemployment, instead of developing and adapting technology for the communities where people already live and work, the NCB's entire effort is directed at stripping the richest veins of coal in the most accessible areas, regardless of social cost. A mushroom settlement at Selby is no compensation for chronic distress in the Rhondda valley or run-down villages in Fife. The NCB is engaging in a crude form of asset-stripping. To treat a whole industry as though it were an accountancy exercise – and to sacrifice whole districts on the altar of gigantism – is not hard-headed modernism but a regression to outmoded fantasies: *it is a planning disaster*.

The pit villages threatened with extinction by the Coal Board are not an atavistic survival from the past. Merging a country setting with urban sociability, uniting work and home, they are in many ways a model of how we might live in the future. With the spread of home-based new technologies, they are a closer approximation to that future than the dormitory suburb. In the use of time, they are a great deal more efficient than those commuterlands whose inhabitants spend three or four hours every day in the journey to work.

It was the contention of the government that there was something un-English or un-British about the strike, that the miners, at any rate those who supported the strike, were destructive, and that their leader was daemonic – a Lenin, a Stalin or a Hitler – at the very least a revolutionary syndicalist, bent on the seizure of power. Readers of this book may be struck, rather, by the extremely limited nature of the miners' demands, and the local, even familial, character of their action. They will encounter anxieties and preoccupations which are the common currency of contemporary life – the difficulties of meeting mortgage payments, or of providing clothes and treats for the children – even if the circumstances in which they appear are exceptional. They might consider the strike not as a conspiracy against the state, or as a threat to public order, but rather as a sustained exercise in collective discipline, and of that capacity for 'community self-help' which the Prince of Wales is currently canvassing as an answer to the disasters of the inner city. The reader will find plenty of examples of that well-known British capacity for 'muddling through' – not least, it may be, on the part of the strike's leaders, and also of the ability to extract enjoyment from apparently unpropitious circumstances (for reasons of space we have omitted an account of the vernacular use of spaghetti when lorryloads of it (sent by the strike's Italian supporters) arrived in Yorkshire). In spite of the disappointments of the strike itself – and, subsequently, a deepening bitterness – the picture that comes from the villages in the year of the strike itself is one of hope, creativity and enjoyment. If communities of such vitality can be crushed, it is not only the inhabitants but the country as a whole that will be impoverished. Having let the planners loose in the inner city twenty years ago, and learnt too late of the environmental and human costs, perhaps they can now be stopped before they wreak havoc on the remaining industrial villages. It might in the end be cheaper.

# PRELUDES

## Best suit, the Afan Valley in 1969
Barbara Walters

Babs Walters lives in the remote pit village of Glyncorrwg in the Afan Valley, South Wales. During the miners' strike she helped to organise a small women's support group for the fifty-six miners in the village, who work at St John's Colliery, five miles away. Her husband and father were miners. The following piece was written after an unsuccessful campaign to keep the Glyncorrwg pit alive.

1 Barbara Walters

I remember the familiar smell of pit clothes. I recall clothes warming, spread around an open coal grate, always ready for the wearer. A grate polished with black lead until each raw, rough, red brick was a smooth, gleaming, velvet black. The proud mantelshelf displayed its wealth of brass in every space of its darkest corners. A coal fire told of a worker's victory and for a time at any rate we allowed ourselves to forget that the coal glowing in that healthy fire had tightened young, healthy lungs. The dust lay in hiding behind a tall brass ash pan out of sight. My mother, always a slave to her men and the pit, washed and patched these clothes regularly, and just as often scrubbed the backs of daily washed bodies. 'My best suit' my father would announce, his eyes looking for me. He knew

I hated these clothes, dulling the grate, dirtying the hearth. 'Best suit' he'd say, preparing to go to work, 'what do you say, Peg? For with these' and he paused so that his words could take effect, 'without these clothes, there wouldn't be any others.'

Idle trams stand scattered around the pithead, some already giving life to tufts of green grass. Scores of others, ugly and empty, lay upside-down one above the other on a roadway that had once housed people in neat rows of uniform houses which had been placed as near as they dared to the pit surface, and not more than a yard away from a black river. High on a man-made platform the black, stencilled shape of a wheel stood pathetically still, as if waiting for someone or something.

No lone horse strained at the chains of a tram, no shout of 'lookin' for a start, gel?', no ageless whistle, no voices hiding behind black faces, 'down here gel, there's plenty of room'. I began to remember much of what I had forgotten a very long time ago, about boys who had left school at 14 as I had, who had put on those heavy working boots and even wore them after work, 'breaking them in' they would say. Small-framed little boys who felt ten feet tall after their first shift at the coal face, boys who spat with gusto their first dust-filled spittle through pursed lips, the lips that managed to hold on to a stump of woodbine even as they talked. All this was part of a first day, when they deliberately left their tell-tale eyes unwashed and slashed back their hair, their symbols of manhood. So it was that the nearer I came to the coal tips that had stopped growing, the harder it was to swallow my Celtic emotions.

I could have sworn that I heard the sound of Welsh English being spoken, that I could see near and dear faces peeling away from the inner darkness of a pit cage, their hobnailed boots greeting the surface of the ground and sending sparks into the morning air. They were familiar-faced ghosts hitting the pit's daylight with talk, talking about things that could have been or should have been with such earnestness, telling the world of their profound convictions, even if those convictions were sometimes centred around a game of rugby football. Pit talk. So much wit. So much craft. Thomas lost half his ear in an accident. Searching for his half ear in the coal dust, the ambulance man was offered all kinds of substitutes including a chew of tobacco. But I, in my imagination, saw Tom holding his bleeding ear as they laughed and joked while searching. It was only with time that I realised that this was very much part of the closeness between pit and village, and this kind of attitude they had was developed with experience and wisdom. So Thomas did not become Tom ear-and-a-half; it was decided with a show of hands that 'eighteen months' would be a far better name indeed. Voices – voices of men who loved to sing, enjoying their own sounds, lending words to any tune at any time to suit almost any occasion. 'Now then boys' they began,

'Empty box. Empty belly.
Empty tram. No coal ready.'

Every note of music would be given its full value, every word an added
meaning, each man in his own persuasive tongue calling on his inner
man, pleading for his voice high or low to reach its own forte, and then
with prize-winning awareness the rendering ended,

'I can hear the haulier coming
Tell him full next time.'

Now, when the pit's hooter no longer speaks, no early morning buses
take men to work, no steam engines disturb children asleep, we no
longer waste our time making grates a gleaming, velvet black. 'All
this is gone in the name of progress' they said. We still have one
factory. I wonder if anything will happen to that, and if so what kinds of
words will be used to describe that kind of progress. The sounds of our
village are changing but I am suspicious of what may come and of what
may remain. Our black river seems to be louder as if it is announcing
that it is going to get cleaner every day, and birds sing as if each day is
Sunday. Why should I feel so sad at the sight of this uninhabited pit?
Can one honestly cry for what one had dreaded to live with?

By climbing a rough, stony slope just a short way from the pit's
surface one can walk along a mountain road and view at close hand the
progress of forest greenery. The straight lengths of trees are changing
the shape and colour of our mountains. I watched a butterfly darting in
and out of long spiky grass which hid wild whinberry bushes and almost
obscured tiny trees. I followed a sheep path that I knew miraculously
found its way from one village to another, and here, cutting into the
mountain, were the blue scars of old level workings. Here, too, were
old farm dwellings that held memories of a farmer's wife's white
aprons; her six foot sons; warm milk and brown eggs. There were old
stables that had sheltered pit ponies, well-fed ponies sought after by
children on Sunday walks. How good to remember that only one horse
had remained to strain on those cruel chains when our pit closed. The
mountains played tricks with my mind's eye as their curves danced in
and out of the sky's edge. How small one is made to feel as mountains
soar away from each other only to meet once more. Here was a feeling
of completeness. Here to me was home. I wandered back into the fold
of the mountains, back to where man had formed huge slabs of
concrete into buildings, now empty. The silence disturbed me. A
massive framework of steel hung over a railway line. Under this
fearsome, grimy shelter that sealed off the light of day was a railway
wagon, resting. Once it had been destined to be filled with shining
clean coal. Now the wagon, like the buckets that hung overhead, no
longer waited to turn to be filled. Those huge iron buckets had carried
pit muck from the surface of the pit to the highest point of the

mountain to overflow into unsuspecting young streams. A silent pithead with not a wheel turning; it should have been a hive of activity. Now, it was like a gaunt toy octopus, all its tentacles immobile as if someone had forgotten the key. Amid the debris were twisted steel bars and bold, heavy chains. They lay there waiting to be salvaged like cruel torture instruments of some medieval age, but in fact they were implements of the twentieth century that had failed to tame the coal faces beneath the earth. How many young lives had been wasted in the taming of coal faces was a memory one avoided. 'Some day perhaps,' I spoke to my ghosts, 'a polite historian in his remote world searching for truth will say what honest fools we've been.' My mind drifted around unused forest roads — men on the moon — briefcases with no plans for our tomorrow's children — what to have for dinner tomorrow and so on as I went home. The big wheel seemed to be seeking answers in the sky, but I was *glad* the coal tips had stopped growing. My small son walking beside me asked, 'What's the matter mam?'. 'Nothing,' I answered, 'a bit of coal dust has gone in my eye.' If the ghosts of the past were watching, they had every right to mock me as I left behind that reservoir of nothingness.


# Horden Colliery, Co. Durham*

Huw Beynon, Ray Hudson and Dave Sadler


## Horden and the background to closure

The Horden Colliery is situated in the south east of the Durham coalfield. This was the last part of the coalfield to be developed. While most of the pits in Durham were sunk in the mid-nineteenth century, Horden first drew coals in 1904 and it is one of the few pits in the North East sunk in this century. Blackhall, to the South, and Easington and Dawdon to the North were sunk at the same time. In the inter-war period Horden, under the control of the Horden Coal Company, emerged as the largest mine in Britain with three shafts and an extensive surface operation involving a washery, brick works and coke works.

Nor is this ascendance merely an historic one. It was in 1960 that Lord Robens, newly appointed head of the National Coal Board,

---

* This chapter is based upon a report which was prepared for the Durham mining unions at the Work and Employment Research Unit at the University of Durham in 1985.

travelled to the North East and announced, on a boring ship off Blackhall, that there was enough coal beneath the North Sea to guarantee a future of over a hundred years for the East Coast mines. This claim was substantiated in 1965 in an enthusiastic report in the NCB's house journal *Coal News*:

> Vigorous North Sea exploration by an NCB boring tower over the last seven years has revealed that at least 550 million tonnes of workable coal lies in the undersea coalfield now being 'attacked' by Durham coastal collieries. It will be enough to keep 20,000 miners who work in these pits working for many years to come.

The article commented that reserves in the areas of the Blackhall-Horden-Easington collieries totalled 200 million tonnes. In 1974, under the newly agreed Plan for Coal, this complex of pits was pointed out as being central to the NCB's investment strategy for the area. Horden was a key pit in the plan to deliver almost 2 million tonnes a year of blended coking coal to the new British Steel Corporation complex on Teesside. At that time the future of coal mining in Horden, and South East Durham generally, seemed secure.

This view was supported forcefully in 1977 when the NCB launched a recruiting drive in the area, focusing upon the Horden and Dawdon collieries. The campaign was aimed at recruiting 'experienced miners' who had left the industry in despair in the 1960s. 'Come back into the top league' read the copy; 'Come back to Big Pay' it continued; 'come back to a secure job'. The coal industry, and Horden Colliery, was totally secure, 'the demand for coal is greater than ever'. This was the message then. And it convinced people. Horden was not a 'Victorian hole in the ground', it was a modern super-pit. While pits in the West might continue to close because of exhausted or limited reserves, Horden on the East Coast was a pit with a future. It was a pit which attracted new recruits; it was a 'receiving colliery' for transferred men from closed pits in the West of Durham. It was a pit with a future. This was the view developed by the NCB in the area. It was a view which was generally accepted by the people who worked at Horden and lived in the village; it was accepted by their trade union representatives.

In 1985, however, after the strike, the NCB announced the closure of the colliery. Horden – in NCB's 'newspeak' – was to be a 'manpower reservoir', a function it would share with Bates Colliery in Northumberland. In these pits 'the men would be given the opportunity to transfer to the high-priority pits to facilitate redundancy on a one-for-one basis'. There would be 'no compulsory redundancy' but, in the words of the Area Director, pits like Horden and Bates were a 'cancer' which needed to be cut out if the area was to survive.

This is quite a change. And in truth it does not come completely out of the blue. The signs were there well before the strike began. People look back ruefully to the closure of the Blackhall Colliery in 1981. This pit had been linked to Horden, and it had also been promised a long life. There the lodge committee had cooperated as the NCB asked for a run-down in manpower to improve efficiency. Barry Chambers remembers how:

> 'On the day that the last of the men involved in the run-down were transferred we were called in to Team Valley to be told that the pit was going to close – on the very last day!'

In his view, the Board played a 'dirty trick' on the Blackhall men and they then proceeded to play the same trick on the Horden men. 'It's like a domino effect along the coast. They closed Blackhall then moved the men to Horden increasing their costs and putting the burden of the pumping costs on to them as well.'

In spite of assurances to the contrary, it had been clear for some time that Horden had something less than 'super-pit' status in the overall plans of the Area board. And there were a number of reasons for this. To begin with, as we shall see, the collieries of the south-east of Durham experienced greater geological problems than had been anticipated by the Board, and these problems were exacerbated by the increasing amounts of water which seeped into the pit from the limestone which overlays the coal seams in Durham. This water problem increased in scale as the NCB closed down pits and pumping stations across the region. The pattern of run-down in the County (*twenty* pits were closed in the 1970s) increased the pressure – of water and costs – in the pits that remained open. This pressure became all the more intense after the collapse of the coking coal market in the later 1970s. Like the geology, steel production never lived up to the NCB's plans, and with the change in BSC's ordering policies (away from Durham coal and toward imports) a crisis was created for domestic coking coal production. This crisis revealed itself in Durham in the closure of Blackhall and the subsequent closures of Boldon, Eden, Houghton, South Hetton and East Hetton. Pit after pit; each of them a coking coal producer; each of them closed for reasons of 'safety' or 'exhaustion'. Read against this list, the closure of Horden (the last major coking coal producer in the area) seems entirely predictable. And it is this which rankles most with the men who work at the pit, their trade union representatives and their families.

As the crisis developed, the men at Horden asked questions. What was the future for the pit? Was there a 'hit list' and were they on it? How important were the losses they were making? Didn't the closure of Blackhall and the transfer of men to Horden make their pit vulnerable? To these questions they received repeated assurances to the effect that the pit was losing money but it was 'within budget'; that there was no 'hit list'; that there were no plans to close Horden in the foreseeable future. The people at Horden look back on these words with some bitterness.

Their claim is a simple one: the NCB tells lies as a matter of course and their management have behaved in a deceitful manner towards the workers' representatives and the agreed consultative machinery. Many men who work in the pits are now convinced that the NCB's main area of expertise is in colliery closures. To this task they have developed numerous engineering, economic and psychological skills. One man put it like this: 'I'm convinced there's planners up there not planning to mine coal but planning for to close pits.'

To 'outsiders' this might appear an overtly cynical or exaggerated view. At Horden men repeatedly point back to particular incidents which lead to this conclusion, to agreements made with the Board and to statements made by the Board's representatives. These claims – made by reasonable men who would describe themselves as 'moderate' politically – are disturbing ones, which require investigation. In themselves they raise important questions in relation to the manner of the operation of one of the country's major state-owned industries.

## Consultation

In October 1981 the year that Blackham closed, the NCB announced its intention to withdraw Horden from the area of the pit known as Zone 6 where faces had been developed in the E seam. At the meeting of the pit's consultative committee convened on 1 October 1981, Tom Callan, General Secretary of the Durham Miners' Association, expressed his complete surprise at the decision. Zone 6 was seen as the future of Horden Colliery as the source of bulk output of coking coal. Already rumours were circulating around the village to the effect that the pit's future was in doubt. Gordon Proctor, the NCB's D District Production Manager, was at pains to alleviate these fears. He explained the problems encountered in Zone 6 (two faces, E80 and E81, had encountered water problems) but added that:

'The colliery was certainly recording a financial loss and it was imperative to increase production . . . production of the G seam (in Zone 6) could not be expected before 1983, and in the mean time a concentrated effort will be made in the seams currently worked to raise output to 3,000 tonnes per day. There were sufficient reserves in these seams to employ current manpower for a further ten years. There was no plan to reduce manpower.'

The trade unions were unhappy with the situation and expressed the view that decisions were certainly being taken by the NCB without prior consultation, and that these decisions deeply affected the future of the colliery. Nevertheless, the trade union representatives were reassured by the statements of Mr Proctor, and also his reaffirmation of the fact that the reserves in the G seam in Zone 6 were clearly 'in the Horden Colliery take'. Also the statements to the effect that, although Easington Colliery *could* work the G seam 'there was no plan for Easington to work any section of this seam in the next fifteen years', and that 'subject to the "E" seam being left sterile' there was every hope that the G seam would be dry and workable from Horden. Their confidence in the future of the pit was bolstered further by the assertive words of Mr Atkinson, the Area Industrial relations Officer. The rumours and worries, he said, were based upon a misinterpretation of events: 'There were reserves for ten years' production with the present level of manpower. . . .' Worries about the pumping costs increased by Blackhall's closure were also unfounded: 'this had been discussed at Area level and full cognizance taken in both budgets and appraisal of results'.

In response to the worries expressed by the General Secretary of the Durham Mechanics – Mr Tom Bartle – Mr Atkinson could not have been plainer. While no one had guaranteed manpower levels – because no one could

> 'The production manager had said that there were existing reserves for ten years with the current level of manpower. There was no plan to run down manpower at this colliery, and nothing had been said about job losses in the next ten years – the production manager had said that if a wrong decision was made now this could result in job losses in the future.'

He added, however, that in spite of the union's protestations and suggestions, 'the subject for discussion is a management decision'.

Five months later, at another special meeting of the pit's consultative committee held on 5 March 1982, the Board reported back on these developments, with a Five-Year Working Plan for the colliery which was presented on a wall board. Mining would continue at this pit in *four* seams over the period. Beneath the overwhelming optimism of this plan, a worry was expressed about the future of the Zone 6 reserves. These events were to become the subject of detailed boundary changes, conducted by the Board without consultation with the trade unions. In 1982 it was clear that Easington Colliery had been allowed to work the G seam in the Zone 6 area.

With relation to this development, the Board expressed a general reluctance for Horden workings to enter the Zone 6 area above the workings of the neighbouring Easington Colliery. The Board pressed the view that Easington Colliery had not to be endangered and pointed to the need for 'information obtained from developments and boreholes over the next 3-3½ years'. While the union representatives at Horden expressed impatience over these delays, the Board's Five-Year Plan seemed to offer an assurance that time was on their side and that there were extensive reserves available before Zone 6 was mined. So, while the union representatives pressed with questions on Zone 6, management made reassuring noises about Zone 5. This area of coal had been ceded to Horden from the reserves of Easington Colliery as a token exchange for the Zone 6 take. Easington had experienced enormous difficulties in mining in the Zone 5 area. At Horden, however, the Board seemed optimistic and pointed to the possibility that 'the drift currently being driven from seam "E" to seam "G" in Zone 5 could continue to the seam "J"' thereby offering a serious expansion in the pit's reserves and more time before Zone 6 reserves were explored. Even without this, the pit had a Five-Year Plan and the minutes of the meeting record how Mr Proctor reassured the union representatives with the opinion that:

'there were reserves from existing seams for five years plus – they afforded ample time to get the information required and to decide what seams are to be worked [in Zone 6].'

When pressed on this by Mr Tom Bartle of the Durham Mechanics who suggested that 'the closure of Horden may be imminent', Mr Proctor was categorical in his denial, and Mr Atkinson added that:

'there was no threat of an early closure, although eventually all pits must close. What was being said was that care had to be exercised as Easington Colliery had the greater resources and therefore had a longer production life.'

The worries expressed by Mr Bartle, however, extended to the other union representatives present. Everyone had a sense that the Board was not being straightforward, or even honest. The assurances seemed too pat. Lodge officials knew that the men in the pit were extremely worried. Stan Langley of the Durham Miners' Association felt that the Board was: 'sowing seeds of doubt in the minds of the work-force by means of propaganda to

precondition them to the possible closure of the mine'. Further-
more, Tom Callan was sure that 'economics had a large part to
play in the current situation'. This view – that the losses
attributed to the Horden pit were the essential background to all
the discussion of the pit's reserves – was supported by certain
references to markets and reinforced by the Board's insistence on
the need to shed manpower. The Five-Year Plan had, as its
immediate aim:

> to boost output from 2,500 tonnes a day to 3,000 tonnes per day.
> This would reduce the envisaged financial loss by £5 million.
> Manpower for the Horden/Blackhall mine would reduce (by redun-
> dancies and natural wastage) to 2,000 in the next eighteen months
> thus further reducing the loss.

The Board added that: 'If manpower saving schemes were
introduced then further reductions could be obtained – *a
reduction of 100 men would result in the loss being reduced by £1
million.*' (Our emphasis.) Within all this, though, the Board's
representatives were bland in their assurances. While all pits
closed at some point Horden's early demise was not being
planned. All that was required was time to investigate further the
strata in the Zone 6 area.

This investigation, with water problems in the G seam,
eventually led the NCB to announce its decision (made some
months earlier) to cede the whole of the Zone 6 reserves to the
Easington Colliery, thereby severely limiting Horden's future
development. As Tom McGee, the union's engineer, stated in
June 1983 when he investigated the decision:

> 'The Coal Board believed that there could be undue risks to
> Easington Colliery associated with the Permian water if the High
> Main (E) remained intact and the Yard Seam (G) was exploited. This
> appraisal by the Board induced them to change the boundary line
> between Horden and Easington Collieries. . . . This change meant
> that 3.6 million tonnes of High Main reserves and 3.3 million tonnes
> of Yard Seam reserves would be removed from earlier estimates of
> Horden Colliery future reserves.'

While Mr McGee accepted the Board's view that 'Easington
Colliery takes priority over Horden', he was unconvinced that
'leaving the High Main intact and working the Yard Seam after
fully exploiting the Low Main from Easington would present an
unacceptable risk to Easington Colliery'.

McGee's point was clear. There was no need to redraw the
boundaries. No colliery would proceed into Zone 6 until such
time that Easington had completed the extraction of coal from
the Low Main seam. However, this was likely to take between

ten and fifteen years. Horden *could* enter Zone 6 at that time. If Mr Proctor's assessment of the other reserves in the colliery was accurate, it was simply a question of planning and not one which required boundary revision.

This, however, was not to be. Once again, it seemed, the Board's assessments were not correct. The situation was spelled out to the union representatives at a consultative committee just three months later on 14 September 1983. By this time the situation had become 'so severe' that the Area Chief Mining Engineer, Mr Burn, 'had not yet made any recommendations to the Area Board'. He intended to read a 'prepared statement' with a view to receiving 'constructive comments'. The tone was very different from two years ago.

The pit was losing money; pumping costs were £3.5 million per annum; results in the E seam were 'extremely disappointing': in the face of this there was only one 'realistic plan', and this looked different from the Five-Year Plan discussed earlier:

> There had been good faces in 'F' and 'G' seams. . . . The best plan would be to concentrate production on four faces in these seams with associated developments – this should produce 3,000 tonnes per day. However, to arrive at/near this break-even figure on this tonnage would entail reducing manpower to 1,200.

Mr Burn was clear that

> 'implementation of plans must be carried out as quickly as possible . . . there must be evidence in this financial year that attempts were being made to reduce losses . . . no colliery had a guaranteed life . . . the smaller the number of men employed the longer the life of the colliery.'

This 'new realism' had clearly affected Mr McGee who said that while he would

> 'like to say that all reserves would be worked, in the present economic climate this was not possible – elsewhere in the country, collieries were being closed. Today the Board had given an indication of the road to follow to attain a near-viable situation.'

The unions agreed. The Mechanics Lodge Secretary, Derek Gray, discussed the mechanisms of reducing the manpower by 500. In reply to his questioning the Area Chief Mining Engineer reiterated that 'the acceptable figure would be attained if the output was raised to 3,000 tonnes per day, and manpower reduced to 1,200 men'. He added: 'if a positive proposal was not submitted in the short term then there was the distinct possibility of one being enforced from other channels.'

The plan was accepted. Horden went through a manpower

rundown. There followed a period of quite intense discussion of problems over the organisation of production in the pit. In this it was clear that the men and their union representative were intent upon achieving the 3,000 tonne target set by the Board. They had agreed to cooperate with Mr Burn's arithmetic and with it the prospect of a secure future. However, Mr McGee's appraisal of the pit's reserves signalled a major problem: 'It is likely that the G seam in the area currently being worked will be exhausted in about five years. The F seam also has about five years' life on the area currently being worked.' Cost-effective the pit may be. But without a settlement on Zone 6 it would be cost-ineffective and short-lived. This was the situation in early 1984; before the strike which affected the Durham coalfield for a twelve-month period.

# The Doncaster Panel, 1969-84

Dave Douglass

Dave Douglass is pit delegate at Hatfield Main Colliery and a member of the Yorkshire Executive of the NUM. He is joint author of *Miners, Quarrymen and Saltworkers* and author of *A Miner's Life*. The questioner is Guy Boanas.

2 Dave Douglass

Panels exist for the four areas of Yorkshire – North Yorkshire, Barnsley, South Yorkshire and Doncaster. As to the focus of the panels – I think they started either in the War or just after the War and they were very strictly governed to be simply a place where the executive members of the NUM could report back to the branches on the subject of the executive meeting – and that was all. Anything other than that is totally unconstitutional and in fact there's no place for the panels in terms of the official structure of the Union.

The panels are composed of the branch delegate from each branch, usually the secretary and some-times a committee member or another branch official. Usually not more than four people from each branch attended a meeting.

The panel meets after every executive meeting unless there's an emergency meeting. A branch can call an emergency panel meeting if it gets the signature of another two branches.

*Q   Can you tell us how picketing worked before the recent strike?*
D   The general pattern of events is if a colliery has a local dispute and goes on strike then the custom is that they have to be on strike for a fortnight before it comes and asks for support from another pit that's not involved. The reason for this being that if they're going to settle a week after you've come on strike then you've all lost that money for nowt. So they have to be serious. What usually happens, however, is that pickets start flying out all over the place straightaway – before you get the chance to talk about it. Normally they have an emergency panel meeting and they report back to emergency branch meetings and then take a mandate from that.

*Q   Why are the panels important?*
D   What the panels became – particularly in Doncaster – is a kind of a junior miners' council with representation based on just one region and the panels would quite unorthodxly discuss matters of mutual concern, joint policies, formulate joint action so that they could vote as a block and organise their own policies before they went to the Yorkshire area and to the council – so, for example, the Doncaster area would have a block way that all the branches would vote at the same time.

They particularly came into their own in the 1960s. The Yorkshire area at that time was dominated by right-wing leadership and the panels were used more or less as an alternative assembly and through the 1969 unofficial movement they were used as the organisation for the running of that strike – the 1969 strike. There was a general inertia in the Union through the 1950s, through the period of the oil boom and the 'nuclear era'. Coal was an anachronism and really it was just a matter of hanging on until you got your pension and the Union didn't have any will to fight. They were really getting out of touch with the rank-and-file – although the ordinary rank-and-file member also believed this gospel of doom for a long time – in fact until the unofficial movement launched the big strike in 1969 and that gave people the confidence and gave them some fight.

*Q   How did the 1969 movement begin?*
D   It's hard to know where it all came from. Many people have pointed to the signing of the power-loading agreement which made a national day wage as opposed to the local bonus schemes and led to a disparity of wages with, say, Kent earning 92 shillings a shift and Nottingham earning about 90 bob a shift until you got to Durham where they got 74 shillings working on the coal face – in all something like 83 and threepence for working in the Yorkshire coalfield. With the signing of

the National Power-Loading agreement the top earners stood still while the bottom earners caught up. What it meant was that a man working on the coal face in Nottingham, Scotland, Durham, wherever, earned the same money for his effort which then gave them a national identity and made them realise that whatever progress was going to be made had to be made through the national union.

In terms of actually putting teeth into it – well, there were lots of other disputes. There were unofficial disputes in Yorkshire, the most important one being about the fall back rate – if a collier when he went to work and there was no job for him on the coal face, if he had to work elsewhere, his money it dropped down. Now this caused a whole series of unofficial strikes in Yorkshire.

*Q   How were the panels involved in this?*
*D*   Well the panels more or less coordinated the actions. Once a strike started at one pit or another then the pit would come to the panel to request support for its action.

In the 1960s there was a general feeling that we had to go for a wage rise or the surfacemen's hours or whatever. When the strike occurred – it occurred around the question of surfacemen's hours – the surfacemen were still working the hours that had been imposed on them after the 1926 defeat, whereas the hours for underground workers had come down to seven and a quarter hours. And when the strike happened, it happened around that issue. Now the strike didn't exactly succeed outright but what it did do, seeing it was in the middle of wage negotiation, was to make the Coal Board give the biggest wage rise, percentage wise, they'd ever given since long before the War. Previous to that time they'd gone in for pennies and ha'pennies and stuff like that.

With that victory, plus the constitutional victories which were won within the Union to change the rules of the Union from a two-thirds voting majority to a 55 per cent majority to declare strike action – it sort of paved the way for the activities that happened in 1972 and 1974.

All of these methods of spreading the strike reached a peak in the mass picketing of 1972 – the picket line was still sacrosanct in those days. The whole perspective was the domino effect. We expected the strike to spread like that in 1984.

*Q   I'm just wondering to what extent the Doncaster Panel becomes involved in these quick picketing actions before authorisation from the area?*
*D*   It usually happens first. If it's a local issue, one of our agreements, the first thing you do is to seek the support of the Doncaster area.

*Q   Did the panels take any early action over the closure of Cortonwood?*
*D*   Before the Yorkshire area decided to support them? What they did was to put it on the agenda as to what action to take on Cortonwood. Now there were several other items on the agenda. There were a

number of other pits on strike. Because whenever you have an overtime ban it's only a matter of time before it leads to a strike. Because there's all sorts of frictions start happening with an overtime ban and demarcations as to what's ordinary working time and what isn't. And it inevitably leads to management sending people home. And once they've been sent home, there's a natural instinct to try and spread that strike once you're on strike. So there were three or four irons in the fire at that particular time. Cortonwood was only one of them. So I came back and reported at a mass meeting at my branch as to what action to take. And I was told that we had to support Cortonwood, support the workshop which was threatened with privatisation, but not support two of the others, that we thought were irrelevant. One was over snap time. We thought that was irrelevant and would even lead to premature action. In fact the whole thing was premature action, because we wanted the overtime ban to continue really until the following Christmas. That was the object of the exercise. And that's why the Board knew it had to act. We were getting to a point where the scales were starting to tip, as the fuel got used up. Now they had to take action otherwise they couldn't string it out.

There had been a major dispute before that over Dodworth. Over the question of a man that was sacked for hitting an offical in the grounds. And that strike stopped Barnsley, half of North Yorkshire, and was spreading like wildfire. But it was one of these situations where the Council delegates were dead against the strike, and to my view, the men were all in favour of it. And I supported that, but my pit wasn't on strike; the pickets were coming to my pit. But the delegate from Dodworth was against it, and it was his pit on strike. Now I thought it was just the shot in the arm that we needed, but other peole thought 'No, no, it's premature, you're jumping the gun. . . .' People were that frustrated you see, because we'd lost the bloody Lewis Merthyr vote and we were all ready to go into action over that. The first thing that come along were this bloke's case which happened to be a good case, actually. But if it were a lousy one they still would have had a go to show the management they were still ready to fight.

# 2 RUMOURS

## Interviews, South Wales miners at Porthcawl, July 1983

These interviews are a small selection from a series of video-tapes made by Television History Workshop at a holiday caravan site, during the Miners' Fortnight, July 1983. The film, though completed then, was not shown on Channel 4 until October 1984 – long after the start of the strike.

### Arthur Belmont, retired miner, Clydach Vale, Rhondda

*Q   What do you think about the possibility of a major confrontation after Ian MacGregor comes in?*
AB   Well I hope it don't come. As I said it's not the right time now and this government knows it, but I'm afraid confrontation will come between Scargill and MacGregor. It's Maggie's idea of putting two bulls together to fight. But if common sense is used I don't think there will be a strike. I hope not, because if they do that will gain them the whip to slice the pits you see. Suppose it's up to the young men working there now not to me, I hope they take some bit of advice and see to it – but don't come out on strike because they've got good wages today, good wages today and conditions are better.

### Ivor Evans, Cwm Colliery

*Q   Why are they closing the coke works at the colliery?*
IE   Well, same reasons they give in any sort of pit. No sale for the coke and I know I have seen them myself and a tremendous amount of other people have seen them, twenty-five tonners coming in, that's twenty-five tonne wagons by the way, full of coke and a stream of wagons day in day out, afternoon, morning they come in continuously right into the coke works and out, and now they tell you they're shutting the coke

works which to me, there's more there than what meets the eye. It's not, in my opinion, a sale of no coke there's something else brewing there which hasn't come out in the open yet. . . . The men that's working there – and they'll tell you it's the finest coke that's in Great Britain. So to say they can't sell the coke is all lies. As simple as that. They're short of repairers now. Colliers can't get on the coal. There's plenty of coal. They say the machines would break, right, conveyor pans, chains, belts, now that's not the miners' fault. Its the management's fault, that's their trouble. Yet the colliers get the fault, you read the papers. It's the management's place to see all the maintenance, everything else should be done on off shifts.

*Q What do you think has been the impact of things like the incentive bonus scheme on the coal industry?*

*IE* A wash out. Now we are a very good pit as far as safety and accidents is concerned. Men in headings and drivages, those men have got to go like lunatics to try and earn a bonus. Some are very keen on safety, others will say 'Well, look, we'll get a bit more' – get a bit more coal until eventually there's accidents happening owing to the incentive bonus.

*Q Has the incentive bonus scheme had any other effect?*

*IE* The boys on the surface they works as hard as anybody underground. They've got to fill the timber, they've got to handle all the muck – they does most of the donkey work, the surface boys, and they only get 40 per cent of the bonus. So if you get (underground) £40 a week bonus those boys on the surface are working – and I've seen them, they're working really hard – they'll get about £10. It's wrong. So the boys on the surface – and they're all disabled miners that have come up from underground, and how some of them does it I don't know – they'll get £10, and you'll get £50 and £60.

*Q What are the bonuses like in Wales compared with other pits like up in Yorkshire?*

*IE* Well their bonuses are fantastic en it? You get the miners' coal book which is out once a month, it'll give you the records of the bonuses of all the collieries. They're all different.

*Q Why do you think Ian MacGregor has been appointed Chairman of the NCB?*

*IE* Well – what did Scargill say – he's the hatchet man. Look what he's done to the steel works. . . . The *South Wales Echo*, they'll tell you, they're going to cut half of South Wales in the next five or ten years.

*Q Do you think the men will move to other pits? With closures?*

*IE* No. No. Men that's 50 or over they won't go. They'll take the pittance and that's all they're having, this redundancy money. You read the papers they're getting £20,000, £22,000 redundancy money. I read one paper, over £42,000 redundancy money. The most they've ever had in a colliery is £8,000 and lucky for having that, and that's the most they've had and they've been put redundant. . . . My own brother, he

## The Miners' fight is your fight

THE MINERS are fighting for all of us. In South Wales 100,000 men, women and children depend directly or indirectly on the coal industry for their livelihoods.

Without its pits South Wales will be devastated. Engineering factories will close, road haulage firms collapse, railways will be torn up and docks filled in.

The markets for steel, gas and electricity will shrink. Unemployment will ravage the steel mills, gas depots and power stations.

## We need Welsh coal

Without its industry, South Wales will be unable to pay for public services. Hospitals, clinics, schools, transport and housing will all deteriorate even more rapidly than they are at present.

The country needs **more** South Wales coal, not less. We produce anthracite, as well as prime coking and steam coals which are becoming increasingly expensive on the international market.

The British Steel Corporation, for example, imports over 1,000,000 tonnes of foreign coking coal a year into its Port Talbot plant, despite the fact that the steelworks is situated right next to Western Europe's largest untapped reserve of prime coking coal.

## Investment, not closures

Similarly, the country is short of 1 million tonnes of anthracite a year. Yet the Coal Board is **closing** South Wales anthracite mines when it should be expanding them and opening new ones.

The South Wales coal industry needs investment, not closures. It needs jobs, not longer dole queues.

Our fight is your fight. By supporting the miners you will be ensuring that this country retains its own vital supplies of fuel. Without these supplies, we shall once again find ourselves at the mercy of multi-national oil companies and foreign governments.

Published by National Union of Mineworkers (South Wales Area) Sardis Road, Pontypridd and printed by Cymric Federation Press, Neville Street, Cardiff

Designed by ................................... ...... by Cardiff

3  Pro-strike leaflet put out by South Wales NUM which circulated throughout the coalfields

had 40 per cent pneumoconiosis. He failed to work and because now they can let you finish on what they call ill health, they gives you 500 quid. Now that's about five weeks' money and that's what he gets and he don't get no more than 500 quid which is bloody ridiculous for a man with 40 per cent pneumoconiosis.

*Q  Do you think there'll be industrial action over threat of closure?*

IE  Well, I would say yes, there's got to be. You take Maerdy. We're being told that Maerdy is the next on the list. Now we've got to try and protect some of the jobs, we know the men fifty and over, well, I can't see all those getting to another colliery, they will take the redundancy some of them, not all of them. Well, you've got to fight for these jobs haven't you? Look what he's done to the steel works, look what he's doing to Colliery Coke Works! Look what he's done to the brick works! He'll close them all. They'll close the pits but they'll have a fight on their hands this time.

*Q   So you think there will be widespread support for action?*
IE   Yes, yes yes. That will be guaranteed. That is guaranteed. You'll have the Scottish miners out, you'll have the Durham – you'll have everyone out. They have guaranteed us full support – if South Wales comes out and collieries are closed we'll support those and they will support us.

*Q   If it comes to industrial action do you think government legislation to prevent secondary picketing will have any effect?*
IE   None whatsoever. It'll try – but they'll have no effect at all, not on the miners. This time they will all be together not one or two.

*Q   What do you think about the question of current stockpiles of coal?*
IE   Fifty-six million tonnes was in the paper this week. Well. Read the paper next week there will be 83 million tonne stockpile. A month ago there was only 22 million so . . . you know take it as it comes like – it's all lies like. They have got stockpiles, it's obvious they've got stockpiles, but not the figure they are saying like. Definitely.

*Q   How about imports?*
IE   Well, we're having coal in from South Africa. We're having coal in from France – of course those governments subsidise the mines out there to fetch the coal over here, see. Ours don't. Now then they say it's cheaper for them to get coal from South Africa and from France than what it is to produce it – in your own collieries. We are trying to stop it.

*Q   What do you think about Arthur Scargill?*
IE   Well, let's put it this way. Cwm Colliery once a year gets a big do in Porthcawl for retired miners and – I'm not trying to brag colliery up but – the union there they makes a good do for the men, women and gives them a good night out and makes a presentation to retired miners, could be a miner's lamp, OK, flowers for the women and all that – Scargill spoke there two years ago and I'll say this, I'd never met the man before, I've never met him since, every word that he said in Porthcawl? – we had the dinner and dance – every word that he had said in there two years ago have come true. He said these collieries would close. Not only he was there, there was a lot of other management of the collieries there and Scargill . . . spoke extremely well. He made statements regarding stockpiles of coal; this colliery will close, that colliery will close – and they are. Every word that he said has proved right up to now.

*Q   What do you think are the prospects for young people?*
*IE*   Impossible. No work at all. There was two good factories in our area. Clark's shoe factory and [UNCLEAR] they were the biggest two factories anywhere in the area, two years ago they shut the two of them. Clark's moved their factory out to Ireland. It had got blown up so much the talk is they're coming back to us in the Rhondda Valley now. Two years all these boys that used to work for Clark's some of them are still out of work, these are good men on machines and they haven't done a day's work since Clark's moved. They're hoping that Clark's will come back there, that is the talk. Clark's is coming back there and they will employ them back, the 200 or 300 people they'd employed there, and these boys are waiting for them to start up again. But there's nothing else at all around there. Not a job anywhere.

*Q   The present government have advised people to pack their bags and move off to find work. What do you reckon on that?*
*IE*   Pack your bags – where are you gonna go? You can go round England, you can go anywhere you like, everybody's on the dole, so you're not gonna get anywhere are you? There's no work in Wales, South Wales has had it. You go to England, I've got relations in England they tell you straight there's no work up there so where are you gonna go? If you get a bike, God knows where you're gonna have to go to look for a job maybe in Scotland. You won't get nothing around here and you won't get nothing in England. They are worse off than we are in some parts out there. You take Liverpool, take all the steel works that have been out there, take all the docks they've closed so where are we gonna go from there looking for work. They tell you get on your bike and look for work. Three parts of those are millionaires, we're not.

*Q   Has your colliery changed recently?*
*IE*   Well. Let's put it this way, we've had one general manager but in fifteen years we've had about six managers which is one manager for colliery, one manager for the coke and then a general manager over the two pits. The manager that's there now, he goes down underground at 7 o'clock in the morning and he don't come up until 5 o'clock in the night. Every day I've never seen a manager like it – he's doing his best to try and get things going. For the other managers, I don't know much about them, but this one, he's underground more than any manager and I have been there best part of forty years.

   I've had a living out of the colliery mind, not a good one, I got a living there. I've got a brother can't walk full of dust. I've got a buddy had his arm off in the colliery, his father got killed in the colliery, his brother broke his back in another colliery, so the colliery have done nothing for him has it? I've had a living, a pittance of a living put it that way. These boys as far as some of them are concerned – they could close all the pits. As far as I'm concerned they can do what they like man. They'll tell you you go for a dust board. They'll go to Cardiff and go before a board. . . . They'll tell you after thirty or forty years underground you have got dust insufficient to affect your health. A fortnight later you are dead. You have a post mortem on you and you'll find you died through silicosis. I know one person he went for a board, he had his letter back – a slight dust on your lungs insufficient to affect your health in any way, a month later he died and we advised his widow to have a post mortem on him. They opened him up – died through pneumoconiosis. If I died tomorrow I promise you my Mrs would have a post mortem on me.

*Q   What's your impression of the mood in the coalfield at the moment?*

IE   All right, we're happy-go-lucky sort of people, you know, we take things as they come until they tread on your toes, and then when they tread on your toes it's time to start, en it? I've been close, very close to it like. As it is now – I say we're easy going, don't tread too hard, but when they do tread we'll tread back, simple as that, and we'll be on the loss, they'll be on the loss. They say they've got this 56 billion tonnes stockpile, my opinion it'll soon be needing it too.

### Derek, Dai and Luke, Britannia Colliery

*Q   Luke, can you describe to us what the situation is at the present time in the pit that you're in?*

A   Well, the pit that we're in now are making a tremendous lot of profit. We're averaging about £60 to £70 bonus a week and they're on about closing the pit. That's – the left-hand side of this – the L9, there's no end of coal which we could develop straightaway off it. But the executives in 1981 have given it away.

Britannia is not exhausted whatsoever, never. We've got the finest face at the present moment in the country. And we all know it. And it is an embarrassment to the executives by this face producing so much coal. So they're going to close it and just shut everybody up.

*Q   What do you think the reason is?*

A   Well the reason is because the union employed an engineer. This is what they try and bluff us with. But he's closing the wrong colliery down.

*Q   Why do they want to close the pit that's making money, Dai?*

A   The reason why the union are closing our pit is to salvage another colliery.

Because they've got our reserves.

But it's all been given away in 1981. They should have told us in the beginning like what was happening. What really happened, we fought for three years to save our colliery, we came up and down to Porthcawl on several occasions up to London, lobbied our executives – and there was no mention of closing the colliery down. It was making a profit of £160,000 a week, we worked off a deficit of nearly 2 million, all that in six, seven months. And like I said we was coming back – down to

Porthcawl to lobby our executive, then they still didn't tell us the pit was shutting. We was under the impression that Margaret Thatcher was closing it but no it wasn't, it was our own bloody union.

We should have realised in the beginning when they closed Bagshot and Baghot Washery – and they was washing our coal. They closed Baghot Washery down, we should have realised then in 1981 when they closed that down, Britannia had got to go. Cause they're not paying all that money to haul to another place to be washed.

They close pits left, right and centre now because we didn't listen to Arthur Scargill in the beginning. If we had every miner obeying Arthur Scargill there'd be no pits closed now. That's the only true union man you can have out is Arthur Scargill because he appreciates they close them, he's the only man that knew and the only man that shouted at it, that they will do it, nobody took no notice of him and now they're just doing it.

*Q    Why didn't you think that people took any notice of Scargill?*
A    Well I think maybe that if he had put it on two different ballots about closing pits and pay rises, they might have had the vote to come out on pit closures. Everybody would have been out.

*Q    Do you think that has been a setback, nationally, for gaining support for opposition to closures in future?*
A    I think we're not having much support from England, English collieries, because they're earning fantastic bonuses up there. They're earning much more than us.

Well this is it, isn't it?

As regards up to England, yes, that's where we lost the majority vote. If we wasn't on this incentive scheme – bonus lark – we'd have every pit out in South Wales. Every pit out in Great Britain. Cos if they're earning tremendous bonus up there before – well before ever we bloody started earning bonus.

You see the most of the votes is up in England. They got about 55 per cent of the vote in England. There's Wales, Scotland and Kent and Durham. We only rate about 45. We vote to strike, they vote against it cos they have fantastic bonus. They've just opened Selby Colliery; Siddal said, on the late national news, we're not only closing them, we're reopening them. What happened a week after he opened it? The bloody place flooded out. So that's so much for his bloody bragging.

*Q    If there was any other kind of work available would you prefer to go and do that?*
A    Where? There's none here. She's not starting any trainees so there'll be no plumbers, there'll be no colliers, there'll be no, what shall I say, there'll be no turners, steel turners, when the country is on the end of its decade, which I think it will take a decade to pick back up, she'll have no trained men or skilled personnel to start the country back up. She'll put them all on the dole.

Take my son now. She'll learn him to be an artist. Draw on the dole.

How to draw his dole. And that applies for nearly 3 million people in this country. But I believe it's nearer 4 million now.

What work am I going to do outside the coal industry? I've done twenty-five years in the pit. That's all I know is pit work, so I'm not going to get a job anywhere else am I? Cos I don't know nothing else only the industry that I'm in now. So I'm buggered to do anything, only work coal. I'm too bloody old.

*Q How are the conditions?*
*A* I think nobody likes to work down a colliery. I mean everybody has their own skill. I mean you get a brickie, you can get a welder, I'm a miner, so I'm an A1A man, I'm on top money so they can put me anywhere and I'll do any job that's underground. The roads, bookings, face work, packing, turning, anything you want I'll do it as long as it's underground at the face. But I can't do any other job – well, buggered like isn't it? Or do a brickie job I'm buggered at that, but underground I'll do any job that's there. And nobody can't fault my work.

Not a very pleasant place to work but it's a living. It's what you were brought up doing isn't it? It was good enough for our fathers so, well, I wouldn't say it's good enough for us now cause we're a bit more educated and there are quite a few miners down there, coal miners who got university degrees. High school scholarships and whatnot and they can do other work but the thing is when they close the pit down what's outside for us? Cause the government has stopped all our other industries.

*Q What about your sons, would you like to see them working down there?*
*A* No. Well, this is one thing which was brought up at the last meeting we had. She's not closing the colliery down she's closing the environment down. Like there's no employment for our own children. Not just as miners but as skilled men on top of the colliery. Skilled men down the pit but also you've got the backing of our skilled men behind you and working on top of the pit to give us the essential supplies we need. Like electricians and fitters, to assemble all these cutting machines and they need to be in a position where they can be, how can I put it, more educated than men working in heavy industry outside. But the way the government is doing it now, it's cutting everything down, there'll be nothing left for the skilled men on top of the pit or underground.

Well I got a boy now, he just sat his O levels, and he's waiting for the results. There's nothing round so I told him to stop in school. Save hanging about, hanging about the road and the streets. I said 'stay in school'. He's sitting now for this engineering course, he's thinking for that. I said 'you won't go down the pit, there's no way you'll go down the pit'. Never go down the pit. Maybe stop on the dole for the rest of his life as far as I'm concerned. He won't go down the pit.

*Q Do you think the coal industry will be privatised?*
*A* No, definitely not. Our fathers worked for that. And they killed our fathers, private enterprise. They killed our fathers, they won't kill us.

## Roy Walters, Tower Colliery

*Q   What do you think has been the impact of the incentive bonus scheme on the work-force?*

RW   Well, the incentive bonus scheme was only put there for one purpose and that purpose was to divide the work-force. I'll give you an example. After 1972 strike, an old Coal Board director named Wilfred Myrion, he wrote a letter to then Derek Ezra saying that the only way that the power of the NUM is going to be broken is to bring an incentive scheme back in so that right-wing leaders in right-wing areas can then get the power back in their hands which was brought in with the help of Mr Lord Gormley. Half the work-force rejected it in the beginning, but he managed to force it through and it has done what it was put there for, to divide the work-force and we won't be a united work-force until this incentive scheme is gone.

*Q   Do you think that there'll be opposition in the future against closure policy at all?*

RW   I can't see us having another strike this year with pit closures because I can't see these areas which are running £200 a week bonus week in, week out, bringing home more money than I have on top, that they're going to vote for a strike over a pit in South Wales.

*Q   What's your view about Ian MacGregor being appointed as Chairman of the Board?*

RW   Ian MacGregor's only been put there for one thing hasn't he? He was appointed by the Tory government to do a job in the steel industry which he's done, and he's been appointed now to do a job in the coal industry, to butcher it. That is what he's going to do.

*Q   Why do you think that has become government policy?*

RW   They can't really go about to denationalise the coal industry because they know that that would cause uproar. So their way about it is to close the pits down one by one so that the coal industry is really at rock bottom with just a few pits in the high production areas to keep about 75 million tonnes a year turnover but then especially down in South Wales, they'll go into privatisation in a big way with the oil companies investing a lot of money in it. So all they're doing is preparing things so they're going to gain out of it in five or ten years' time.

*Q   Why do you think the recent ballots against, for instance, the closure of Lewis Merthyr pit weren't successful?*

RW   The reason why it wasn't successful was because miners in other areas are earning big bonus and they're not prepared to sacrifice their money to support us down in South Wales when we don't earn hardly any bonus at all.

*Q   There was an argument that Ti Mawr was on it last legs anyway in terms of reserves, etc. What's your view on that?*

RW   Well that's a funny thing because Lewis Merthyr and Ti Mawr are

## Another run to Notts with food. May 1984

Packed up grub bought out of the £20. It surely would have been easier to take money but didn't think. Tins, shampoo, soap powder and Sanitary Towels – that's all I could cope with. Large shampoo to split. Huge soap powder to split. Stopped again by our 'fairy brigade'. The rotten swine tipped everything out of the topbox until they came to the towels. Ah hah. What's this then? Step back, a look of horror. Oh joy. No more fingers in the box. Wonderful! (They are scared of S.T.s – great stuff. Must try and utilise this.) Gazing on tins, shampoo and the now broken bag of soap powder I gritted my teeth and with a 'thank you officer' I collected stuff together, mounted bike and rode on my way.

Distributed stuff. The look on their faces. It is well and truly worth the hassle. How can they 'against the odds' stay so solid, the lovely Notts women. I am with you but I must do MORE. Had to do a post haste back home. I've neglected my own a bit. My eldest boy looks ill. What does he eat except what we give him? Not much I shouldn't wonder.

## To let. June 1984

'Mum, my flat is to let.'

There stood my eldest son. He could not cope anymore. I now had to face the fact he would be 'returning home'. I cried when he left here but he was 23; and here he was again. I knew my 'dining room' would be his bedroom. That was where I went to write and for peace and now that was going. But I had to accept the inevitable: if he couldn't come to mum who could my striking miner turn to? I'd no bed, so went out to get an inflatable rubber bed.

When he said 'and now my flat is to let' I decided it was a sign that wasn't going up in my house, heart or mind ever. We are *not to let*.

## Arthur's Flyers. June 1984

Lance rang. I already knew he was one of 'Arthur's Flyers'. How are you son? Well mother, well. Mum, you know that fire my dad mentioned? O.K. for us to have it? Yes, get your father-in-law to pack it up.

Lance, can I go picketing with you? Silence –. Lance are you there? Whistle through his teeth. Mum, women *shouldn't go picketing*. Rubbish. Mum, er, it's not right for women to be on picket lines; the police are violent and they don't care who they hit. Yes darling I know . . . will you take me picketing? Mother joined together, all the coal comes up at Ti Mawr. Two years ago they closed Ti Mawr Colliery and they told the men to go over to Lewis Merthyr, there's ten to fifteen years' work there, and you'll be allright for that period of time. That was only two years ago and all of a sudden after two years, there's no workable reserves left.

*Q   Do you think the policy of joining pits underground is part of a broader policy?*

RW   The NCB now, in South Wales, they're trying to get a big programme through in joining pits up. The only reason for that is to close one complex down.

*Q   Is that a deliberate way of running down the industry?*

RW   Yes, because immediately they join us up in Maerdy then there be something like 230 surface workers in Maerdy Colliery which would have to go on the dole.

*Q   Is it likely that redundancy payments will get larger with Ian MacGregor.*

RW   Well it has already started. The redundancy payments now are good. They're a lot better now than they have been for a long time. And I suppose that when he gets in that he will ask for higher payments again which is one way of demoralising the people over 50 and they will turn around and they will say, well we've worked for thirty years, forty years in the pit, if we go to 60 we only get £500, we can have £21,000 now or £30,000 or whatever the case may be, they're going to take it, and you can't blame the men for taking it.

*Q   How does that square with the union policy that there should be no closures other than on the grounds of exhaustion or safety?*

RW   That policy was a policy passed by national conference but it hasn't been upheld since it's been passed. I should imagine ten or twelve pits were closed in Great Britain since that has been passed and it's not because of exhaustion or because of safety. It's just through economic reasons and I feel that our National Executive, it's time that they woke up to this and they started to fight it and not just let it happen.

*Q   Do you think that there will be a fight over that issue?*

RW   No. My personal opinion is that there won't.

*Q   Why not?*

RW   It was turned down five months ago. I don't think anything has changed from then until now. We knew five months ago that Ian MacGregor was going to be appointed as Coal Board Director, we knew then he was going to be appointed now in September 1st, so nothing has changed and i don't think anything has changed the minds of the work-force. the Tory government and the Coal Board have got the biggest thing on their side and that's the media, which influences a hell of a lot of people when you read the *Sun* and the *Mirror* and the *Mail* and the *Express*. They would rather believe what they read in there than what our union will tell them. Arthur Scargill said back last year that there's seventy pits to close in Great Britain, everybody laughed at him. But now the Coal Board have admitted that themselves. There's seventy pits going to close but have they put it in the paper that Arthur Scargill was right? No, aha, they're too clever for that.

*Q    What are the kinds of things that people are talking about here, over the fortnight?*

*RW*    The men who I've spoken to from the pits, when we've got into conversation – the one point that comes to everybody's lips every time is the incentive scheme and what it has done to the union, dividing us. And that has been our main topic, and talking to a miner from Derbyshire last night, you could see the different attitudes, that he's allright, he's having good bonus, why should he worry about us? As far as he was concerned, the incentive scheme was a marvellous thing. So after just speaking to him you could see what it had done.

*Q    What do you think the union strategy will be in the near future?*

*RW*    That is a very difficult question to answer. I hope that they will try and resist the pit closures that are going to come when MacGregor takes over. But whether they go about it in the right way or not is a different thing. If they are going to start holding ballots again, then I'm afraid we're going to lose. The only way, the only strategy is a strike. Forget about your ballots, forget about all the talking, the only strategy if the pit is nearing to close, or pits are nearing to close, is to come out on strike and get the rest of the coalfield and start picketing the pits out. That is the only way you will get miners out on strike now. The same as we done in 1981, we went out picketing and they come out and supported us. That was the one comradeship that we have got left is that a miner won't cross a picket line, I believe.

*Q    Have they got the conference decisions on bringing the men out on strike?*

*RW*    No, the only conference decision which has been passed now is that they intend to hold another ballot which I think is wrong. We've been rejected once in a ballot massively over the closure of a pit and the NCB will use the same tactics, they've got everybody on their side, the media, the television, they'll have everybody on their side to influence the men, and a ballot just won't come out in our favour.

*Q    Could you just pursue that a little bit? Why should one pit in South Wales be able to bring out the whole coalfield?*

*RW*    Because it's our jobs that are at stake, going back to those men put up a hell of a fight, having a sit-in underground, they deserved to keep that pit open for what they had done, but they were rejected because of the ballot box. I know it's supposed to be democratic, but I don't believe that a ballot should have been held. We should have gone straight out on strike then. The pit should have been called out on the Wednesday, the same as my pit was out on strike on the Wednesday, five of us before anybody else, to go down the coalfields to try and get support. But once the ballot box comes in, men like to have it to hide behind and I'm afraid that's what happened. Our jobs, even though our pit might not be producing as much as they are or earning as much bonus, it's still our livelihood and it's still our pit which we would like to keep open till it's exhausted to have jobs for our sons to come in to.

# 3 START OF THE STRIKE

## Ruskin tapes: How the strike began at Cortonwood

**Mark and Liz Chipchase live in Cortonwood where Mark works at the pit**

*Mark*   I'd just like to put my point of view on how the strike was sparked off at Cortonwood and how the closure were announced in such an underhand way by the Coal Board. And how they did it were, on the Thursday, the day before they announced the closure they had a review meeting at area level which our manager attended. Nobody knew about it. I went to a union meeting on Thursday night and our materials officer said, 'I've had a phone call. It's been announced that Cortonwood's going to close in five weeks.' I said, 'All right Bill', I says, 'load of balls that', because there'd been that many rumours going round the pit that we all knew it was going to close but we expected, maybe two, three four years' time. So I just took that with a pinch of salt, sort of thing, and then, when we went to work next morning, it had been announced that Cortonwood were going to close. And all the men were really happy about it, singing and dancing, they couldn't wait, saying. 'Let us get the bloody pit closed, let us get to a better pit.' And they went home, and over the weekend they realised what it meant. They thought, 'that's my job, that's my pit. five week's time, if they close it, I might end up on the dole.' And I think they realised then that they'd got to stand up and fight that closure. They called a special union meeting then for Sunday morning and had a ballot on whether to take strike action or not. And it were 100 per cent majority to take strike action, as from the Monday.

*Q   Can you remember any of the things people said to you on the weekend?*

*Mark*   Well, they said things like 'Let this pit close, I'm glad it's closing, let the doghole close, let's get to a decent pit.' I don't think they realised what it meant until they sat down and thought about it.

*Q   Can you remember how your own thoughts changed on the weekend?*

*Mark*   I were one of these that thought, 'Well, bugger it, I've had enough on it, let the pit close. . . .' Then I went home . . . and thought about it and I realised that we couldn't just sit back and let it happen. And I think Cortonwood were put as a tester by the Coal Board. I think they thought, 'Well we'll close Cortonwood and see how the men do react.' I don't think they expected us to react as strongly as we did. I think they got a shock, Cortonwood and the government. I don't think they expected a national strike.

*Q   Did people get a shock at the meeting about how strong the feeling was? Did they come prepared to pass the resolution they did?*

*Mark*   After they'd had a couple of days to mull things over and think about it, there were a 100 per cent turn out at Cortonwood which has never been seen before at Cortonwood up to that day. And it were 100 per cent vote for a strike after they'd seen all the implications of what were happening and what they were trying to do. About twelve months previous Elscar Colliery which were about two mile away from Cortonwood closed, and all the younger end of the men were transferred to Silverwood and all the older ones – 55, 54, around that age – were transferred to Cortonwood on the understanding that it had got five year's life left. So they thought [Cortonwood's] going to see us out. They'd been here twelve months, and then they got this bombshell that it's going to close in five weeks.

They said they couldn't sell Cortonwood coal. I think Cortonwood coal's some of the best in Yorkshire. And three years previous to the strike they'd spent millions of pounds developing Dartfield Main, about three mile away from Cortonwood. Also prior to the strike they'd just spent £45,000 refurbishing the baths. And they always said, 'when there's been a lot of money spent at a pit, it's due for closure'.

*Q   When did you first mention the news of the closure of the pit to your wife?*

*Mark*   I rang her up from work on the Friday when it had been announced and told her. I said 'Pit's closing in five weeks – we're out celebrating tonight.' And I were one of them that were glad it were closing.

*Q   How did you feel on the Sunday night when the Cortonwood strike had been called?*

*Liz Chipchase*   I felt better about it than I did on the Friday.

*Mark*   She were upset about it. She were worried about it.

*Liz*   Because we'd been told that our place were closing – that's all we'd been told, we hadn't got a day – and on Friday when he rang up . . . I just didn't know what was going to happen.

*Q   Can you remember feeling at all fearful?*

*Mark*   It weren't so much having two jobs put off at that point. But we didn't know how long it were going to be before their place closed.

*Liz*   You rang me up on Friday morning didn't you, and on the afternoon we had a meeting with our union, and we were told a bit more . . . that we would be there longer than we thought.

*Mark*  And that were worrying, because, with that one over your head, she might be made redundant and I might be losing my job, possibly.

*Q  Did you feel better knowing you were going on strike?*

*Liz*  Yes, that, and knowing that we'd got longer. I felt a lot better about it than when we didn't know anything.

*Q  After the meeting, can you remember what people thought was going to happen? What the result of the strike might be?*

*Mark*  I think everybody thought that we would get support nationally, solid. I said to my wife 'it will not last three months, this', and we all thought we were going to get 100 per cent backing from the rest of the country. But obviously Nottinghamshire let us down and Derbyshire, to an extent Leicestershire, and we didn't get the backing that we needed which we ought to have had from the start.

*Q  Did you start picketing at other pits immediately?*

*Mark*  On the Monday – no. They were not really organised. But when we went to work on the Monday there were a picket on at us own pit. But then after maybe a week then we started going flying and started getting things a little bit organised.

*Q  Did you have consultation with Yorks area?*

*Mark*  I think what it were – we got provided with a minibus by Barnsley area – headquarters – after a week or so. Cortonwood ought to have been solid until the last days. Sadly we had ninety scabs going in. And I were ashamed. Anybody asked me where I worked, I were ashamed to tell them because of these ninety scabs that were going in and it were Cortonwood sparked the strike off. There didn't ought to have been one scab let alone ninety. The majority on the scabs were older than 54, 55 time, they'd been transferred from Elscar and I think, what they were after [was] they wanted to get back and get their redundancy [money] sorted out.

# Ruskin tapes: How the strike began at Hatfield Main

*Dave Douglass*  The executive met on the Wednesday and decided to deploy pickets from the Wednesday . . . over the border as well. Because as you know Armthorpe and Hatfield took off on their own on Monday morning and went to Haworth to dissuade. By Monday night. . . . within one day – within one night we had two pits closed. . . . We had to go up after them and tell them to come back because it were very popular.

*Voice*  We went to Haworth on the Monday night and Haworth was shut and then on the Tuesday morning we went to Bevercotes and shut

Bevercotes as well. A lot of lads that had not really took any notice about the strike, opened their eyes – there were about 400 of us, some from Rossington . . . the majority were from Hatfield and Armthorpe.

Well what we did was – we had what you call a piss-call meeting. There were just a few lads here, there and everywhere. 'Phone calls were made and we decided to go out on the Monday before the executive meeting on the Tuesday to make them think – to make them *know* – how the lads felt. And we honestly believed – well I do – that we swung the Exec. to our way of thinking. Before we were picketing our secretary said, 'You can't do this, you can't do that' – you know – and I mean, Taylor and the works said, 'You can't do it.' But we did. We went out and we closed two pits in one night.

*Dave Douglass*    We'll probably all disagree about this, because we were in different positions. I was on the Executive then. And I'll tell you now, there was no problem about picketing. But the feeling that we had were, we weren't sure if North Yorkshire would come out. To be honest, we thought there'd be a revolt in Yorkshire. So we held the pickets back in case of wanting to get Yorkshire out. Because the position always was to get your own coalfield out before you go and see anybody else. But Armthorpe being like it was, and everybody was on hooks, Armthorpe just said 'Come on, we're going', so half the bleeding pickets went with them. Didn't wait for us. So when we did have the meeting, it was already an accomplished fact – either you deploy the pickets or the pickets will deploy themselves.

*Tony Clegg*    . . . Within three days the police presence was there. And when we went to Ollerton – bloody hell, what a sight! – there were 200 of us and there must have been about 300, 400 police at the bottom of Ollerton pit lane, but for three hours, from 5 o'clock to quarter past eight we did nowt but shove police up and down the lane. . . . We had the advantage of being at the top. There was a big wall at one side and a fence at the other. And we just linked arms and they tried every way to break through that, and they couldn't do it. And behind them there were 400, 500 day shift waiting to go in and the police were shoving us up and down. . . . This was after Cortonwood had been out a week but it was only the third day of the national strike. They weren't Nottinghamshire police. The police were already mobilised to such an extent. . . .

# Interview: How the strike began at Armthorpe

**Single miner, faceworker, 21 years old, born Armthorpe**
We had a mass meeting in here and I believe there were only five

against the strike. There was a couple of old blokes who were near retiring anyway so you might expect that. And a couple of young lads. About five in all against it. Everyone else put their hand up. We were more or less solid.

First couple of days out on strike I remember. This branch first started going into Nottingham picketing and we got a roasting there. We went to Haworth first and Jack Taylor got on phone and told us to come out because Nottingham were having a vote. He said leave it up to vote and see what happens. And we said no chance – if we're out, they're out. It's their jobs and all, sort of thing. So we went picketing. Day shift we got about thirty out. Afternoon shift about thirty out. Night shift come and we went to Hatfield and got some lads from Hatfield to come and from other pits round Doncaster area. And we all got together and had a mass picket at Haworth and it shut pit down. It shut pit down for a week while they had the vote. That same night we went to Bevercotes and shut that night shift down. I thought we had it cracked then. But as soon as they had the vote, and when we started going to other places instead of just one pit and making it shut. It all just collapsed and the two pits went back to work and left about eighty out on strike at each pit.

4 Women on the picket line at Bevercotes Colliery, Nottinghamshire

# Interview: How the strike failed at Bentinck Colliery, Notts

Barbara Bloomfield

Many people have asked why the Notts coalfield reacted so strongly against the strike. In Bentinck Colliery, an isolated pit two miles from the village of Pinxton on the county border with Derbyshire, only twenty-three men out of 1600 came out and by the end of the year that figure was down to sixteen. The three interviews here were taken on 14 October 1985, in the week when the Notts coalfield was balloting on whether or not to form the breakaway Union of Democratic Mineworkers. Between them, Colin Bottomore, Todd Clark and Lennie Harper seem to express some of the contradictions of the Notts miners and in particular the battle between a gut trade unionism and a stubborn unwillingness to be, as they see it, 'led by the nose' by their trade union leaders.

### Colin Bottomore, Branch Secretary, Bentinck Colliery

*Colin, can you tell me what your attitude was at the beginning of the strike and what happened afterwards?*
At the beginning I was for the strike because before the strike obviously myself and the rest of the union committee were trying to influence any strike ballot that might take place. I mean in favour of the strike. I wrote a notice in favour [see page 74] and it was put up on noticeboards and I told people to put some 'steel injections' into themselves and fight for their jobs. That was at the end of February. But when we had the meeting the mood from that meeting was obvious that the men didn't wish to support a strike. Of the 500-600 men who attended the meeting, I didn't hear anyone at that meeting, there was no one from that audience spoke in favour of the strike. The only people that did so was myself and Neil Greatorix [now full time at Berry Hill, NUM Headquarters]. None of the staunch supporters of the strike from this colliery supported us on that day. Some other areas had a ballot and those areas that did ballot at that time voted against a strike, same as Notts, and then of course the attitude hardened against the striking miners because of the violent picketing that took place from the very first day they entered into Nottinghamshire. On the first shift that they came to Bentinck I spoke to about twenty to thirty pickets and came in the canteen and I personally bought them all a cup of tea, we were that close in friendship. And then . . . about half past ten . . . the pub just up the road turned about fifty to sixty pickets out and violence started

immediately they came out, violence toward men walking to work, running men across fields, chasing men in groups, chasing individuals through the gate and shoving them on to the road. And from that moment I said I would have nothing to do with them.

5  Pro-UDM and pro-NUM stickers

Of course, it's history now how the ballot went, 73 I think per cent against supporting the strike. Well the question was asked of me on the rally we had at Bentinck Football Field and I had to reply in all honesty 'What will happen if we have a ballot and that decision goes against your view, would yer support us?' Well obviously I would say yes, of course, I defend your right to have a ballot and then we could have decided that if the vote didn't go the way we wanted it we wouldn't support it. So I made that promise and I kept that promise. Myself, I didn't cross a picket line until after the ballot had been taken. I attended work but I didn't get paid for it until Notts had had the ballot decision, and then I attended work and I got paid . . . but I supported the overtime ban throughout the strike solidly.

*Did you think about resigning?*

Yes I did and in fact I thought about striking on a number of occasions . . . all the way throughout that strike, it hasn't been easy. And though a lot of people say 'Well, you got paid for it' I admit I got paid for it but there's always been a conflict in my own mind between opinions because I would have loved to have supported the men that were on strike but I wasn't elected to support the members on strike, I was elected to support the men at this colliery. And I mean, I'm in a position where I've got close friends who won't talk to me because of it, I've even got members of me own family don't talk to me so I ain't come out of it all nice and easy. It's cost me a lot. It's cost me a lot in regards to looking at meself in the mirror, cos that's not easy.

*Has your opinion about the way the strike was conducted changed since the end of the strike?*

No it hasn't, and my opinion about how it was conducted from Nottinghamshire as well as from the national level hasn't changed either . . . in fact I think both sides didn't conduct themselves very openly and frankly. I think Scargill made a mess from the beginning, I

A meeting will be held on Sunday to report on the Notts Area Conference, and the Boards policy of Pit Closures.

The ballot to be held on Tuesday 8th March is not to prevent South Wales pit closures only. It is to prevent a policy of mass pit closures which the Union believes is about to take place.

South Notts is no different to any other area, some pits in Notts are losing vast sums of money, and if pits are to close because of economic grounds, Notts, Yorkshire, Kent etc. will all come under the hammer.

Bentinck will loose around £7 million this year, who's safe?

Notts area to loose 1,000 men.

Overtime to be cut

Transfers have been taking place in this area for a number of years. We have men in Notts from all over. Who fought for these pits? (No one) the coal first. But transfers cannot take place without pits to transfer men to. Facts are McGregor to take over the chairmanship of the N.C.B. (Why!)

To help the miners keep in employment. I dont think so. To save the coal industry, the steel industry is the proof of the McGregor policy. Thousands on the dole. Whole villages out of work. Fathers & Sons unemployed, this is McGregor, this is the fear in miners hearts. This is the reason the union asks the miners to support their recommendation. Support your union and fight for your jobs. This will be your last chance.

6  At the end of February 1984, Colin Bottomore, the NUM Branch Secretary, was urging men at Bentinck to support the strike. Later he changed his mind

7 'Don't Let A Tory Win The Glory', slogan on banner at an NUM mass picket at Babbington Colliery, Notts, 9 April 1984

think we in this area didn't do what we should have done, we should have gone round talking and explaining what would happen and we didn't. We weren't ready for the ballot. I do wish we had gone in favour of the strike and sometimes I even think to meself, only briefly cos I dismiss it, I wish I'd said 'No thank you very much' and gone on strike.
*Have you and Todd Clark talked about all this?*
Oh aye, regularly. . . .
*Does he think that you did wrong?*
Of course he does.
*And do you think he did wrong?*
No I can't say he did. The only thing was I wasn't an ordinary NUM member. I was elected spokesman but I think if I'd been an ordinary man at the pits I'd have gone on strike.
*Did you see yourself essentially as a person who supported Scargill or who supported the right of miners to work?*
I definitely did not support Scargill during the strike. I was in the opposite field because I didn't like the violence and the way it wasn't

condemned. I didn't like it from either side. I saw limited violence but I didn't like what I saw from the police as well as the other side but I didn't support Scargill because he did nothing at any time to represent the whole of the mining community, he just represented those who were on strike and I didn't support him at all. I supported the lads in this colliery and this area.

*How did you react to the obvious hardship cases that you must have heard about among the strikers?*

We didn't hear of any hardship cases among striking miners, we heard exactly the opposite because obviously the tales that were fed back to me were from people that were working and their attitude was to harden my attitude, see? And I know for a fact that every evening they were in the public house and every dinner so they couldn't have been that hard up for money, them particular strikers we had. It hardened me against them in some respect because of the violence that was used against my wife, because someone stopped my wife in the town and spat all over her and pushed her against a bus stop and some women had to come and help her out.

*And that was because she was your wife?*

Yes, because she was my wife. If people are prepared to do things like that they should do them to me. I'd be more prepared to accept it or to defend myself.

*And these were strikers were they?*

Oh yeah.

*Local?*

Not from here, not from Bentinck.

*How would you describe what you believe in politically?*

I am a true, deep socialist and I would hang Mrs Thatcher tomorrow if I could. I hate Tories. I think there's more to life than profit. But I wouldn't join the Labour Party because they told me I'd got to. I think there's too much labelling people right, left and centre.

*Don't you think you've, in the long run, done more harm than good to what you believe in?*

Well, let me start by saying that the thing I regret most is my part in the organisation of that May Day demo against the strike, cos that's what united Notts working miners against the strike. I was pelted by bricks and grass sods by strikers and it looked as if I was Judas with the thirty pieces of silver. I've been led into a position of being under a great mental and physical strain because I've been in the front instead of following and I've been chosen by people on the other side to be their target, I've been called a 'man without principles.' I wish I'd never been Branch Secretary during 1984. I could have sat at home and been on strike. I think 'well, you're a hypocrite in some ways'. I don't like the place I hold in history. I wish to God I was no longer in it and I'm no longer proud to be a miner.

*What do you think is going to happen at the ballot this week?*
It can only be a matter of conjecture to me or anyone else. The support will come from Nottinghamshire in my opinion. My own view is a contradiction of terms I would think. I would have said six months ago that I would have nothing to do with the breakaway union. But now I'm going to vote for it. Pride plays a large part. I've always thought I had a right to a say in my union.

*What about the argument that you should try to change from within the NUM?*
You can't change from within when you aren't given a voice and Notts aren't given a voice. I believe in the NUM and I don't think this union can exist for any length of time but I'm going to vote for it. Notts has got to be accepted back into the NUM under equal terms until Mr Scargill is prepared to cooperate with us.


## Todd Clark

He used to be treasurer of the union at Bentinck. He went on strike on Friday 13 April just before Bentinck had a ballot and stayed out for the rest of the strike. He was one of only twenty-three men out of 16,000 at Bentinck who supported the strike. After the strike he returned to work and stood for President of Bentinck NUM against two other men. One became a full-time official, the other withdrew and so Todd got in by default and he's been President ever since, even though his politics clash with so many other miners at Bentinck.

I've been kicked out of the union by Roy Lynk but I took them to court the next day and got back in. I made an undertaking to represent any men, working or striking, but my views are my own. And it's worked out pretty well. The people respect my views but after this Friday I shall probably be out of a job. I've just lost me wife, I don't know why, I think it might have something to do with the dispute. She just wandered off into the night and I've got the kids. She supported the strike very strongly, even more so than me. After the strike I said, it's like after the war, you have to talk to the Germans. You can't come here and not talk to people cos I'm outnumbered 1600 to one. The wife couldn't take it.

# TO ALL NOTTINGHAMSHIRE MINERS
# YOU ARE NOT IN THE NATIONAL UNION
## (Confirmed by High Court Judgment on 7 August, 1985)

# ARTHUR SCARGILL SAYS!

**"THOSE WHO GIVETH THE POWER, HAVE THE MEANS TO TAKETH AWAY THAT POWER"** (Presidential Address to Yorkshire NUM, 1975)

**"I BELIEVE THAT THE ONLY WAY YOU'RE GOING TO GET WORKERS' CONTROL IN THE REAL SENSE IS TO TAKE CONTROL OF SOCIETY ITSELF"**
(New Left Review, July/August 1975)

**"NOW I'M A MODERATE AND REASONABLE MAN"**
(Speech at Sherwood, Mansfield, 12.11.81)

**"I WILL FIGHT FOR A DEMOCRATIC UNION WHOSE LEADERS ARE ACCOUNTABLE AT REGULAR INTERVALS"** (Speech at Sherwood, Mansfield, 12.11.81)

**"I SUPPORT THE SOVIET UNION OVER HUNGARY"** (Sunday Times, 10.1.82)

**"I'M NOT PREPARED TO BE A PART TO THESE ATTACKS ON THE SOVIET UNION"**
(Sunday Telegraph 28.8.83, Scargill's Address to Anti War Conference in Moscow)

**"I AM OPPOSED TO SOLIDARITY BECAUSE IT IS AN ANTI-SOCIALIST ORGANISATION WHO DESIRE TO OVERTHROW A SOCIALIST STATE"**
(Iris News, October, 1983, Published in Trotskyist News Line)

**"WE HAVEN'T HAD A SINGLE REQUEST FOR IT"**
(Reply to Question about Pit Head Ballot—Daily Mail, 13.1.84)

**"WE WILL REMEMBER YOUR FACES"** (Blidworth, 1984)

---

# SUPPORT YOUR AREA UNION
# VOTE YES
## ISSUED ON BEHALF OF THE NOTTINGHAM AREA EXECUTIVE COMMITTEE

E. Mellors. Printer, Hucknall. Nottingham

8  Pro-UDM leaflet for the 'breakaway ballot' of October 1985

She used to wind the window down and call people scabs and point the car at people. Since she left me she has said, 'well I looked after you a year while you were on strike' so it's obviously affected her somewhere along the line.

*How do you get on with the men at the pit?*
I get on with most of the men. I didn't picket the pit until the last three months of the strike. I couldn't bring meself to picket me own pit, they knew what they was doing and I knew what I was doing, I didn't think they needed telling. It's no use me standing out there shouting at them to come out.

One of the major things which'll all come to light eventually is the wives. They played a major role in the strike and you'd get a wife saying 'if the rest of men are going to work, you're going to work'. Actually, the wives were the ones who voted, not the men. And I think that's one of the major reasons that Notts carried on working. Plus the fact that Notts is an integrated coalfield, I'm a Southerner, there's Southerners, Northerners. You can't say we're Yorkshiremen or Geordies or Scottish or Welsh. The Midlands miners are from all walks of life and all different opinions. Plus they're the greediest men in this country . . . they'd cut their granny's throat for a tanner. They are the greediest men that ever walked this earth. I've seen men fighting for somebody's shift here and I've seen a man trapped and the men say get someone else to take him out I'm stopping an hour, that's how they are.

The easiest thing for me to do now is to say I'll stop with the breakaway union but if I did that I'd be throwing the credibility I've gained. A lot of the men here respect me for what I did. If I said I'd stop with them they'd make a lot of headlines out of it.

*Are you at all tempted?*
At the moment, taking it that me wife walked out on me three weeks ago and I'm left with two children, 11 and 9, my duty is to look after me children so I was very tempted to say, 'I'll stop with you because of me children'. But looking back on it I owe it to what me children's been through for a year and me wife not to. I'm torn but I can't bring meself . . . I mean, I spoke to me wife on the phone and she says 'If I'd have asked you to go back to work you'd soon have left me' and I said 'well, it never come to that did it'. I thought about it but I don't think I'd have left me wife, I'd have left the industry altogether and looked elsewhere for a job.

*I'd like to come back to some of the things you've raised. Firstly, Lennie said that you were 'King striker', probably the most militant in Bentinck . . .*
. . . Um . . . I'm not a militant striker . . . I'm a level-headed striker. I don't go around chucking bricks and shouting 'scabby bastards' and all that. My idea of being on strike was to diminish coal stocks, push the Coal Board into a corner and then negotiate. Men who go to work

should be told that they're doing wrong but not to the extent of lobbing bricks.

*Do you think you'd have been more militant if you'd have been a miner in South Wales for example?*

In South Wales you had 100 per cent support from every person in your village. Round here if you walked down the town you stood a chance of getting a fist in your mouth. And I think people respected you, when you're a minority people have got a lot of respect for you, and they keep their mouths shut. When you're the majority, you don't have to worry anyway. It's only when you get a fifty-fifty situation where you never know what's going to happen. I'll never forget the feeling I had when I returned to work and you're walking through those pit gates me legs went to jelly and thinking 'oh what have I done now'. I was accepted back on to the coal face and back on the team within no time. They disagreed with me and I used to give them as good as they gave me. They used to come and ask me my views on things and I'd explain but when I got this union job I was sweating buckets. Me first branch meeting . . . very rocky.

*How did you get elected with your views?*

It was quite easy . . . I was left unopposed in the end . . . I just walked straight into the job.

*But didn't some of them more anti-strike people, if you like, go all out against you?*

They threatened a no-confidence vote and all the rest of it but it just doesn't wash. In a democracy they can't use a no-confidence vote. I made an undertaking that black, white, right or wrong I'd represent the people of the colliery. I'm a fair person and I've done me job.

*See, the point that is puzzling me is that I've been to a number of coalfields and feelings ran very high. But here it seems like everyone's able to disagree and yet politics doesn't 'get in the way' of . . .*

. . . See, politics doesn't get in the way . . . people who are pro-strike are in such a minority that they don't pose a threat. People like to look at both sides of the printed literature and you'll find both sides in our canteen. We don't pose a threat, except when [Colin Bottomore came through the door at this moment] the Branch Secretary sees me talking to you [laughs] and panics.

*What did you do when you heard about the strike, I know it's a long time ago?*

It's a very long time ago . . . erm . . . well I was a charge hand ripping when I heard about the strike and a lot of people were pro the strike. Neil Greatorix which is now a full-time official at Berry Hill [Notts Area NUM union offices] was one of my closest friends at the time and a very militant person and he would have gone on strike but the men in the pit voted not to strike and he said he wouldn't. He says because the men at the pit voted not to strike and he supported them but I think it's because it was near branch election time, and if he'd gone the other way he'd have got knocked off.

*What did you do during the strike?*

I supervised fuel. We got a contract with the council to saw the trees down and logged out and took them around to people for fuel and arranged for food parcels and that sort of thing. Sooner than picket cos I couldn't see any profitability in picketing.

*I'd like to come back to this question of women persuading men to go back to work. That's a charge that has been very much refuted by a lot of women and I've never personally heard another miner give it as a reason or an excuse not to go on strike.*

I think you'll find that a lot of men at the pit were under pressure from their wives; 95 per cent of miners are under their thumb. They swear and drink but you see them out with their wives and they do as they're told. I know it goes the other way . . . women took the reins, they were feeding us and organising clothes parcels and they became that motivated that their husbands couldn't come back to work if they wanted to.

9  The Berry Hill Working Miners' Demonstration against Scargill and the NUM on 1 May 1984 (*Nottingham Evening Post*)

*You said your wife was quite militant. In what way did you support each other?*

She had a small part-time job. She fed me, kept house, I don't know how she managed it. She kept us all through the strike. She's kept me going with her views and her agreeing with me.

After the strike she changed.

*Why do you think that was?*

. . . Erm . . . It had the same effect as when you go on holiday and you come back, like post-natal depression, or post-holiday depression. I think it was such a trying time after the strike, it were so good, and then there was such an influx of money, everything seemed to be going right. She didn't seem to have any point to fight for and I think that's the main reason our marriage broke up. She had a new three-piece suite, new carpet and £6,000 kitchen after the strike but she wasn't satisfied. She felt bored.

*Just one more thing, what do you think is going to happen in the ballot this Thursday and Friday?*

It'll be a 70 per cent breakaway vote . . . um . . . the big carrot's out and they'll be spoilt and there's no way the men will go against that.

*Do you think the breakaway union can succeed?*

It'll crash within five years. Because they'll start closing pits around here. It'll be trimmed down to be privatised and people will realise the error of their ways. There's no future in the national union or the Notts union without them being together it's just playing one off against the other and I don't see any future in it. The carrot's there and any man over 46 who keeps his mouth shut and his head down will hope he gets redundancy.

### Lennie Harper

He left the mining industry after his father was killed in a rock fall at Warsop Main Colliery in 1951. He went into the army for six years then became a bus driver for eight years before returning to work at Bentinck.

We had a ballot and we voted by a huge majority at this colliery, I think it was four or four-and-a-half to one to work. And I was one of those who voted to work because I didn't hold with being told what to do, I wanted to have my say. To my mind every colliery comes to the end of its days and everybody has been promised they'd be given a job if they wanted one or they could take redundancy with severance pay, so that was fair enough in my book.

*Did you talk much about whether you should strike or not, bearing in mind that Colin and the branch Committee had recommended you should?*

Only over a pint in the pub or whatever. There was a lot of ill feeling

about it about the way it was developing, 'you've got to do this and
you've got to do that', there's no such thing as you've got to do anything.
You make up your own mind and you vote that way.

*But can you imagine if you were in another coalfield and most
people said 'let's support the strike' do you think you would have
been persuaded to go the other way?*

I don't know. Err . . . I don't believe so. I think I would have still voted to
work, as I said, all collieries run out of coal, if you keep taking
something away it doesn't get replaced within ten minutes, coal comes
in over a matter of millions of years. Therefore it follows on, no coal no
work, you've got to move.

*But given that it's generally agreed that many more pits have to
close and there will be a reduction in the number of miners. . .?*

. . . On the contrary, I believe that coal will become King again, that over
the next ten to fifteen years we'll be down to sixty to seventy super-
pits but after that we'll need more and it'll start picking up again.

*Can you remember what you were doing when you heard about
the strike?*

I were off badly.

*Sick?*

Yes. With a heart complaint.

*You were at home were you?*

I'd been off with it for about six month then. I was down to return to
work you know, just a few more tests. I came off me normal job on to
what we call a light job.

*When you had the meetings before the strike, were there a lot of
people at that time who weren't decided, or was everyone going in
basically the same direction?*

We'd been advised by our Branch Committee and Secretary to vote for
the strike . . . um . . . Colin and Dido, they advised us that they were
recommending us to strike – they were for it, they said we should all
stick together. But the majority of men said 'No, we'll not be told what
to do.' If it had all been done in a proper manner right from the start
then we would probably have got the vote right through the whole of
Britain to strike.

*Why do you think things were so peaceful here when in other
places feelings were running so high?*

Because they wanted the hassle. The strikers wanted the hassle, the
strikers wanted trouble, they wanted to impress on us their will. We
said NO and round here we were in the majority. Therefore, if we
hadn't been in the majority we'd have been in just the same trouble as
they had in Yorkshire. If you knew someone that was a striker, they
played it cool and you played it cool and the thing was never
mentioned. If they did it was just a few sharp words perhaps . . . and
. . . but I never had no bother with anybody.

*Why is it then that people like Colin are still in positions of power*

*at the pit when they don't reflect what the miners think . . . I mean,
can the breakaway union ever provide officials – do you think?*
He's got the rights, it may be he's got a lot of power but he's only got it
while we say he's got it. While I'm satisfied with the way he's doing it
he's in the job, isn't he? I do believe Roy Lynk can get things done, I've
known him for a long time, David Prendergast, personally I've known
them.

*Did you have flying pickets at Bentinck during the strike?*
Yes, from Yorkshire. There was about 3,000 of them out here. The first
day this was a Thursday I think, we came to work after the ballot, they
appeared on the scene about 700 of them. But no policemen. There
was just a narrow line about three feet wide to walk up into the baths
entrance here. They just shouted at us. One jumped in front of me . . . I
walked past him and that was it.

*Did it ever get nasty?*
It never got nasty here. They only ever had one man who was punched.

*I've heard Derbyshire miners who were on strike saying they got a
lot of hassle on the streets, people were calling them scabs. Was
there any of that here?*
No no . . . there's only one that's a bit bumptious here. Shoots his
mouth off and that.

*So how did the strike affect your daily life?*
It didn't have no effect at all. Where I live my next door neighbour was
a striker but that was it. There were a lad across the road who were on
strike and he went back to work, and that's it. See, where I live, it's a
street on its own, it's in the country, it's away from the village not even
near a town and there's only twenty-four houses, it's a mixture, there
was about 30 per cent of them are miners on the street and that's it.

*What was your attitude towards flying pickets?*
Picketing? Well, in 1974 I was a flying picket, I went down to Yarmouth
Power Station and that was just like an holiday. There were no
arguments. If we stopped a lorry from going into Yarmouth nine times
out of ten, he'd turn around and go back. But they didn't get that this
time did they?

*In some parts of the country they did. Did you talk to the flying
pickets?*
Yes. They used to come into the canteen and talk. We got very friendly
with some of them. Seeing as I was working in the baths at the time I
was with them a lot. We got quite friendly, some of them even came
and had a bath. Right? There was no hassle, not when things calmed
down a bit.

*But did you or either side manage to convert anybody from the
other side?*
No.

*And what's decided you to vote for the breakaway union?*
Basically to do with rules, the new rules. I'm not going to be told I've

got to do something. You're not going to tell me I've got to pack up work over something I don't believe in, unless I've had a secret ballot and the majority says. New rules mean – you'll strike if we tell you to strike.

*Why do you think voting Yes will be a good thing for you?*
I don't. But under the breakaway rules I've still got me individual rights. It'll not be a good thing for the mining industry. Eventually in time we may come together again or they may decide to join us. I do believe that a lot of the men in Yorkshire and Scotland would like to join us.

*Are you interested in politics?*
Yes. I was a member of the Labour Party until 1976 while Harold Wilson was in but when they did a U-turn on the Common Market, the left wingers started taking over and forced me to leave the Labour Party. I voted Conservative last time in protest along with 21,000 others in this area, in protest about the Labour Party, when Tim Smith was elected MP for this area, and I've voted Conservative ever since, and I think I'll vote Conservative again, unless Kinnock fulfils what he's done at this last conference. If he can get over Scargill and Heffer and Bernie Grant, and such as that, I'll vote Labour again. I might even join the Labour Party again.

*Does this pit have a reputation in Notts then for being right or left or whatever?*
I should say it's middle of the road.

*Why do you think that is, that some pits are more militant than others – is it because of people coming in from outside?*
No. It's the people who go to union meetings. It's the chosen few. We only get the die-hards to union meetings. I go, although I didn't go on Sunday cos I'm secretary of the local darts and domino league, otherwise I would have been there. But there's an average of about thirty turn up at union meetings out of 1,600 men. If there's something going on, something of interest, you might get 200 but on average it's about thirty and they tend to be the agitators.

*Left or not?*
Labour dominated.

*Do you find yourself talking against people like that?*
No I don't. There's two or three, I think there's about six, there may be more, at one time there was four of us opted out of paying the Labour Party levy. I opted out, I was the second. But since this dispute there's a lot more opted out.

# Memoir: North Staffs, a tale of two pits

Dave Cliff

Hem Heath and Florence Collieries in North Staffordshire are less than three miles apart and are 'twinned' by tunnels underground. Yet during the strike Hem Heath gained a reputation for militancy while Florence miners were reluctant to support the strike. Dave Cliff is a miner from Hem Heath, presently studying at Ruskin College in Oxford.

The 1984-5 miners' strike was slow to spread to the North Staffordshire coalfield, it wasn't until 19 March that pickets first arrived from Yorkshire and South Wales. The response to the picketing was mixed. The local evening paper, the *Sentinel*, carried a dramatic report on the effects of the picketing on 20 March. Two of the five North Staffs pits were at a complete standstill (Wolstanton and Silverdale), partial production continued at Hem Heath and the remaining two were working normally (Florence and Holditch) the report claimed. This situation was to develop over the next few weeks and polarise into a miniature reflection of the Yorkshire/Notts situation.

Much has been written, and many theories expounded, on the reasons for the lack of militancy in the Notts coalfield: poor area leadership, good working conditions, high bonuses, tradition of moderation, no ballot, and the security of the Notts pits, have all been quoted. But many of these reasons do not stand up when applied to individual pits in the North Staffs area. Florence Colliery behaved like many of the Notts pits and Hem Heath, although the strike broke at an early date, showed a degree of militancy that many Yorkshire collieries would have been proud of. The reasons given for Notts failure to strike I shall look at in relation to Florence to see if any can explain the lack of militancy there.

An area ballot held in early March showed that 73 per cent of Midland area NUM members were against strike action; not a single pit showed a majority in favour. Less than a week later, four of the five North Staffs collieries had declared the strike official at mass meetings. The first to do so was Holditch on 22 March. Accusations that the indefinite stoppage vote was taken at a Kangaroo meeting with less than 200 in attendance were aired in the local press. No such accusations could be made of the strike vote at Hem Heath on 23 March: over 600 men attended the meeting and heard an appeal from a South Wales miner to join the strike to protect jobs. The meeting took a vote on whether to make the strike official at Hem Heath; out of the 600 at the meeting less than ten voted to carry on working. In quick succession, Wolstanton and Silverdale Collieries followed this lead and declared official stoppages at their respective pits. A meeting at Florence Colliery to decide the same issue refused to let a South Wales miner address them and by a small majority decided not to take strike action. From this point the numbers ignoring picket lines increased rapidly, until at the start of May the NCB could claim that Florence was working normally.

The differences between Hem Heath and Florence were on a par with those of Yorkshire and Nottingham. Great militancy was shown by the Hem Heath strikers; at Florence those that did support the strike seemed to do so half-heartedly. Before the strike had run its full course (not quite a year at Staffordshire) the majority had returned to work in all the area's pits. No great credit can be given to any of the area's pits overall – no Maerdy exists in Staffordshire. But the relative militancy of the Hem Heath strikers certainly stands out in an area of moderates.

Many of the theories used to explain Nottingham's failure to respond to the strike call do not stand up when applied to the differences between Hem Heath and Florence. Their work-forces are drawn from the same catchment area; the Hem Heath workers enjoy better conditions and bonuses than their colleagues at Florence. Security of employment is far greater at Hem Heath, a local feeling that Florence may face closure in the next two or three years exists, and they both enjoy (or suffer) the same area leadership. These facts lead me to believe that Nottingham's failure to respond might be due to deeper reasons than have been suspected.

The different course the strike took at Hem Heath and Florence can be judged partly from the tally of arrests (many unjustified) at each branch. Hem Heath strikers were arrested at demonstrations and pickets all over the country. To quote each and every instance would take a book on its own to record. Many Hem Heath strikers were arrested picketing their own colliery, the strike was never 100 per cent supported although less than thirty out of approximately 1,600 worked for the first few weeks. Hem Heath men were among those arrested at Florence, Silverdale, Holditch and Wolstanton at the height of the picketing. For a moderate area Hem Heath mobilised a good number of pickets. Florence strikers by contrast were never much in evidence away from their own pit. The numbers of Hem Heath strikers arrested mounted quickly as a bitterness towards those who carried on working developed. This bitterness did not seem to reach the same degree of intensity among the Florence strikers; the picketing by Florence strikers seemed far more amicable and friendly. It was almost as if they expected and accepted that the majority of their workmates were going to carry on working come what may.

The numbers of men returning to work at Hem Heath increased with the approach of the two week's annual holiday at the end of June. To get these men across picket lines the NCB hired coaches, driven by non-union labour, that would refuse to stop at the picket lines. (The coach firm normally used supported the strikers by refusing to cross pickets.) The same tactic was never needed at Florence: the working miners would group together just down the road from the colliery and walk in together with a police escort. The fact that strikers at Hem Heath were being denied the chance to talk to their colleagues who had decided to return to work caused much frustration and, on occasion, led to outbreaks of violence. This had the result of increasing the bitterness of the strikers and portraying the police in the role of strikebreakers. Hem Heath strikers were mobile and devoted to the union's cause; they played prominent parts in all the major demonstrations and provided flying pickets for all the local collieries. The numbers mobilised can again partly be judged from the arrest tallies, on the basis that the more active a striker was the more chance of him falling foul of the law. Hem Heath men were among those arrested at demonstrations in London, Mansfield, Sheffield and Nottingham; they were arrested picketing at Baddesley, Littleton, Lea Hall, Trentham Workshops, Staffordshire House (NCB Headquarters) and various power stations. Florence, by contrast, showed little enthusiasm for organising flying pickets or attending national demonstrations. The militancy of the Hem Heath strikers resulted in near to 100 arrests, eight sackings and five imprisonments. At Florence I very much doubt whether arrests reached double figures and there were no sackings or imprisonment of Florence members.

Why this great difference? One of the arguments used to explain Nottinghamshire's reticence to strike is that of poor area leadership. The area leadership for Hem Heath and Florence was exactly the same. This leadership at first responded to the situation by calling an area ballot and asking pickets from outside to stay away while this was conducted. From this point onwards all initiatives were left to individual branches. The officials at both Hem Heath and Florence called on their members not to cross picket lines, so at this point there was little difference even at branch level leadership. The meeting on 23 March that endorsed strike action at Hem Heath, and Florence's meeting that refused to take this path were the first major pointers to the large differences that existed. Thus it is obvious that area leadership did not play a crucial role here. The argument that Nottinghamshire men enjoyed good working conditions and received high bonuses and so were reluctant to strike is almost completely reversed in the situation at Hem Heath and Florence. Hem Heath's bonus payments taken over a yearly period amount to much more than those paid at Florence (it would average out at at least £10 a week difference). So if high bonuses had an overall effect of reducing militancy this should have been more noticeable at Hem Heath. Florence, being the older of the two collieries and having less spent on investment and modernisation, had working conditions slightly worse than those at Hem Heath, so again this could not have been a major factor.

There is no simple answer to explain why some collieries were in favour of the strike and some against. The arguments presented for Nottinghamshire's lack of commitment seem simplistic and overstated. One aspect that I believe needs further investigation is the role played by management-worker relations. This is one of the points that was glaringly different at Hem Heath and Florence in the build-up to the strike. During the overtime ban that preceded the strike the management at the two collieries reacted in totally different ways. At Hem Heath, if maintenance work that should have been carried out in overtime necessitated the closing of a part of the mine, management took the stance that it was a situation created by the men's refusal to work overtime and so they would not be redeployed to other work. The NUM Branch at Hem Heath took the decision that if any member was sent home due to management's refusal to make other work available then all NUM members would go home. The result of this was that during the whole period of the overtime ban men at Hem Heath only worked three full weeks. In fact, when one section, COSA, refused to abide by this decision of one man sent home all men out (except those employed on the maintenance job in question), it resulted in a one-week strike to make the COSA members follow and adhere to the overtime ban. The effects of the overtime ban at Florence were less dramatic; little time was lost because the management there agreed that if maintenance work needed to be carried out during normal working hours, then men who could not work on their normal jobs would be found alternative work. This fostered a belief that management at Florence was doing its best to look after the workers there. The opposite was true at Hem Heath. Management's hard line attitude created bitterness and militancy, and this was to remain a factor throughout the strike. One question that needs to be answered is did this this type of difference exist between Yorkshire and Nottingham? In other words, were management atittudes significantly different in these two areas?

A second point is the role of branch officials and committees in the build-up to the strike. Union meetings at both collieries were attended by a very small percentage of the work-force, but union business was taken to the pit by some of the committee members at Hem Heath. Wider arguments than everyday issues, such as the amount of bonus paid, were developed by these members. Economic and political debates were everyday occurrences in some parts of the mine. Men who did not bother to attend union meetings were kept in touch with matters discussed at branch meetings through committee members instigating controversial discussions. I cannot say whether this process happened at Florence; it was by no means a unanimous action of the committee at Hem Heath. On one occasion at a branch meeting it was suggested that a newsletter should be started to keep the men informed of what was happening. Several of the committee objected on the grounds that if 'they' couldn't be bothered to attend union meetings then it was not the responsibility of those that did to keep them informed. Some of the committee were less than helpful when approached by men who had not been to the meeting asking what had been discussed and what decisions taken. One answer I heard given was, 'If you'd have wanted to know what's what you'd have been there, don't expect me to tell you if you can't be bothered to get up for the meetings.' There seems to be some evidence that the sections kept informed were the ones that responded most positively to the strike call. Once the strike got under way the imagination of the strike leaders at Hem Heath was used to keep the men occupied and involved in the daily running of the strike. Picketing was varied; transport was provided for flying pickets. Some felt that we should only picket our own pit while we still had men working, but it was quite clear that a day or two spent picketing somewhere else was a great morale booster. This is one area in which I feel the Florence strike leaders failed. Hem Heath's leaders booked as many coaches as were needed to transport any striker that wanted to go to any of the many rallies that were held. Rank-and-file members were encouraged to take an active part in collecting funds that were desperately needed for food parcels. Members who had never been to a union meeting in their lives embarked upon journeys to London and Birmingham to address meetings and appeal for funds. This active participation by rank-and-file members involved them deeply in the issues of the strike in a way in which mere words could never have done. Without further investigation it is impossible to compare this with the way Florence's strikers tackled the problems. The small involvement I had with Florence leads me to suspect that much of the work of running the strike was kept as the preserve of the branch officials.

The men at Hem Heath saw the dispute as their dispute, not a dispute between their union leaders and Coal Board officials – could this have been part of the problem in Nottingham? Much work investigating these aspects must be carried out if the NUM is ever going to stand united against a common enemy.

## Postscript

After writing this chapter on the differences that existed between the two Staffordshire collieries, Hem Heath and Florence, during the 1984-5 miners' strike, a conversation with an old miner now employed at a private mine in Chedle helped to shed much light on the development of the differences. Apparently when the Chedle pits had closed, all those who were transferred to other collieries went to Florence. Chedle mines were notoriously difficult to work, with bad roofs, low seams and water problems. The Chedle mine-owners were harsh taskmasters and poor payers according to the miner I talked to. There was no tradition of militant trade unionism in the Chedle pits as in most parts of the Midland coalfields. The men transferred to Florence Colliery, shortly after nationalisation, found the conditions much better than they were used to; the pay also improved and under nationalisation many of the petty fiddles, employed by coal-owners, to rob men of the money they had earned, ceased. The new world of Florence Colliery under nationalisation was a million miles from their previous lives in the Chedle pits. No tradition of unity and active support for the miners' union existed and the move to the much better conditions at Florence were not going to foster the need for unity. Even though the majority of those who worked in the Chedle mines have now retired or simply left the coal industry, their attitudes and ideas have permeated the majority of new entrants to Florence, thus maintaining the non-militant attitude that kept many working through the national strike, the attitude of things are not so bad here, we're doing all right.

By contrast, the influx of men at Hem Heath Colliery came from Durham, Scotland and, to a lesser extent, Wales, all areas where the tradition of Union and unity were strong. The attitudes that come with these men have to a large extent influenced the role of the Union and the way in which many now see the Union as a common bond needed by all. True, Florence also received some manpower from these areas, but they arrived to work in the overwhelming atmosphere of content created by the Chedle miners' prior move there. I believe that this basic historical difference goes a long way in explaining the divergent courses taken by two collieries that, on the face of things, seem to be much the same. Individuals starting work in a militant, pro-Union environment are quite likely to become strong supporters of that type of collectiveness, while the opposite is true in the case of a moderate, management-orientated environment. Militant work-forces generate future militancy as moderate work-forces generate future moderacy – this seems to be the case at Hem Heath and Florence.


# Agit-prop: Delegate's speech at Hatfield Main

Dave Douglass, Branch Delegate


On Saturday 10 March Hatfield NUM called an emergency branch meeting. Cars with loudspeakers on top had toured the villages calling everyone to the Welfare Hall in Stainforth. The night previous, being a Friday, the packed working men's clubs had had the evening's entertainment interrupted by Committee men, announcing the emergency meeting, and urging that this would probably be the most important meeting of their working lives.

When Saturday dawned, the village of Stainforth was awash with men. In the hall the bodies packed shoulder to shoulder in innumerable ranks from the foot of the stage to the back walls. The double doors were thrown open, and men packed in and overflowed out into the car park.

In the roadways the traffic inched along in single file as miners' cars lined both sides of the road and filled every side street. The mood was mixed, though nobody doubted what the meeting was about.

David Douglass, the branch delegate, speaking without the microphone which he explained stopped him talking because it used up one of his hands, addressed the massed ranks of the miners in a volume only a decibel or two below a shout.

'Everyone knew this day would come.
It's here.
There is no place to hide; we have it to face.

The decision is the most important one we've ever made . . . or will ever make in relation to your future.

I warned at the last meeting, and the one before that, that the stocks of coal were running down so fast, the balance was shifting in our favour.

There cannot be more than a few months' coal left at the power stations. I warned that if they were going to move, it would have to be soon.

Well, they've made that move, although in fact they've been trying to provoke us into action for weeks. We've been trying to get you to resist that provocation and get your shifts, even as late as yesterday on 75s.

Half of Yorkshire had been laid off! Men treated with utter contempt and the union had been told outright lies.

Cortonwood is the acid test of loyalty to this union, fail this test of loyalty, abandon Cortonwood and this union might just as well close down lock, stock and barrel.

Because if we don't back the union, there is not the slightest reason why the management should listen to us or take any notice of us whatsoever.

The union has no strength without you! So it's not just a fight for Cortonwood.
IT'S A FIGHT FOR WHETHER OR NOT YOU HAVE A UNION.

Cortonwood is an attempt by the Board to establish the principle that pits will close on economic grounds.

If we accept that Cortonwood can close . . . because its coal's too expensive, then we can accept that ANY pit can close on economic grounds.

I want to remind you.
That *this* pit, this time last year was losing six pounds per tonne MORE than Cortonwood is now!

Remember that MacGregor has stated he can see no justification for the Doncaster coalfield to stay in operation.

Doncaster's coal is too expensive, roughly *half* of Doncaster's pits produce coal DEARER than Cortonwood's.

I DON'T THINK OF THIS AS A FIGHT TO STOP CORTONWOOD CLOSING, IT'S A FIGHT TO STOP *DONCASTER* CLOSING.

Don't anyone think because we only lost 1½ million pounds SINCE JANUARY, that Hatfield is safe. A single swift does not a summer make! [laughter]

Hatfield *has made a profit*! ONE WEEK . . . IN TWENTY-TWO YEARS!

OURS is among the lowest in the country and we are one of Britain's most persistent loss-makers [Shout 'You've got to be good at something!']

Last year we were number thirteen on the Board's closure list of twenty.

CORTONWOOD is an outright challenge.
It's not been put forward for review, just 'closed middle of April'.

The trail of Cortonwood closure is a trail of lies and deception.

When Elscar was being run down, the men were offered SECURE futures at Cortonwood. They were told they would see their days out at Cortonwood. . . . THAT was in December . . . now they are told their days will end in a couple of weeks' time.

Cortonwood's Silkstone is among the best valued coal in Britain. The pit has operated until recently just two faces; just before Christmas a third face was opened. The Board explained that Cortonwood's markets had improved.

Imagine the situation at the pit. . . . When the Secretary is walking up the road, and the manager calls him up to the office: 'Mick, I've some bad news, sit down. I have to tell you that Cortonwood ceases production April 1984.'

The Employment Protection Act says, by law, the union must have prior consultation BEFORE a decision of that sort is reached.

The Redundancy Payments Act says, by law, ninety days' notice must be given before serving of redundancy notices.

But the Tories don't care about employers breaking the law and riding roughshod over the miners.

WE are told to have faith in the Colliery Review Procedure but THEY refused even to bother with it on this occasion. Not that we've ever had a review in our favour yet.

IT'S OBVIOUS THAT THE BOARD CONSIDER THIS UNION AS A PAPER TIGER THAT CAN BE IGNORED AND MEN MANIPULATED AND PUSHED AROUND.

[Shouts 'What we gonna do about it?']

That's why this isn't just a fight for Cortonwood.
Nor even for Hatfield. But for the right to have an effective union to represent you!

[Sustained applause]

It is also the immediate prelude to a massive pit closure attack upon the Doncaster coalfield in its entirety.

The problem is immediate!
And the problem is NOW!
It requires an immediate and radical response!

[Applause, stamping]
There is Bullcliff.
It is joined underground to Denby Grange. Development work was under way at Bullcliff to give them work until the year 2004.
What was planned was to give the other Bullcliff men two faces to work in Denby which would tide them over six months until the development of Calder Drift.
Stupidly and selfishly Denby men refused to allow Bullcliff men to take over those faces.
The Board's response to this internal argument was to say 'right, Bullcliff is totally closed . . . now!'

NO CONSULTATION.
NO REVIEW.
THE PIT IS CLOSED.

OUR action, regardless of the internal squabble, is to prevent the writing off of that huge lump of reserves at Bullcliff.

THAT ISN'T ALL . . .

At Ferrymoor Ridings the Board, with the union's agreement, started to construct a washery complex. As usual, because it was specialist work, an outside firm of contractors was employed in its construction. Now when we've approached the Board about manning the washer, we are presented with yet another fait accompli.
The washer we are told will be manned by an outside private firm . . .
NO MINERS . . . it will be private.

I don't need to spell out the implications of this. . . .

IF IT'S A WASHER TODAY, IT'LL BE A DRIFT THE DAY AFTER AND A DEEP MINE THE DAY AFTER THAT!

We have been warned of the possible denationalisation and the return to private coalownership.

WELL HERE IT IS.

THIRTY-SEVEN YEARS AGO. THIS UNION DEFEATED THE COALOWNERS AFTER TWO CENTURIES OF STRUGGLE.

I HOPE NOBODY OF *THIS GENERATION* OF UNION MEN IS GONNA ROLL OVER AND LET PRIVATISATION COME CREEPING BACK!

[Shout 'never']

If anyone needs reminding what the coalowners were. . . . take a look around the graveyards in Durham, Northumberland, Barnsley and Wigan. The acres of monuments to our dead killed in their thousands. And the little kiddies, blown to kingdom come for the owners' greed.

If you think that it was just because it was a long time ago . . . take a look at the countries where the mines are still privately owned and look at the treatment mineworkers have received there.

The enormity of the threat posed to us all by the Cortonwood closure in particular can be seen by the fact that of fifty-six pits in Yorkshire . . . twenty-one operate at a loss, and about fifteen at a bigger loss than Cortonwood.

IF YOU LET THAT ARGUMENT GO UNCHALLENGED AT CORTONWOOD YOU HAVE AUTOMATICALLY CONCEDED THE OTHER TWENTY-ONE PITS.

The threats have already been made.
The Board, after spending £50 million on Houghton Main, have announced their intention to close it.

Fryston has more untouched seams than touched. But there is to be no development, when work is finished in the existing seam . . . that's the end ot it.

Manvers. The branch was called to a meeting with the area director and told 'If the pit isn't in profitability by July, it will close, and don't think you're going running to the review board . . . because it's not going in.'

Dodsworth. They had originally agreed to numbers of men being transferred to Redbrooke next door, the branch have repeatedly tried to bring forward names of men, the Board refusing to discuss it. With Dodsworth closing date coming closer and closer there is a strong indication from the Board that there is no place anywhere for Dodsworth men and compulsory redundancies are just about here.
All the while I'm telling you this . . . and I'm trying to get over the seriousness of this situation and I'm trying to give you the reasons why this battle has to be fought . . .

I AM ACUTELY AWARE OF SOME PEOPLE IN THE ROOM WRIGGLING AND SQUIRMING TO FIND A WAY TO SURRENDER THIS UNION. TO STICK THEIR HANDS IN THE AIR AND SAY 'THANK YOU MR MACGREGOR . . . A KICK IN THE BALLS . . . THANK YOU SIR. . . . THE DOLE QUEUE, THANK YOU SIR'
Take what we're given
Eat Shit!
And the current running is

STRIKE PAY
STRIKE PAY
BALLOT. BALLOT. BALLOT.

When it was the overtime ban it was 'Why cooperate?'
'Why change shifts?'
'Why double back and have Friday off?'
Because some men actually didn't approve of the ban, they wanted it to

collapse, make men lose money, cause discontent and get back to a quiet life of seven shifts a week and bugger you jack I'm all right!

Now it's any locker we can pick up . . . to stop the resistance to closures.

There are few people who have fought harder on the question of strike pay than me, but the simple fact is we have no provision for strike pay.

Just weigh the matter up yourself – 56,000 miners at £15 each per week comes to £840,000 PER WEEK!

The union would be bankrupt in two or three weeks and I mean FLAT BROKE. No offices, no staff, no compensation department. Nothing.

The trouble is, a lot of people think the multi-million-pound pension fund is money in our bank . . . it isn't. We can't even say where it isn't spent let alone where it is. That fund is 51 per cent under the control of the NCB and they aren't going to give it to you for going on strike.

BUT PEOPLE ARE USING THE QUESTION OF STRIKE PAY AS A MEANS TO GET THEMSELVES OFF THE HOOK . . . AND RUN AWAY FROM THIS STRUGGLE.

At the end of this report I want those people who believe in surrender who don't believe in fighting for their jobs . . . to get up and say so JUST LIKE THAT.

The question of how to play it, of what arrangements are going to be made we will take. . . . BUT AFTER we've decided to fight, after you endorse this report. A man who's prepared to fight FIRST and ask the details after I have time for at this meeting.

As an anti-nuclear campaigner, I'll tell you I find the attitude of the Doubting Thomas's rather like the Civil Defence syndrome:
It goes like this:
'There won't be many survivors from a nuclear war . . . but I'll be one of them.'
So you do nowt about nuclear war until you're blown to a pile of radioactive dust.

You can think what you want about that attitude. But if anyone thinks they mun dee nowt about closures because yours isn't going to be one of them . . . must think again!

The best pal of that attitude is the philosophy which says:
'Let it close and we'll go somewhere else.'
That was the philosophy which closed down whole areas. It's the reason why Northumberland had six pits left when it had sixty. The reason why Durham had a dozen or so when it had in excess of 100. It is the reason why some areas no longer exist at all!
And think on this,

When our pits are closed up yon, *we* came to Yorkshire.
WHERE IS YOUR YORKSHIRE GOING TO BE?
THERE IS NO PLACE LEFT TO RUN
WE BACKS ARE TO THE WALL.

People have been talking about eating grass

[shout 'I thought you smoked that', general laughter]
I'd rather eat grass and fight to maintain our dignity and self respect . . .
THAN TO SURRENDER TO THATCHER AND THE BOARD AND LEARN TO EAT SHIT!

[Cheers, stamping]

The decision to oppose closures was made yonks ago . . . reaffirmed
half a dozen times and in the individual ballot in 1981 when Yorkshire
voted itself powers to take strike action if any pit or workshop was
threatened with closure other than seam exhaustion . . . THAT BALLOT
RETURNED 86 per cent in favour.

[Shout 'That was then!' Countershout 'Shut up, you', general hubbub to
the right of hall]
I take my mandate from this branch. This branch has never voted less
than 70 per cent in favour of action against closures.

[Shouts 'That's not true! Your telling lies!' Countershouts 'Last week
you were a militant, what are you this week?'
Shouts 'Them figures is wrong.' Countershouts 'Shut up we're
listening.' 'Chuck him out.'
Chairman: YOU'LL GET YOUR CHANCE. YOU'LL GET YOUR CHANCE, CARRY ON
DAVID.]

I wish you'd make your mind up what side you're on.
We've had umpteen mass meetings in here and on each occasion the
policy of resistance was endorsed.
So that's why I voted in favour of strike as of Monday.
If I've done something wrong. . . . Somebody better tell me how I've
done wrong. This pit is NOT FOR SALE!

[Cheering]

If you want to lift that mandate committing us to action. . . . You won't
just be committing industrial suicide, because let's face it, you can
throw your own job away any time you want.
YOU'LL BE COMMITTING INDUSTRIAL *MURDER*.
BECAUSE IT'S THE JOB OF THE BLOKE SITTING NEXT TO YOU YOU'LL BE THROWING
AWAY AS WELL AS YOUR OWN.
I WANT A VOTE, ENDORSING THE VOTE I MADE . . .
ENDORSING THE DECISION OF COUNCIL . . .
TO STRIKE FROM MONDAY . . .
LET'S HAVE THAT VOTE FIRST, THEN WE'LL TALK ABOUT DETAILS AND PROBLEMS.

THIS, BROTHERS, IS THE LAST DITCH BATTLE OF THE MINERS' UNION.
IF YOU MAKE THE WRONG DECISION NOW, YOU'LL HAVE THE REST OF YOUR LIFE ON
THE DOLE QUEUE TO REGRET IT.
AS YOU KNOW SCOTLAND AND WALES ARE WITH US FROM MONDAY.
KENT AND POSSIBLY DERBYSHIRE WILL BE JOINING OFF THEIR OWN BAT AND THE
REST WILL BE PICKETED OUT.

THE FIGHT BACK HAS STARTED LADS.
LET'S GET INTO IT!

[Sustained applause]

Brief speeches of support for the action and then a vote is taken.
Five vote against, everyone else in favour.

# 4 A STRIKE DIARY

## Brookhouse, South Yorkshire

Iris Preston

These are a few extracts from a 100,000-word diary which Iris began writing on day one of the strike.

10 Iris Preston

### The beginning. 6 March 1984

Today my sons are on strike, both work as miners at Brookhouse Pit. And it is no good you putting this journal away – the situation isn't going to change, so you might just as well write it again.

*Today my sons are on strike.* Oh God, I put my pen down, sat back and thought about it. Oh God it can't be so. They will have no money, no job, nothing. We must have a 'Round Table' conference, surely they will both see that I'm entitled to that. The lads know I will not see them starve, so we must talk and talk about both points of view, but in my heart of hearts I know they are both responsible lads and sensible, and that neither of them will have made the decision without first thinking about it.

On my way to work driving behind hundreds of exhaust pipes (I ride my motorcycle) it really 'hit me' my life would maybe change, I had responsibilities not just as a housewife and working mother, but to workers everywhere, it is now time to 'stand up and be counted', but journal, I don't want to stand up and be counted. I would just like to go my own 'sweet life', deep inside I know I am wrong. But maybe they will be back to work next week, anyway we'll see what comes out of our 'Round Table Conference' which will be held on Sunday.

## Round Table Conference. 11 March 1984

To the boys an 'Excuse for a bloody good Nosh up'.

All present and correct. Donna, Lance, Tarrance, Chris, Les and myself and not forgetting the 'sticky-fingered bid' Lindsey, plus one ugly cross-bred collie terrier.

Lance opened the conversation between mouthfuls of roast tater and Yorkshire pudding, putting concisely the case for striking. 'We're out and we're staying out until Pit closures policy of the NCB are scrapped, and the Plan for Coal is accepted.' I didn't understand either of those two policies. Oh Chris, where has your head been, two boys involved in the hardest dirtiest job and you know nowt – well not quite true. I knew that their job was dangerous so I just didn't talk about it – why, because I was afraid to face reality. I never wanted to face the fact that things could happen below ground but now I must. The more I listened to my sons the more I realise what little I know, and must now educate myself. Listening to my sons made me realise I have been the proverbial ostrich, also the knowledge that they have amazed me. I did not know my lads – and inside I was ashamed. By the time lunch was over I was committed – should have been many years ago. I love my sons but had not thought that loving and doing went together. . . .

I see my sons' faces across the table. Tarrance's eyes twinkling as he saw comprehension in my eyes – 'Now Mother bas, watch which cudgel thou picks up.' Lance 'I reckon we've got a tiger by its tail here. Oh bloody hell, what have we done. This were 'er who was going to "talk some sense into us". You know Tats, maybe encourage us to scab.' I'd never heard the word. Blackleg yes, scab no. I wasn't, I wasn't. I just wanted to talk to you.

## Trouble. March 1984

In Nottingham lives my brother, his wife and two children. Geoff is a motor mechanic at Thoresby pit and like quite a few NUM members in Notts came out on strike, roughly in Notts half were out and half stay in.

I am proud to say my brother was out, one of the minority and really out 'against all odds'. As I write this I am determined to give them every support I can so this will mean frequent trips to Notts and phone calls. Lots and lots of communication and if possible some positive help.

I have some annual hols so will arrange to 'trip over'. In the meantime I will ring.

- Hullo Pam, everything o.k?
- Well yes – I suppose so.

- Come on. What's up?
- Nowt much. (Ha! Get yourself over a.s.a.p.)
- Pam, o.k. if I pop over?
- Yes love, when?
- Tomorrow.
- Yes, that will be great.
- Night Pam. I'll be with you. Bye for now Pam. God bless you, see you tomorrow.

I could tell that things were not just right. But what? Was it the strike? The pressure? Her voice sounded dead and tired.


## Run To Nottingham. March 1984

Thank goodness – weather decent cold but manageable. A woolly knickers run. One pair of warm drawers, one pair thick tights, plus thick knee-high socks and jeans. Tophalf: one tee-shirt, one blouse, one sleeveless jumper, one huge sleeved jumper, one jacket, one motorcycle padded jacket, one thick scarf, thick gloves, one cotton thermal type helmet plus cycle helmet. Very fetching, the whole ensemble! Hope I don't want to 'go' on the trip – there is so much clothing I will never get it all off in time. Pack a few goodies in the topbox and on my way.

Crisp freezing day, nose frozen, happily cycling away. Notice a couple of signs 'STOP POLICE'. Took no notice. Ollerton roundabout, pass police station, village shop – stopped for some bits and bobs. Not a soul in the shop. Greeted the shopkeeper – 'You're not very busy.' No, well 'they' are only in at certain times. 'They' turned out to be working miners' wives who were escorted by the police, or rather the police were there. Must encourage more talk with the shopowner. 'Oh, I'll have a packet of those.' Do you mean that the wives of strike breakers have a certain time to shop and are guarded? Well, sort of. And this seemed to be the set-up. Strike breakers' wives used the shop at certain times when the police were in the vicinity. While I was chatting away in came a strike breaker's wife. She asked who I was. 'Visiting relatives,' I said. She must have assumed they were a strike breaking family and she let forth with both barrels. 'How did you get past the police?' Said I never saw any. 'Oh, bleeding strikers, don't know when they are well off. If they want to starve let them. I'm not giving up what I've got. I'd have left my old man if he'd become a striker. I'm not stopping in the house 'cause I'm not afraid of them.' Who aren't you afraid of? 'Strikers'. Why, have they harmed you? 'No.' Well, then why be afraid? 'Well I'm not. I've heard they hit the women.' Inside I was horrified at the atmosphere.

Police poked its head inside the shop. 'Are you all right?' Yes, said woman and shopkeeper simultaneously. 'Who are you?' Just visiting. Who? Relatives. Who? Brother. Where? Around the corner. Now comes the nitty gritty. Where round the corner? Birklands Avenue the name, why officer? I want to know. I replied, why officer? 'It's my job to keep law and order.' Why, is there some trouble? Insisted again 'Who?' Then it was 'Is he a striker?' I moved towards the door. 'Get on your way.' This is a free country isn't it? Revved engine up and away. Turning the corner I saw a Panda car following me so I went all around the estate to shake it off and slipped myself and bike up some back entry, waited half an hour and proceeded to my brother's. I never mentioned the incident to them, they have enough problems without me adding to it. Pam was working but Geoff was in. We discussed the strike; up to now they have received no financial help, but he seemed strong. Geoff gave me the why's and why not's; we spoke of Spencerism – God, what's 'Spencerism'? – and how he would not have that at any price. but he is down-hearted I can tell. Poor Geoff, I can only love you all and hope. When Pam arrived home we hugged, but she is quieter than usual, the strike is obviously hitting this family hard.

I left them and set off back home, around the same village shop. Police, lots of them. I stopped by and asked a young man what's happening. 'Nowt – this is like it now round here.' Are you a miner? 'Yes.' Are you on strike? 'Yes.' Good lad, what's your name? But before he could give it to me there was a sickening 'thud' and four police officers surrounded him and beat him with truncheons. I am crying as I write this, his scream will stay with me for ever. All I could shout was 'What's your name', 'Leave him alone'.

It is 1984 and I work in the courts of law and the incident doesn't gel with my job.

## Early strains. April 1984

My eldest son is still living in his flat and he comes home for meals and brings me two ton of washing every week. 'Cleanliness is next to Godliness' so I'm told, but with the amount of washing I get I think I'd rather have a heathen. He broke his wrist so is claiming sick and won't accept anything from us, he looks tired and wan. We cram as much grub on his plate as possible but that won't give him peace of mind.

Always the same reply. Are you all right son? Yes Mum, I'm fine. But there is now gentle hints about returning home. I must admit journal I value my privacy and am not too keen on the prospect of my son returning home and it is for selfish reasons.

We are very much alike in temperament so that could mean a battle of wills and to be honest I don't want it but I must tone myself to his needs, if needs be. He hasn't said directly yet, so cross that bridge when you have to.

## Ollerton roundabout. May 1984

I set off in good spirits. It had rained in the night but it was a lovely day. I particularly remember the fresh smell in the air and I felt exhilarated and glad to be alive and free. My damn wing mirror had worked loose again, so got out adjustable spanner and tightened the sodding thing up. Slipped the spanner into my inside pocket, mounted up again and was away.

Nothing untoward happened though the police were there, but it was a wonderful day. There was the STOP POLICE signs as I neared Notts but I just ignored them. After all I had nothing to be afraid of and wasn't unduly worried.

Then the stretch of road to Ollerton roundabout and behind me the police (where the hell did they come from?) and the siren. But unconcerned I tootled along. Next minute there 'they' were in front and stopped me.

> – Now then, didn't you see the stop signs.
> – No officer.
> – Are you blind then?

Oh. I was told to 'get off my bike lad' and put it 'over there'. By that they meant in the middle of Ollerton roundabout. 'Stand it up.' The ground was soft from the night rain and the stand spike just embedded itself in the soft ground. I wrestled against the back wheel and the wet ground and gave that exercise up as a bad job and let it fall on to one of the officer's feet. By now I'd worked myself up into a lather. These police seemed so aggressive and menacing. The officer who was the recipient of my bike let forth such sweet words. I was flabbergasted. He could have got a PhD in languages. Still rolling words from his lips I was ordered to 'remove my helmet lad'. He grabbed me. Take off your helmet. Happy to oblige officer, I said. I still wasn't unduly worried, I was only visiting my brother. 'Hey sarge, we've got a bird 'ere.' Standing before me was a huge officer – white shirt, red hair and bloody evil looking. 'Undo your coat', and there in the inside pocket was my adjustable spanner. Explanation followed which was totally disbelieved. All I heard was 'offensive weapon'. No! No! Explained about my mirror again. Oh Yes. By now I was frightened, *really* frightened. Get over there, pointing to an AA hut. Are you going to arrest me? Shut up cunt and get over there. What offence have I committed? Just get over there whore! And then it dawned; *it* was going to search me. Oh God No. Can I have a policewoman? Just get over there.

I stumbled across the road toward the hut. As I went up those steps into the hut I felt a thud on my back. I think I was kicked in the back – only a kick could have been delivered with such force. Are you searching me? I want a policewoman. Get your hands on that wall cunt. Spread those legs.

About one to one and a half hours later 'It' came back into the hut and said 'You still here? You can go.'

### Health or wealth. May 1984

Well journal, I've had a turf out of all clothes that were not needed. Will be sold and the money will go to my families in Notts plus I have a silver charm and a gold watch and a ring. This will be 'haggle with the jeweller's' time.

Not bad, not bad. £20 for the chain and ring. I know he robbed me but needs must. Two good food parcels there.

Had to visit the doctor's. She and I had a long talk on the 'Miners' Strike'. She said I'm knocking myself out, my nerves are shot to pieces. My reply was the government and the law system and otherwise have shot my nerves to pieces, not the Miners.

11 The role of the police: black miner expresses his opinion

. . . er, there's no room in the car, it's full. Really? My son is prevaricating. His mother picketing! Shame and all that rubbish. Lance you had better get used to the fact that the women are here to stay and what's more, where you are we should be.

The request for the fire was significant. There was already a heating problem plus no money for bills. Donna suffered from eczema which left her nerve ends open and she felt cold when others didn't. A full canister and a spare must go, with a pre-dated cheque for more canisters.

## Adoption. June 1984

During my contact with Notts I sort of 'adopted' people. Somehow I couldn't stay on the fringe – my heart ruled my head. It always has and it always will. Listening to women talk I realised fairly early on that the spirit is willing but the flesh is sometimes weak. Just a little problem could send a miner over the picket line and it was now that I decided I would alleviate the little hardships in a mining family. So, journal, on a visit. I found a family with a newborn baby. A 'strike baby' as they came to be known. I knocked on the door. 'Can I come in lass?' There before a nearly burnt-out grate and a lovely baby girl on her knee was my friend, and tears were rolling down her face. 'What's up lass?' She replied 'and you can fuck off too'. Come on darling, what's the matter? And it seemed all the pent up emotions, frustration and hate against the system and government and the NCB poured from her. My beautiful baby; look at her, look at her. And she lifted the beautiful little dress to expose rags that were being used as nappies and her grief rolled down in huge tears down my lively friend's face. And I never spoke, it was all there.

## A rally at Kiveton Park Workingmen's Club. 14 November 1984

At the invitation of Audrey Gilbert during a telephone conversation I visited Kiveton.

Starting with the journey. Needless to say I got lost. I can't direct a match on to a matchbox but managed somehow always to arrive. Like many people in Yorkshire at this time (e.g. miners, black people, motor cyclists, of which I was – plus a *Person*?) wearing badges, I was stopped. It wasn't a new experience for me (see my search at Ollerton roundabout), only my sense of humour got me through but will not *ever* get me through the feeling of being unclean and degraded. Anyway, I was stopped – must be my big behind, – there 'they' were. They had been following me up for what seems ages. This dawned on me when they didn't pass me which they could have done so easily, me on a 49cc. cycle. All the time their lights dazzled in my mirrors which I hate, it throws me off balance – not got the best of eyesight.

They swung round me, waved me down to stop and there they were – four of God's creatures, and 'invited' me in their usual courteous way to get off my f. . . . bike (my bike was not simulating any such movement). 'Good evening officer, anything wrong?' Always the pit villages were policed by these 'friendly little darlings', the best in the world, I've always been told. Inside I was scared to death. Four coppers, lonely road and darkness – not conducive to a good feeling. One opened its mouth: 'Where the bleeding hell are you going?' (must join his charm school). My mouth froze; the tone of his voice told me one wrong move girl and you will be a guest of her majesty (small capitals) tonight. 'Visiting friends in Kiveton'. Oh yeah! Here it comes – Is your husband a striking miner? No officer, he works for the MOD. Always seems to take the pressure off a little when I mention not a striking miner but an MOD worker. Not much change in this lot, it was going to be tougher than usual. 'Friends, what friends?' Pulling rank, I said the local councillor. Little did I know the local councillor was the dreaded 'striking miner'. Audrey is a parish councillor. There was a definite difference in the next Oh yeah! Hastily, I went on (by this time I was covered in perspiration fogging up my glasses and swamping my armpits); 'yes, a parish councillor. I'm taking some knitting patterns and photos of my grand-daughter (I can't knit a stitch) to her.' Messers Charming & Co said get that topbox open. Shaking like a leaf I inserted key and swung box lid open. There covering all my goodies was an open packet of sanitary towels. The officer's hand was poised for the 'search' (they throw everything on the ground wet or not and leave you to clean up the mess). Its face was a picture! He stepped back in horror, 'Get on your bike you fat cow.' Trembling all over, I couldn't get it started. Thank you officer, I'm just on my way. All the time I had visions of my topbox in the hands of the law – arrested, no job and maybe a dreaded search. In the box were photos of police brutality, next arrangements for picketing. The S.T.s had been a quick inspiration. Having been stopped before they had become part of my 'First Aid Kit'.

## Visit to adopted group at Grimethorpe. 10 November 1984

We met at the Forresters at 5.45, two carloads. Arriving at 7.30 we met the group. It was Grimethorpe Women's Action Group meeting night. The men of our group were asked to leave which annoyed me. They had come straight from work, no tea, and to be asked to leave didn't seem too 'nice' to me. They seemed a well-balanced group though. There are two groups; one section wants more action, which they seem to provide, 'solidarity' I heard it described as and they also do the food parcels. The other group provide clothes and single men's meals and soup kitchens. Made a point of getting to know the women and discuss their hopes, joys and disappointments and present needs. There is an urgent need for a fire guard by Mrs Joy Roberts. Heard what some families were existing on – £11.95 for wife, husband, two children. This is the year 1984 and it's ludicrous. On this Tuesday night it was cheap food for sale. Some of the bread cakes were taken back for early morning breakfast to meet the 'solidarity' workers. I took some photos. The women mentioned a butcher in the village who had supported the miners all though the struggle. To quote 'if ever a lad wanted a medal it were 'im. He's been great 'e 'as'. They need shoes, children's clothes and bed linen. Men's trousers, etc.

Going back to the 'strong action group'. Betty was telling us that her father came from Wales with six children and because of his union activities was made a 'corner man', one of the hardest jobs in the pit in those days. He died old and gaunt before his time. His daughter seems to have carried on the 'old spirit'.

There was a visit from the Cudworth women asking for support. They spoke to the men of our group. It seems that their men eat at the 'Grimey soup kitchens' but I feel they need the security of a support group. We left around 9.30. It was hissing down. P. dropped me off at home. On the way home he asked me if I wasn't 'too trusting'. We discussed this at length. The meeting seemed successful; anyway see what comments are made on Thursday.

On my arrival home I thought about the needs for Joy Roberts' fireguard. It is little things that tend to make miners return to work. The pressure from a wife just turns the tide. If I could knit the fireguard I would sit up all night, but she will have that guard come hell or high water.

### The festive season. 11 November 1984

*Christmas* – a change for some. It will be a 'criticalmas' for some of the miners. I feel so deeply and wish so much for the families. One can just hope.

### Union meeting support group. 15 November 1984

The fireguard was brought up again and a male said not to take up individuals' needs. He has a lot to learn about really caring for people. Little problems in a family could up pressure. Result, a miner crosses the picket line.

### On the phone. 24 November 1984

A full morning of telephone calls. Rang Anna re the loss of my keys and a mention of the fireguard still received resistance. But I am committed to my sister's need in the coalfield and if I have to buy it myself she will have it.

### Going to the CND meeting. 24 November 1984

. . . Audrey gave her speech and was heading for the door. I asked chairman if I could read the 'poem'. I read *A Miner's Mother Laments*; there was complete silence at the end and then applause. They were crying and once again the chairman called for a collection which collected £60-£70. I asked Audrey for £10 for Joy Roberts' guard and she gave it to me willingly.

### Visit to Ireland for Sheffield Women Against Pit Closures. 30 December 1984

I have had time to think and evaluate this trip and want to record the impressions I got and remarks made by the Irish women.

One of my visits was to the Battered Wives' Refuge where the women had had all the disasters and unhappiness that human beings can inflict on each other. I remember them very clearly asking me what right had I to come over here and ask the Irish to help the miners. The question for a second threw me. But if we look at the question it is right. The Irish are still now experiencing what we are only recently experiencing. The police state, and poverty, and riot squads, and yes – what right do we have?

I explained the similarity of their position to ours. Two wrongs do not make a right and they were hostile and every right to be so but I put forward the miners' case, their reasons for the strike and hoped that these women would try fairly to see that both situations are 'government made'. At the end of the session I promised these women I would go back to the coalfields and work for the unity of the Brits and the Irish together. All was quiet for a few moments and then it happened. Questions and more questions and the hostility vanished, and the links were made. We are together fighting the same cause – 'Justice'. The best accolade was 'You will always be welcome by the women of Belfast.'

Also important is the link made by us with the Irish. The more links the women make, the stronger the bonds and as the strands tie together and become stronger so do we. I will keep in touch to maintain those bonds.

## Notes forming maiden speech or much burning of midnight oil

Reasons for keeping a record of this speech.
    (1) My first political speech.
    (2) Used it in Ireland.
    (3) Maiden speech.

Good evening Brothers, Sisters, Comrades.

Just an ordinary housewife.
Mother of two miners.
Before strike. I like many other women would see family off to work or school. In fact did all usual jobs women do for their families.

Involved in no political activities.
excepted *never* voted Tory.

But in March 1984 that existence changed.
I had two striking miners in family.
One is married with a baby (my grand-daughter) and they exist now on £9.50 per week.
My eldest is single and receives no financial help.

Both sons started at pit not long after leaving school, looking for a *SECURE* future.
There have been in this dispute many incidents (no doubt many of you experienced the same) which have caused us to feel frustrated and angry. And maybe changed your life.

One stuck out clearly in my mind.

The day my eldest returned home to live.

lived in his flat five or six years.
he had struggled along on no income to stay in his flat and keep his independence.

That day he returned he cried and said Mum after all these years had to return home.
I'm beaten and only have you to turn to and now my flat is *To Let*

It is sad to see your own crying. Knew then, more had to be done to help not only him but there would be thousands like him.

But what –
I joined a Women's Group SWAPC

gave history:

This group started just after the strike started when Brookhouse and Treeton came out. Sheffield group is a thriving, active group
– providing   money
             clothes
             food
             pickets and help to seventeen pits
List pits.
   Brookhouse, Fence w/shops, Treeton, Dinnington, Kiveton, Thurcroft, Kilnhurst, Manvers, Wath, Maltby, Silverwood, Manton, Cortonwood, Cadby, Shireoaks, Barnborough and Elscar.

We come from all walks of life. Each of us adds to dimensions of group. Not regretted one single min. Haven't had time. Been too busy.

We fund raise. Speak at meetings.

But I still realise that there are many flats like my son's that were *to let*. Unlike miners who have gone against their union where the *to let* sign has already been hung up.

But not for us.
That sign will never be hung up for us.
*To Let*   Thatcher's government starve our lads back to work or any
           miner back to work against his principles.
*To Let*   this government take away workers' right to a union.
*To Let*   any government takes away people's rights and our liberties.
*To Let*   (very important) the legal system take away our right to
           freedom of choice, our right to justice.
Dig deep and support your brother.
*To Let*   the miners work and fight against unemployment.
*To Let*   them have pits in which to work. Campaign against pit
           closures.
*To Let*   All have a right to a union.
*To Let*   us have Justice.
You must show your solidarity with miners and their families.
Whichever pit you decide to support. Cherish them. Because you are cherishing your own futures.
Thanks meeting for having me etc., etc.,


**GCHQ Rally to Cheltenham. 26 January 1985**

Miners need cash and I continue to collect. We marched or rather I 'lalloped' behind the Society flag, a comrade and I carrying the Women's Group flag. Oh joy, oh joy. Tis blissful on a freezing day to carry the banner. Almost surpasses the joy of rolling the bucket. We plodded across the mud at Montpellier Park to be met by barrages of buckets for the miners. My God I thought, there is competition here. On the way up a man was shaking the hands of the marchers. That's Norman Willis, I was informed. A most unprepossessing little man. Right! I thought. I will see if he will contribute to my tin and have verbal intercourse with him. Oh dear, got rather carried away. He dumped some change in my hand and said 'You put the money in.' To say I was astonished was an understatement and instead of giving the usual thank you I said 'Can you spare that really?' He turned towards me breath reeking of booze and asked me why. So out it all came: by not fully supporting the miners by calling an all out strike he's one step forward and three back actions. In fact once I'd got going I was quite eloquent and rounded it off by saying 'Oh well you're on the platform this afternoon with another stand down leader and lets see what happens. You are all pissing in the same pot but remember this Willis, It's got to be emptied without spilling it and your actions have proved neither of you are capable of that, so how can we expect you to be strong on the issues of supporting the miners or the workers.' All that said in one breath.

While the others went in to listen to the speakers I stayed outside to collect for the miners, getting the usual hassle, continuing to put the miners' case forward and competing with what seems like hundreds of other collectors. The speeches were relayed outside and I listened to Kinnock who gave a good speech but in my opinion no intention of keeping to it and not really meaning what was said.

The first aid lady was concerned for me. I was so white and so cold that she asked to inspect my hands. They were 'dead' and she ordered me to the first aid tent to have a hot drink, but I could still walk and the box was only half full and I wanted to catch as many as I could coming out from the meeting and fill the box. We all trooped back to the coach. But just before this two coppers kept following me around so I did a quick nip into the loo, waited until they had gone and then continued collecting. It was a change to see them without truncheons and made this remark. A woman overheard me and said 'rubbish, the police do not carry truncheons'. I tried patiently to explain that it was normal for the police to police the pit villages and pit heads with truncheons drawn and I offered her a bed at my house and a couple of nights on the picket lines which she refused. Collected on the coach going back.

## School. 7 February 1985

I had arranged to go to my youngest son's school.

He had had a school mid-term report which was appalling. English Lit. was abhorrent to him so the result was failure to attend school and lack of homework in all his subjects. Result, this report from school.

I also wonder if this strike has not affected him too. He has two brothers on strike and I feel this situation worries him and this is why I feel justified in including this write up in the journal. I reasoned and argued with him over this report and have managed to get English Lit. dropped from his curriculum but he still has another subject to take. But what?

As the strike has gone on so mothers and wives have found difficulties outside the financial area and my 16-year-old son is one of the many who have found this dispute difficult.

## Tying ends together. 16 February 1985

This week I've written several letters to friends and supporters of the dispute.

John and Dorothy received two letters with enclosures – leaflets. A letter to Maisie enclosing poems and a thank you letter for the money. Whether this letter should have come from the group I am not sure. I'm an individualist and though I will work with a group I tend to want to do my own thing on certain things. So the result is letters treating the donors as my friends because that is what they are.

Barry and Adele plus leaflets, Belinda Jones thought I left page 2 out. What a memory! A letter to Trevor who sent me a gift of some sheets. To Pierce some stickers and poems.

This Saturday distributing of leaflets didn't happen. I rang Carol to say I would be late only to find that they hadn't been picked up yet. What organisation, it annoys me. I rang the printer, then rang Jim who wasn't in. Rang Jim Sunday. He will pick up leaflets and bring them to the group.

On the Saturday I received some clothes from Belinda. I also in the week received a letter from Cudworth Women's Action Group thanking me for a donation but it was not my donation, it was from my friends in Buckingham. I feel grief that Cudworth are without much support and will try to donate whenever I can.

I can't remember who else I've written to.

## Discussion in the Community. 2 March 1985

The Camera. This is now being used at nearly every pit and

known as 'big brother'. The miners resent it. Even some scabs – they feel it is another intrusion and restriction in their lives.

They were not sure whether it recorded continuous movement in the pit area and put it on film to be used against them.

The women felt it could take photos of the homes of miners near to the pit.

This pit has a public path running through it from one village to another. The camera restricted people from using this path.

The old people of the village expressed a little fear of it.

Most of the community was disgusted by the use of this camera and felt it was not just put there to protect NCB property as the complement of police was heavy and not much damage was done at this pit.


## Delegates vote to return. 3 March 1985

Today is my birthday and almost one year ago today my boys and the miners came out on strike. Journal, I have been putting this recording off and even now it's pained me so much to write about it.

We saw so much courage from the miners and their families. But back to recording in chronological order. We saw Sue off in a taxi and hoped she was able to catch the early train, then watched the news on T.V. for the delegates' vote on a return back to work vote. Inside myself I hoped they would stay out but I also knew that they could take no more of the hardships, arrests and brutality that was shown and given to them. My sons' faces flashed before me and the faces, some gaunt and haggard, of the miners, flashed before me too.

As soon as the news came through my son rang me. Stoic as always he has accepted but reiterated that his pit might now close.

I asked myself, many times, why the other unions did not support the miners. Cannot they see that this could be the end of fair play, fair pay and decent working conditions for all except the chosen few. Are they so blind or so afraid?

I feel leadened by the results. I can understand the reasons but cannot bear to think of the consequences. My own union, the CPSA, is in jeopardy and like many there are redundancies which now that the miners have returned will escalate and the 3 million that are unemployed will be higher. So much for Maggie's 'we the Conservatives hate unemployment' speech. The operative word there is 'hate' unquote.

I rang John and Dot – they both knew I was upset – and told them it is now inevitable that at least half the Yorkshire coalfields will be unemployed, the whole of Kent, some more in Wales and

Scotland. A sad day in our history. We must somehow overturn this disaster. There is two years before an election but I predict here and now that somehow or other this government will do everything in its power to put off this election and jobs and pensions and wages will go up just before the elections. They will keep the Iron Hand going until then.

In 1983 I knew nothing of politics. Never voted Tory but that was the extent of my politics. Now it horrifies me, the knowledge gained through this strike has opened my eyes, but some of it bewilders me. How and why have we let it happen? Ignorance must be stamped out. The dispute is over but the struggle continues.

My own sons knew the meaning of the word solidarity in its fullest sense and stayed out. They have stood tall. I hope the world remembers them and all the others. The results of their loyalty will not be forgotten by the NCB and now pray every day that they will be alright and no harm will come to them.

My solidarity with the miners will surely bring some repercussions for my own job. Anyway, that has yet to come. In the sea there are ripples, anyway, let's wait and see and not be too pessimistic.

### March back to work. Brookhouse. 5 March 1985

My son rang me (or was it the other way round?). He asked if I would be marching back; wild horses and broken legs wouldn't have kept me away.

I got to the pit around 5 minutes to 9 to see 400 miners, wives and families assembled. So much for the NCB and the media's portrayal of only 218 still out on strike.

Lance was there. He seemed cheerful and we hugged and kissed and I cried. My son comforted me, it should have been the other way round. I grieved for him and all the others.

We marched alongside of the men, up that drab and dreary lane where all the trees and bushes had been removed to afford as little protection to the pickets as possible, even in the middle of a roundabout. There was recent evidence of horses' hooves. The NUM banner and WAC banner were in front, my heart was like lead. When we got to the top the men stood on one side and clapped and cheered the women who had stood so courageously alongside their men during this long and arduous dispute. I looked toward my tall son and saw tears in his eyes, he knew that this return heralded the closure of his pit and the long year with all its encumbent hardships had almost been for nothing. The beatings, the near starvation diet, meant little to my 26-year-old son without *full* victory. He said he was proud of me and that he had the best mum in the world. My lovely son, it is I who am proud of you and all those who stuck it out.

On the march back a young 21-year-old said 'What am I doing marching up pit here?' Son, it is because you are a democratic young man and not as the government would have us believe and the media portrayed – a mindless violent young man. Though your lodge voted to stay out, the majority vote at the delegate meeting was for you all to return and this is why you are marching up pit here. His reply was 'it don't ease the pain though, does it'. All of you who haven't stood with these men remember that reply. It speaks for itself.

Kathy was there at Brookhouse to march with the men. I will not forget it was not her pit and yet she was there. Thank you Kath and all of you who came.

Carol and a few of the others walked in with one of the women who had been on strike. I saw Gary's mum there, Audrey, in her buscrew uniform. She too has supported a striking miner all through this dispute. Her job is also in jeopardy. Ridley is privatising the buses here in Sheffield. God, what a country! NHS, Waterworks, BRS, there won't be anything left. Pete then brought me back to work. I just made it back in time; in fact a few minutes late, but my mind felt 'bombed' and during the day I realised more and more that the NCB could take more risks with my son's life.

Journal, I have put off writing this painful episode until the 24 March.

# 5 RIOTS

## Mansfield, May 1984
Bobby Girvan

I think it was 14 May, it was a sunny day and we went down to Mansfield and it was a lovely carnival atmosphere if you like, it was brilliant. The thing that got me, the television cameras were there, there were a few drinks and that and singing and that. Arthur Scargill come on. We were told to get back to the buses pretty early, cos the one driving the bus wanted to go. But the thing about it was that the camera started setting up when half the people had gone and we went walking up the road towards the bus and the bus had gone and we were sitting on a grass verge and then I seen something and I couldn't believe it cos I'd had a few drinks and it was like watching one of these science fiction movies, like a dark cloud coming over the place. You just saw the police coming out of the streets from every . . . you hadn't seen a policeman all day . . . on horseback, they were just getting anybody. It was pandemonium! And they were getting nearer and nearer to us and I thought, What's going to happen? Some of us went running down the road to see what the trouble was and I went to speak to this copper to see what were happening. One of them got me against the wall, another policeman grabbed him and asked him what were happening, and he says, oh he's all right this lad is. This copper went and stood with some of the women so they wouldn't get hit because they were just going mad. I see policemen get on buses, pulling people off, knocking hell out of them with sticks. As I went down the road I kept ducking and diving out of the way. I see a young schoolgirl coming round the corner with a satchel over her shoulder and a horse went flying by and knocked her flat. I went to pick her up and got kicked on the shoulder as a policeman were running past hitting people. And as I got up near the crowd there was people chucking stones and that. I never felt so frightened or so angry in my life when I seen what I seen. You've got horses, then policemen, then people chucking bricks and from what I could see in the middle of it, three or four, probably six policemen kicking hell out of a youth of probably 17 or 18. He managed to stagger to his feet and his face was covered in blood and that and one of them . . . it was like one of these African executions, he got his stick out about a yard long and whacked him across the face with it and the ambulance men was angry and was effing and blinding to the police and they had to put that young lad in an oxygen tank for about 20 minutes before they even moved him and I've never seen a sight like it. And I never thought I would pick up a brick in anger but that day I did. I was totally disgusted with what the police were doing. I'd heard things that they'd do. I'd seen one or two incidents on the picket line but never anything like that.

## Grimethorpe, October 1984

Harold Hancock

Now, after thirty weeks of strike, after thirty weeks of managing on less money than a single man gets on supplementary benefit, thirty weeks of riddling coal for our fires – each bag takes one

12  NACODS won't support the NUM strike. Pickets at Bentley
Colliery, South Yorks break the news to Maureen Page and Jill Fox

and a half hours to fill, and we have to have coal because 95 per cent of us have solid-fuel central heating and cooking stoves – after all this we are suddenly confronted on the coal stack by hordes of trucheon-wielding, riot-helmeted police with dogs. Men, women and kids are punched, kicked and arrested for picking coal to cook with and to keep warm. Many of them are left bleeding and bruised.

This happened on 12 October (nineteen arrests). On Sunday 16 October it happened again: 120 riot-clad police against sixty or seventy people, mainly middle-aged men – most of them with bad chests and unable to run – and women and kids. There were twenty-eight arrests on this occasion.

Monday 17 October was a different story: the police were confronted by quite a few young men: we were not running away any more. Confrontation took place on the tip – miners versus police. For a brief time we had shown that the people of Grimethorpe had had enough. The police station was stoned, and windows broken. By three in the afternoon the top end of Grimethorpe was sealed off by 300 riot police; by 11 o'clock nearly 600 riot police were running amok in the village, clubbing anyone within arm's reach. The next day, Tuesday 18 October, people in the village were running a gauntlet of foul-mouthed obscenities, mainly levelled at women and young girls, from police officers still clad in riot gear.

I make no apologies or excuses for the actions of myself or my fellow miners, here in Grimethorpe, for what happened. As I said at a public meeting on Wednesday 19 October, husbands, brothers, fathers and sons have been killed at Grimethorpe Colliery. This village has had its share, if that is the word, of fatalities; men have paid for the coal lying on the coal tips with their blood, and morally the coal is ours. And we will win, through principle, determination, guts. We will obtain an honest and just victory.

Grimethorpe has now returned to its former way of life. But, with a few exceptions, the determination to stay out till we win has grown; the number of volunteers for picket duty has grown; and so has the support and good will of trade-unionists all over the country. We in this close-knit community have been bonded closer together by the anti-strike tactics of the police and the Coal Board.

Since the trouble in Grimethorpe, the removal of coal from the coal tip, temporarily stopped by the NUM, has started again, but on a reduced basis: it goes only to the local carbonising plant, Coalite Supply Smokeless Fuel, and to old-age pensioners, schools and hospitals. The picking of coal by striking miners is non-existent because of the continuous police presence. Would-be pickers are dissuaded by various methods – police dogs off the lead supposedly being exercised are not the least of these. There are also constant police patrols, NCB security patrols. Video cameras fitted with intensifiers for use in the dark have been installed on the winding headgear. Resentment of the police presence on the tip is voiced by the strikers every day. To them, it is oppression, and, although a lifetime in a mining village limits your knowledge of oppression, retaliation seems instinctive. The brutality of the riot police drafted in from Southern counties has left deep scars on the minds of the people of this village, and an inheritance of hatred and mistrust of the local police. This hatred will take until long after this strike is over to heal – not months, but generations.

# 6 SELF-HELP

## Upton, the Infants' Support Group
Iris Knight

### The Upton and North Elmsall Mining Dispute Infants Support Group

The miners' strike had entered its third month before our small group began to function. In our village we had one group giving food parcels to single miners and putting on one hot meal every three days for all miners and their families. Another small group run by Labour Party women put on hot meals every two days for men only in the Local Welfare Hall.

The problems were that there were too many women and not enough for all the women to be fully involved. When Colin Ward and his wife, Lyn, who owned the local fruit and veg and frozen food shop went out of business due to the strike and offered the shop to any miners' support group, rent free, about nine of us decided to take them up on their generous offer. We had a meeting to decide how best we could use the shop and what part of the mining families we could help.

It was decided by all the group that we should start a nearly new shop and the families who had babies and children under school age were the most needy. The reason for this was they did not get free school meals or clothing grants the same as those who had children attending full-time school. The first thing was to get clothes and household goods to stock the shop. This we did by going from door to door in the village asking for anything nearly new that they did not need. The response was very good and we soon had the shop full, ready to open to the public.

Before we opened we got in touch with the Oxfam charity group who gave us advice on how to set out the shop to our best advantage. This advice proved very good. We also contacted our local sewing factory for the loan of a couple of clothes racks to display the clothes. These were given without hesitation.

The next step was to advertise in the local free press what we were doing and for the miners with infants to come to the shop

13 The group's badge

and register their infants so we could find how many we had to cater for.

In two weeks we had the funds to be able to start giving out food parcels. On our register we had thirty-eight babies under the age of 1 and 100 infants from the age of 1 to school age. When it became known who we were and what we were doing, some of the local traders gave donations of baby powder, baby cream, powdered milk, feeding bottles, dummies and canned baby food, all together about £200 worth. This with the food we were able to buy with the shop takings got us off to a good start.

We then had a meeting to decide who would do what. In the administration of the group, I was elected the Group Secretary and Spokeswoman; Lyn Ward and Dorothy Stancliffe were elected Group Finance Administrators. Then we made a shop roster and all the group did as many hours that their family commitments would allow. This system worked very well and the shop was attended to at all times.

My husband, Clifford, and Terrence Stancliffe not only helped to give out the food parcels they also renovated pushchairs, prams, cots and bicycles to give to the families in need or sell to raise funds. Colin Ward not only gave his shop to the group he also gave his van and did most of the driving. He helped every way he possibly could. As a group we did not get any opposition at all; everyone gave us as much help and support as they could.

The reason our group ran without problems was the way we all found satisfaction in what we were doing. We were more like one happy family, in fact we were mostly related in one way or another and if we were not related we were very good friends. It made us all aware of the needs of other people. Before the strike we were all too much in our own tiny family units; in our own small village everyone knows everyone now but before the strike the new families were isolated; now they are part of the community by the way the villagers, young and old, bonded together in a common cause.

The food parcels were given out every Friday afternoon. All our group members helped on the distribution of food parcels. The babies received powdered milk, rusks, washpowder, baby cream, talcum powder, soap and canned baby dinners. We gave out these parcels on a request basis as feeding bottles, shampoo, dummies and such were not required as often as baby food, etc. The infant food parcels were more or less the same each week; these consisted of cans of beans, soup, rice pudding, a jar of jam, a tub of margarine, six eggs, a choice of breakfast cereal, five pounds of potatoes and fresh fruit when funds allowed.

We had to keep the parcels within the cost of £4 as the Social Security could and would deduct money from the miners' Supplementary Benefit. It was very hard work and long hours but when the young mothers told us that they could not manage without our help it made it all worth while.

We also ran raffles, a tombola, darts marathons, bingo and everything we could think of to raise funds to keep our group running. Lyn Ward, Dorothy Stancliffe and I did the shopping for the group. We went to the Cash and Carry warehouse. This we were able to do with the use of Lyn Ward's trader's card, this enabled us to keep our food costs down considerably.

During the strike a young boy died digging coal on our local disused pit tip. His name was Paul Womersley and he was 15 years old. I was interviewed by the BBC to explain how difficult it was to pay funeral bills when on strike. I knew first hand of the grief and distress of the boy's parents as I have known Walter and Lily Womersley most of my life. A few days after the interview donations for the Womersley family and our group came in with every post. I answered all the letters thanking the people for their donations and support. This was the beginning of many new friendships with groups and individuals all over England. We had group meetings every Monday evening to keep all group members up to date with the financial state of the group, letters of support and donations, group activities such as collections, fund raising, rallies and marches.

All went well until near Christmas then things seemed to slow up and money became scarce. We wanted to give more than usual but no way did we have the funds to do so. This made us all dispirited. Then one week before Christmas we had a phone call from the Women Against Pit Closures Movement of which our group was a member. We had to pick up £900. It was like an answer to our prayers. We could not only give half of it to the other groups but we could give extra and buy each child a toy. We could also put some money in the bank; our group also got a £500 donation from our friends in Richmond which put us on a firm footing once again.

When the group went on rallies and marches, Mrs Barbara Robinson had sole control of the running of the shop as her family commitments did not enable her to go away because she had a sick husband. As the strike went on, rallies and marches got more frequent. They were very good because we were able to meet many of our friends and supporters as they often marched with us.

We always had a lot of police hassle whenever and wherever we went on marches or rallies. The worst that I have ever witnessed was near the end of the strike on a Union Solidarity march from Hyde Park to Trafalgar Square. The police created a bottleneck from Downing Street on to Trafalgar Square. It was plain that they did not want us to hear Arthur Scargill's speech.

During a scuffle between police and marchers, a well-dressed woman who was not on the march, just shopping, was pushed very hard by a young police constable. 'Young man', she said, 'you have not only no manners you have no parents either.' I have never heard anyone called a bastard in such a dignified way. The constable was so taken aback he just walked away very red-faced.

Our main benefactors were the Richmond and Twickenham Unemployed Worker and TU Centre in Surrey. They collected money for our group every weekend. They also collected clothes and household goods for us to sell in the shop. Sometimes they delivered them or they invited some of us to spend the weekend with them in their homes. They came up to Yorkshire to see us and get first-hand information of our strike and struggle.

Without their help I have no doubt many mining families would have starved. The Thatcher government provoked the strike not only to smash the Union but to divide the people of the South from the people of the North. In fact the opposite happened and many groups formed a strong bond of friendship with supporters not only in England but all over the world. Many women came to their senses during the strike and are now playing an active part not only in their own family life but in their right as individuals who can make a contribution to their own future. Many have found that politics play an important part in everyday life and have become actively involved in the Labour Party.

The strike is now over. We as a support group are still very active and will continue to do so because by no means is the dispute with the government and the Coal Board at an end. We may have lost the first battle but our fight for the right to work must and will go on.

## Group members

Mrs Iris Knight, miner's wife, three married daughters, four grandchildren, two boys, two girls.

Mrs Dorothy Stancliffe, miner's wife, one 9-year-old son.

Mrs Lyn Ward, shop owner, one son aged 16.

Mrs Barbara Robinson, miner's wife, four daughters, four sons, nine grandchildren, six girls, three boys.

Mrs Ann Cox, miner's wife, one son, two daughters.

Mrs Ann Macadoo, miner's wife, one daughter 10 months old.

Mrs Mary Nock, miner's wife, one son, two daughters.

Mrs Allison Walker, miner's wife, one son 1 year old.

Mr Clifford Knight, miner, married to Iris Knight.

Mr Terrence Stancliffe, miner, married to Dorothy Stancliffe.

Mr Colin Ward, shop owner and lorry driver, married to Lyn Ward.

## Plans for the future

As a support group we learned the hard way, that you must not sit back and just let things happen. If things are to change for the better we must get involved and help to improve and procure a better future.

To do this we must attain the education we will need. Many of us attend conferences and adult further education college courses at weekends. We have also become active members of our local Labour Party. We have kept up our contacts we made during the strike; these I am sure will prove valuable in the future. We must be ready if anyone in our community needs assistance and we must ensure the Labour Party's victory in the next election. It is the only way to make sure that the working class get a better chance.

As members of the Women Against Pit Closures Movement we will fight tooth and nail to stop the Coal Board putting thousands of men out of work. We are a big army and we will be ready when we are needed again even stronger than before.

I WISH EVERYBODY IN
**CANNOCK CHASE**
A VERY MERRY CHRISTMAS
EXCEPT 'FOR
**TONY MORRIS**
Who's a dirty fucking
**SCAB**

ADMIT ONE

Olney Labour Party
BEER and SAUSAGE EVENING

Olney Working Mens Club
9 NOVEMBER 1984 8 P.M.

tickets £2 or £1 OAP/unemployed

THIS TICKET IS REDEEMABLE
AT THE BAR FOR ONE PINT
OF BEER OR TO THE VALUE OF
**60p**

NATIONAL UNION OF
MINEWORKERS—(South Wales Area)

**OFFICIAL
PICKET**

G. REES, General Secretary.

BETHEL BAPTIST CHAPEL
CONCERT IN AID OF MINERS AND FAMILIES
BY COR MEIBION MAESTEG A R CYLCH
CONDUCTOR GWYNNE WATKINS ACCOMPANIST MRS EIDDWEN THOMAS
ARTISTES LYNNE MORONY, RAY MARKS   BRIAN JONES

PROGRAMME

| | |
|---|---|
| CHOIR | CHOIR |
| SOLDIERS CHORUS | SPEED YOUR JOURNEY |
| O ISIS AND O SIRIS | EVENING PASTORALE |
| GOD'S CHOIR | JOLLY ROGER |
| ARTISTES | ARTISTES |
| CHOIR | CHOIR |
| MYFANWY | JACOBS LADDER |
| LLANFAIR | STOUT HEARTED MEN |
| ARTISTES | ARTISTES |
| CHOIR | CHOIR |
| BANDITS CHORUS | EVENING PRAYER |
| COMRADES IN ARMS | MORTE CRISTE |

HEN WLAD FY NHADAU

14
Self-help: different
groups find their own
ways to raise funds
(with thanks to Kevin
Machin)

# Hatfield Main Welfare Organisation

Bob Hume

It's hard to know where to begin, writing our part in the miners' great strike; where young and old miners stood shoulder to shoulder, becoming experts at picketing, lobbying, collecting, debating, rallying and, yes, battling and protecting each other.

My duties were preparing and providing dinners and food parcels with my own wonderful team of 'Women In Support' along with Arthur Wilkinson and Brian Jones.

Back at the beginning, it became obvious this government was intent on a confrontation with the miners, to smash the NUM and start a massive pit closure programme; the signs had been there for a couple of years and those who had the industry at heart had been saving ready for the conflict. With the arrival of 1984 I was asked regularly 'Will we go on strike?' and with millions of tonnes of coal stock piled everyone realised if we did strike it would be a very long affair, unless of course we were going to use a different ploy this time instead of 1972 and 1974; possibly withdraw all safety men which any self-respecting miner would know would mean trouble ranging from hours to days in various mines, then ask the 'general public', 'do you want a coal industry or not?'. This wasn't to be, and we came out on strike officially Monday 12 March 1984 with 96,000 coming on strike.

Tuesday 13 March 1984. 109,000 on strike. At our colliery, the secretary, Peter Curran, said he didn't want me picketing this time but on the welfare side. So with the help of our local Citizens' Advice Centre we began by getting the Social Security forms filled in and sent off.

Our lads were out picketing, Coventry, Ollerton and sadly on the Thursday 15 March 1984 a South Kirby picket was killed, heralding the taste of what was to come.

Our NUM funds were under threat so certain measures had to be taken. Our own NUM HQ was under threat.

Monday 19 March 1984. Nottingham's miners going into work with police protection (that was disgusting), our lads were picketing Notts IF they could get there. They were being arrested even while travelling there and we were kept busy informing Brodsworth (our local HQ) so the lads could get bailed out as soon as possible. Then we would have to notify the pickets' families they would be home late.

With tea provided by our own Hatfield Main Football Club and a small amount of money coming from Brodsworth we scrounged a five-gallon tea urn from our local Old Folks and 'eureka!' the lads had a pot of tea going in and coming back.

The women's groups were becoming more and more actively involved and other unions were beginning to send in funds. The third week found more and more pickets being injured or arrested; it was very bitter. Fourth week and ASLEF/NUR and TGWU were giving us more support. I repaired an old Burco boiler at the Welfare (Stainforth), bought some plastic cups and powdered soup and 'eureka!' the lads were now being spoilt with a cup of soup. Fifth week and our local traders were rallying to our support. 'Pats Plaice and Royal Fish Bar' were providing fish and chips suppers to our pickets at the Pit Lane. Pickets were going to Lancashire and one of our own centres was providing thirty to forty dinners for our pickets.

On Friday 13 April 1984 our women got soup, pie and peas ready for our pickets. We now had a second-hand cooker but being limited to only 13amp only two rings could be used, but we were steadily progressing and more funds were arriving from unions, Labour Parties and individuals every day. At this time soup kitchens were springing up due to our Women In Support at Thorne, Moorends and Broadway. We were now making our pickets a couple of sandwiches each, to take with them; our single lads were driven to go picketing because they got no help whatsoever. Ninety per cent were fully in support of the strike, but the others were *driven* on to the picket line by Thatcher in order to get a bite to eat.

Seventh week and we were getting often ten of our pickets arrested every day. Eighth week and we were able to provide forty or fifty dinners, trouble was we had up to 200 pickets very active, but eventually we would have everything we needed.

More and more support was arriving and on the Monday we were able to make food parcels up for our single lad-pickets also 'the Centre' (bless them) provided up to eighty dinners. At that time we were arranging to wash some coal at Hatfield for pensioners and the team was provided with sandwiches. Our local butcher, Andy Riggott, was providing 5 to 7lbs of meat every week to make a few dinners for our pickets when they returned.

Another local trader, Wintermans Newsagent, was providing 200 cigarettes for the pickets every week right up to the end of the strike, which was a typical gesture of support our local traders were giving us, after all, our survival was their survival and they were aware of the fact.

On Thursday 17 May 1984, I bought 10 bags of spuds £25, rice pudding, onions and carrots, I took four bags of spuds to Thorne Kitchen, the remainder to the Centre who provided us all with a wonderful stew and pudding on the Friday (18 May 1984), that is just a single instance.

Our pickets going to the Wharfs and Steelworks, one of the

lads was arrested for having a novelty police hat on, while he was sitting inside a car, such was life. At this time I went to see Don Becket Freezer at Doncaster and arranged a deal for our kitchen, onions, veg and chicken, etc. I also went to see a butcher at Thorne and arranged with him to provide some very cheap meat to sell to our people.

My own Hatfield Miners Kitchen Women: J. Standish, D. Hulme, B. Plummer, P. Vanstone, P. Jones, J. Bell, L. Betts, L. Yeardley, C. Grant, D. Fullerton, Sue and Carol Wood, B. Foster, N. Wakefield, were now in full swing, making some stew and packing twenty loaves into sandwiches and as though this wasn't enough we decided that on June 9 1984 we would but a buffet/disco on and invite all the wonderful people who were providing us with funds for our kitchen and food parcels. This was a great idea and was used more and more with greater and greater success, very hard work, but worthwhile.

11 June 1984 my women were now providing 200 dinners in our Welfare which took 30lbs of meat a day, a bag of spuds, two stone of frozen veg, a soup or pudding and all of this remember still on two cooker rings, with the help of two gas rings this was the magic these women provided. Dot Hulme (my dear wife) doing the cooking (and loosing two stone in weight during the strike) things were to get even more hectic as within a week we were up to 300 dinners.

We sent buses to Wakefield Miners' Gala on Saturday 16 June 1984. I was kept busy fetching spuds, veg and meat, making out our accounts and always looking for a better deal. More funds meant more food from Travis Cash and Carry, more food parcels to be given out and on 23 June 1984 we were able to give out 127 parcels. J. Brookes and J. Maine would peel for me 1½ bags of spuds DAILY. P. Killeen would make gallons and gallons of tea and coffee, B. Jones would clean the Welfare floor at the end of the day. Arthur Wilkinson was on duty at the Welfare night and day always available to pickets and on the welfare side.

Len Childs of Cheshire NGA came to visit our kitchen and he and his good wife Margaret became regular visitors and staunch supporters right through the strike and hopefully for ever, he wrote the best letters I've ever had the pleasure of reading.

11 July 1984. Dockers made a strike effort. A German camera team filmed our pickets and the kitchen, leaving me £100 for the kitchen. On 20 July Dot cooked 45lbs of bacon for dinner with fruit pie and custard to follow. With other unions giving more and more support we felt Mrs Thatcher was being told 'We shall not starve'.

On 11 August we gave out 273 food parcels, my aim at this time was to provide a dinner and food parcel to everyone, then I would feel more satisfied for these wonderful, dedicated people hell bent on securing some guarantee of future jobs for our young people in this area.

Atkinson our local baker would give us all his surplus bread, etc. on a Saturday evening, this we would share out to up to 100 families, we had many many thanks for Mr Atkinson.

Then we came to 21 August 1984 . . . what a sickening sight, two scabs went into work at our own Hatfield Colliery, arranged with the police and some terrible scenes occurred. One man soon came out again, but Mr Tommy Freeman who had only been at the pit for a short time, after having already sold one job at the Steelworks, stayed in, may he burn in hell.

At this time we were using fleets of vans to convoy the pickets to the various destinations. I got permission to send all the kitchen women and children to Beach Home Holiday Park for 27/28 August for a day out; and at the same time we could fit a cooker unit with the view to getting a full cooker in action. This bit of organising proved a great success all round.

Scunthorpe Bonneyhale Mushrooms joined the fight with their support right to the end. Central Club at Stainforth gave me £200 for groceries on 30 August 1985 which enabled us to have a roast pork dinner, apple pie and custard on the Friday, each dinner costing 39p per meal . . . that was a magic the women provided.

NUPE Camden sent £200 to our kitchen and we arranged a Broadway v. Stainforth rugby match for our pickets. One of our lads, C. Sadd, broke his collar bone and I cracked a rib (but a great time was had by all!).

ILP Leeds District began supporting not only our kitchen but many others also; support was beginning to flood in and NUPE Camden adopted our colliery, I remember going down to the pit with Peter Curren and two senior shop stewards for NUPE (Rose Head and Ted) the manager happened to be on the premises when we arrived and Peter said hurriedly 'pretend they are my Aunty Rose and Uncle Ted'. When we asked if it was OK to show them around, we completely fooled the manager, he immediately escorted us politely off the premises. Rose didn't help instantly getting in an argument about 'Privatisation and Nationalisation'.

On 1 October Dot and I went to Camden and stayed a week with Rose Head (senior shop steward), she had arranged about twelve meetings for us in the five days, all over Kentish Town. The reception we received at all the various homes and council yards, etc. were out of this world, the reception and interest shown was unbelievable, with promise of financial help to be increased. Also at this time we were thinking what an awful Christmas our children were going to get; so we took this opportunity with the capable guidance of J. Suddaby and Rose Head to ask these people to adopt one of our children for a present if they wouldn't mind; the response was all the help we would ever need.

When Dot and I arrived home a meeting had taken place and I was now the Treasurer of the Hatfield Main Christmas Appeal Fund and J. Standish the leader of the Welfare Women had had a baby boy Christopher, very nearly born in the kitchen. This woman only lost two weeks attending in the whole of the strike; that was the calibre of the staff – unbeatable.

The Children's Christmas Appeal was launched on 8 October with a very generous £1,000 anonymous donation followed by £50 from R. Howe Builders and £210 from Hatfield Main Football Club. On 13 October we had another buffet/disco for all our supporters and began to advertise the Christmas appeal.

D. Abrahams visited us yet again; he was spending more time with us than at Three Bridges and he was (and always will be) very welcome. At this time there had been a bombing at Brighton, so it seemed a little strange when Derek showed up with representatives from Brighton/Bognor Regis ASLEF/NUR, among them a happy chappy called John Flowers, and Harry Brown and wife really ought to take a bow.

On 22 October I went to the Dunscroft/Hatfield Parish Council meeting with Elaine Robe and another woman from the Broadway Kitchen seeking some financial support for meals; and listened to the longest speeches/excuses by the so-called 'independents' as to why they could not help. One mile from our pit head we were refused support and yet we were getting it from Brighton, Leeds, Bognor, W. Sussex, Immingham, London, Bradford, Doncaster and internationally. Stainforth Parish Council had decided to give me permission to buy £200 worth of food per week on condition we bought it from the local traders. Many thanks for their help. To Dunscroft/Hatfield Parish Council, perhaps you will learn later the error of your ways.

30 October and toys were starting to arrive from Grimsby, M.S. Games, etc. The Christmas party had been agreed on for the whole area of Dunsville, Hatfield, Broadway, Stainforth, Thorne and Moorends for all striking miners' children whom we estimated at some 2,000. It would be some task but with the women as the hard core we assembled councillors and women from the respective kitchens. We were going to plan something for the kids of the area which would be beyond comparison. Broadway Hotel, Dunscroft Social Club, Stainforth Welfare Hall and Moorends Welfare and Thorne pit club would all be putting on a party on the same day at the same time. This we would do with presents for all children and Santa Claus coming up from

London (Camden NUPE).

At this time I was paying £1,500 for food parcel food and making up, although the numbers were gradually increasing as things got harder.

Friday 9 November the Riot Police ran amok through our village even kicking an old lady's door in (Mrs Barton, now deceased, God rest her soul). I have a copy of a letter sent to Mrs Barton by the Deputy Chief Constable which reads:

> I note that you are now aware of what took place in Stainforth on the day in question and can assure you that officers coming into the South Yorkshire Police Area in relation to the current problems *are now* subjected to close control. [our emphasis]

10 November and we put another buffet/disco on with the Conlin Duet and a young lady called Sharon Maid, a great little lass who played organ. Once again people came from London and all over Britain.

We organised an inter-kitchen darts tournament on 15 November; something must have went wrong because our lasses won, and it wasn't a fix.

22 November we were now receiving regularly from D. Abrahams and Brighton ASLEF/NUR clothes and toys. Each Saturday we were giving out 700 food parcels which we valued at almost £5 per food parcel, a lot of cash, which despite Thatcher's statements represented a lot of support for our cause.

I was sending cars to Hull to pick up toys and Jim Miller of Priory Place gave us £200 or £300 worth of toys. Liverpool Tobacco Union and London Tobacco Workers' Union were adopting through photos our children, with a view to sending a present straight to that particular child for Christmas.

We were now feeding an average of 500 per day at our kitchen at this time. For the next couple of weeks things became really hectic, buying and wrapping up presents. Once the kitchen women from all over the area had made up the dinners, done the washing up and cleared away, they then went into parcel wrapping until 9.30 p.m. then early the next day they were on with the dinners again, all without the slightest payment. This kind of working-class solidarity the Tory Party could never hope to understand.

At this time the BBC arrived to make a film about life in the village during the strike.

We arranged another darts match and this time Thorne Women won.

We sent four men and two women to Grimsby and Cleethorpes speaking and collecting on 8 December. They all did very well. The Bawtry Forestry Commission offered us some huge Christmas trees which we gladly accepted and took to the various venues and everywhere was being trimmed up.

## The Christmas party

When the Christmas party finally came, we had 2,000 children all receiving at least one present each from Santa Claus. Theirs was a lovely party with games, prizes and entertainment at each respective venue. The cost was well over £9,000, all of which had been provided by the unions, councils, Labour Parties and individuals the length and breadth of Great Britain as well as Australia, Greece, Germany, Holland and France.

Apart from the presents the children were receiving from Santa Claus, Bradford Trades Unions supplied every child with a present, NUPE Camden sent hundreds up from London and the Imperial Tobacco Workers Union in Liverpool and London had adopted hundreds of our children and sent private parcels to the various individuals. To all those individuals from all walks of life we owe a massive debt of gratitude which in all probability we will be unable to repay, but God bless them all.

People from a number of unions from all over Britain came to the parties to witness these children whose parents had been on strike for nine months, having the time of their young lives (which doubtless they will remember for the rest of their lives).

## Christmas

We were only too aware that it was going to be hard, so we made up a special food parcel for every household at a cost of £10. This time we added a chicken, and gave out a record 1,000 parcels; our collectors had proved their worth in London, Cleethorpes, Scarborough, Leeds, Bradford, Doncaster as well as the voluntary donations from abroad. It had been a year of dedicated work: our Welfare Kitchen had supplied an average of 300 dinners a day, 1,500 per week at an average cost to our funds of 39p per meal. Dot, Josie, Brenda, Pauline, Julie had made it possible with a lot of hard work. Joey Brookes and Jack Main had peeled some 5 tons (12cwts) of potatoes. Some 5,500 food parcels had been distributed at a cost of £22,000.

What price the friends we had? The Three Bridges Secretary, D. Abrahams, who came up to our Welfare from West Sussex one night to give a beautiful present to one of our children.

15  Saturday night out and social clubs: Barnsley and South Wales

Another time he came up I met him at the railway station and collected baby clothes and £40 cash off him, half an hour later he set off back home. Harry Brown of Bognor/Brighton ASLEF/NUR who despite having had an operation just before the New Year was on the telephone to our Welfare to be with us on New Year. John Flowers, Secretary of Bognor Regis railwaymen, happened to be with us the morning after the buffet, so ended up firstly sweeping up and then scrubbing with the rest of the team.

1984 we survived, with hardships it's true, with injuries, some of them serious. When single lads get nothing at all and a married couple only £8 per week, yes, you suffer. But our spirits were almost as high as when we went out nine months before. Our only fear for 1985 was that we should not be sold out; we were prepared in our area to fight closures to the very end, to try and save our villages and have employment for our children.

### New Year's Eve

We brought the New Year in with a disco/buffet . . . knees up, for all our kitchen staff, pickets and visiting friends; the night and early morning came with rousing 'here we go's', the Red Flag and Never Walk Alone. At that time we felt invincible.

Meantime, fuel supplies were getting very low, our own people were always on the scrounge for wood and coal to try and get some warmth together to combat the oncoming cold weather. Our own Hatfield Welfare had no heating which would become a problem.

We had started a campaign for second-hand warm clothes and shoes; as usual, people responded magnificently, so when the people came in for their dinners we would have any clothes or shoes laid out on benches for them to pick through. Remember how we are a very proud people, who have always worked for needs, now reduced to this by a very vicious government. They would swallow their pride because the cause was much greater.

On 2 January 1985 we re-opened our food kitchen after having enjoyed a very restful Christmas and New Year; me and Dot personally had everything we normally have had at Christmastime supplied by my son, brother, sister and cousins. We are sure other families rallied round in the same way.

On Thursday 3 January we were back at Travis with a hired box van buying groceries yet again for food parcels which on this occasion was to include six eggs and a loaf each.

We were still receiving late presents from Greece and France and these were being randomly selected from age groups and collected or sent to the boy or girl who had been lucky. One sad note which struck us deeply was the fate of a beautiful sledge which had arrived. The random selection gave it to Dave Smith's child; unbelievably that very man became one of our hard core scabs.

At this time BBC were filming the Welfare side, the food buying, packing and giving the food parcels out and Travis the cash and carry refused to cooperate because of possible consequences if shown on TV. I thought them very unreasonable after the thousands of pounds we had spent there, so we approached the Gateway at Dunscroft and Kirk Sandal who gladly would supply us with everything we needed at a very reasonable price and would welcome the publicity; they were as good as their word, thank you Mr Briggs.

The Coal Board were sending their *Coal News* to every miner's house costing a fortune in an attempt to persuade our lads back to work.

At this time the Scarborough Miners Support Group, led by Jean and Barry from the Flower In Hand Hotel, were in full swing and would be, right up to and after the strike ended; they would call every Wednesday (in a hearse of all things) piled high with food and always with money as well. The group joined forces with J. McGuinness, Scarborough Labour Party, and

16 An unusual fundraiser: pavement artists for striking miners, Nottingham City Centre

Labour Party Young Socialists, also Plaxtons workers all of whom proved to be gems.

This was a very sad time for us, a steady flow back to work had started, and much more personal to us was the sad death of our own retired miner, Jack Main, who had peeled so many stones of potatoes and had been tragically suffocated due to a fire at his home. A very very sad loss to us and our whole community; rest in peace Jack, you were one in a million.

Funds were still coming in regularly to provide dinners, food parcels and bread. Our regular visitors were still coming from various parts of the country bringing money, food and clothes. Meantime our lads were being convicted for picking coal or picketing offences; many of them were sacked even before being convicted of anything. The screw was being steadily turned.

On Saturday 2 March 1985 we had another great buffet/disco enjoyed by our friends and the pickets, and the women . . . I reckon, had they been on the Titanic, they would have lifted it out of the water.

On Sunday 3 March our Executive voted to go back to work even without an amnesty for our sacked lads. Our branch who were still 97 per cent solid behind our union prolonged the return for another 24 hours but inevitably it had to happen and we had to be men enough to accept it, no matter how distasteful that was going to be. This was only the end of the strike, the fight goes on. The children went to Scarborough and had a wonderful time, reuniting all those friends we had built up throughout the strike. This is only a brief account of the great strike and people of this area.

June 1985

# 7 LETTERS FROM THE COALFIELD

## Letters from Frickley and South London

Allan Lowe and Keith Proverbs

*FRICKLEY COLLIERY, SOUTH ELMSALL, YORKSHIRE*
3.10.1984

Dear Mr Lowe

I would like to thank you for your efforts regarding the selling of papers and posters to provide food for our food kitchens. It's really heart-rending to think that people who live hundreds of miles away from Yorkshire can feel for us. We have passed your name on to the lady helpers and they send you a very big thank you.

Keep the good work up and we hope this fight will lead to a wonderful victory.

God bless you and thanks very much
K. Proverbs, Branch President


*OSLO COURT RESIDENTS' ASSOCIATION*
*Colliers Wood, London*
8.12.1984

Dear Mr K. Proverbs

Thank you for your letter dated 3.10.84.

Your letter has been the only personal reply I have received during the dispute and it left me feeling very proud and honoured.

I have a bunch of acknowledgments and receipts from Barnsley and elsewhere but yours is the letter I am most proud to show.

My friends and I have tried our best to help and have been on every demonstration in London, lobbied the TUC in Brighton (I actually got into the Conference Centre there on a phony telecom visitor's pass and heard Arthur's speech), visited Snowdown Colliery in Kent, sold *Yorkshire Miner* and the Orgreave posters and have money deducted at source from my wages.

As you can see from the headed paper I am chair of a small residents' association in Colliers Wood, South West London. I also chair

**17** Great correspondents: London dustman Allan Lowe (above) and Frickley miner Keith Proverbs (right)

the Wimbledon Branch of the GMBATU which officers of my union are trying to close down. I am a member of the Labour Party and a divorced dustman with two fine young sons.

I want to wish you and yours and all of the magnificent men and women in your community everything and more that you wish yourselves and thank you for fighting to preserve the fundamental trade union and human rights for the people of the country.

The enclosed £10 is my personal gift to you and your family. I know it's not much but it should buy a few comforts.

Yours fraternally
Allan Lowe

*FRICKLEY COLLIERY*
15.12.84

Dear Allan

It's now 6am. I have just come off the Frickley line and I shall have a nap then start to get some coal from the tips at our colliery. Anyhow thank you for your letter. I feel so humble and find it hard to put it into words my sincere thanks for your gift to my family. I shall drink your health on Christmas day.

I see from your letter that we have your 100 per cent support in our fight against pit closures. I shall post your letter in our strike headquarters where we deploy 400 pickets per day and it will inspire their determination in a morning.

Thank you for the photographs of you and your lovely little children. Will you please convey our sincere best wishes for a very good Christmas to your friends who have signed the greeting card.

God bless you all
Keith Proverbs

*OSLO COURT RESIDENTS' ASSOCIATION*
28.12.84

Dear Keith
  Thank you for your letter (15.12.84). I took the liberty of photocopying

it and so sympathetic groups as diverse as London Borough of Merton Housing Officers and the Socialist Workers' Party have copies to show the lies spread by the *Sun* (most importantly) and the rest of the media in the south are nothing more than that. *Lies.*

People are confused down here Keith, so it's up to us to keep on telling the truth, and we have bit by bit, little by little, one by one. When we explain this government's premeditated provocation, people come across. It's been hard, but it's working. I think that's why there hasn't been much reported lately.

Historically the miners and their families have had the courage to fight not only for their own industry but for all of us, even though it has meant community division, tears, anger, blood and death. Thanks again mate.

God bless the men and women of Frickley and all striking miners and their families.

Yours sincerely
Allan


*SOUTH ELMSALL*
1.1.1985

Dear Allan

Once again thank you for your letter dated 28.12.84. It's now New Year's morning and we are getting ready for our picketing duties which start at 4am on 2 January 1985. We have had notice from the police that there will be around 400 police there to get two scabs in. The number of cops don't bother us really as we are used to it now. May I say on behalf of my wife, Annie, and myself a very big thank you for your £5. I feel so humble but pleased for your gift. Allan, I hope you and your children had a wonderful Christmas and I wish you a very happy New Year. May I say the response we have had from the London people has been very good and I can understand what you say in your letter about the media, i.e. the sickening *Sun* newspaper, and it must be hard to get over to certain people down there but please, please keep trying as you are the only people who can do it for us.

Allan, as you know I am Branch President at Frickley Colliery and our lads, every one of them, are standing firm and solid behind the NUM to ensure a victory in our struggle.

Allan, I have shown our lads your letters and they all say a very big thank you from the bottom of their hearts.

Keith

*OSLO COURT RESIDENTS' ASSOCIATION*
4.1.85

Dear Keith and Annie

I received your letter on Friday the fourth and like your other letters I shall have it copied and placed on my works canteen noticeboard and shown around my flats and elsewhere.

As you know from our telephone conversation on Sunday, I am trying to organise a small party to visit your village and colliery in the near future.

My mother who is 69 wants to join our group. She came with me and others to Burgess Park in Southwark, South East London, for the women's march where filthy ignorant Metropolitan Police officers pretend masturbated on the roofs around the Elephant and Castle as the ladies walked by. Of course I shall bring my two sons and my best mate, Bob Charlton, who is treasurer of our RA and who has done a lot to help the miners' cause.

Keith please don't feel humble, my friends and I are in total awe of you brave people. I want to thank you and Annie and all the men and women up and down this nation who are fighting the most wicked, ruthless, industrial and social vandal to have ruled Britain for many years.

I have a Yorks Area NUM badge which I always wear and I am very proud to do so.

Allan

*SOUTH ELMSALL*
5.1.85

Dear Allan and Children

. . . Allan when you decide to come up to Yorkshire and to our house, I shall take you on a picket line and show you our soup kitchens and show you where we are digging our coal to keep us warm. This morning I went to my committee meeting and at the Miners' Institute there was 1,200 men all standing there with their cheeks in their hands waiting for the doors to open as the women's section was giving every striking miner a sack of spuds. I wish you could have seen their faces, they beamed with delight. Anyone would have thought they were getting £100 a piece. It was a great sight.

Allan, you mention the filthy Met boys and TV plus the Press. I have been involved with all three of them but we have a ruling never to talk to the lot of them. It's no good for our cause.

By the time you get this letter it will be week 44 and we are still stronger than ever in this very vicious battle with the powers that be.

Allan, find enclosed a small badge. Allan, I have got a Yorkshire tie for you.

Hope to see you soon
Keith

*OSLO COURT RESIDENTS' ASSOCIATION*
25.1.85

Dear Annie, Keith and family

I'm going to make this letter brief because hopefully I shall be in South Elmsall some time on Monday. There will be five of us if that's all right. They will be my mother (she'll be 70 this year), my two sons, Bob and myself.

Now I know we will be unable to all stay at Number Forty-Seven, so, will it be possible for us to be dispersed or use a local hall or something?

On Thursday, pay day, I took a collecting bucket to work and when 'the money was up', I began collecting. The dustmen were all on a flat week, roughly £86, but I still managed to get almost £40.

I shall be seeing a local Labour Councillor for a 'few bob' and also be going around the flats before I leave to make the total up a bit.

The problem I have with my own relationship with Frickley is that other groups like the Merton Trades Council and the Resource Centre and others is that they are already committed elsewhere by twinning. Therefore the support I can expect from them is small. I do help them though Keith so I shall expect a little effort on their part.

Anyway, Bob and I are honoured by your gift and we will wear your ties with the same pride I wear the Yorks Area NUM badge.

My final comment, to say that your letters never bore me and I would love to hear about your family and your job as a Branch President.

I will sign off now, hopefully see you on Monday, hope you can arrange everything for us.

See you soon, we'd rather be pickets than scabs.

God bless you all
Allan, Bob and family

*9 OSLO COURT*
1.2.85

Dear Keith and Annie

I must make this message a note because I want to mention something about the last three days while they are still alive in me.

All of your family and community made my mum, children, Bob and me almost embarrassed by your fantastic hospitality. Reincarnation!

Well, if it happens I want to come back as a Yorkshire miner.

When we arrived at Colliers Wood, mum and me had a couple of beers (Robert and Tony were laying in Number 4). Then we went to the Resource Centre where I gave Tim a tie. I told him it was from you and he was delighted.

I will write properly soon but knowing how you are forced to live on £6.45 a week, I wanted to get my note quickly posted.

Bob, Allan, Robert and Tony

*SOUTH ELMSALL*
2.2.85

Dear Allan

Thank you for your letter. We are pleased you travelled all right and thank you for the gift. Again we are pleased you enjoyed your stay with us even though you did not see too much excitement on the picket lines. May I say a very big thank you to all the following people for their wonderful donations to our soup kitchen or Grog Shop. All our committee send their sincere thanks for the cash donation and the snap you brought up as well.

Thanks again to the following peple:

The Grove Vale Dustmen
Merton Resource Centre – Tim Mills
Councillor Siobhain McDonagh and Friends
Oslo Court Residents – Bob and Friends

I see the talks have broken down again. We think the next two weeks will be vital to us all. We think the scabs will sneak back in larger numbers. That's why we are having a General Meeting to appeal for mass pickets at our pit. Allan I hope Bob got home all right. We noticed his team won at football. Tell your Mam, Annie hopes she enjoyed her stay with us. Our little dog has missed your little children as well.

Well Allan I'll close for now. Same as you, I'll write again soon.
God bless you all

*9 OSLO COURT*
5.2.85

Dear Keith and Annie

Keith, I'll make sure Siobhain gets a copy of your letter and if you would like to (I don't want to turn you into the Postmaster General) write her a short note. She lives quite near me. Siobhain will be out on strike tomorrow and we shall be marching behind the Merton Trades Council banner and we are all hoping for a good turn out.

I was really 'sick' about missing the Sunday march but Tim and others from the Resource Centre were there and told me today how the 'Old Bill' overreacted. I would have been proud to be with your lads in the 'ruck'. It was great they weren't charged with anything because they could have found themselves in the front line of the latest twist in this struggle.

Watching the proud return, the men and women, banners and branch brought tears to my eyes. LBC on the Brian Hayes Show today did a phone vote on whether the Miners' Strike had achieved anything, 70 per cent rang in and said it had and only 30 per cent were negative and remember this, the vast majority of people that can listen at that time in the morning are the idle upper- and middle-class business people and ill-informed housewives who read the *Sun* or *Mail* and their husbands rotten *Evening Stardard*.

The news today is ambiguous and coupled with your letter, I kept getting the feeling that Frickley may not have gone back but as I won't be sending my letter until Thursday things should be clearer by then. Keith, Bob and I will continue to help until you are back and earning, so tell Annie not to worry about that. If the Strike went on for three years, and I was still employed, I'd still be there.

Regarding the Community Watch cozzer, I couldn't give a tinker's cuss what his thoughts are about my community and posters, if he can't handle it, bugger off, that's me. My neighbours trust and I hope believe and respect me, so that's all that counts. I don't know until he spells it out on Wednesday night but I suspect it's just another ploy to get us to grass on each other, but rest assured I'll let you know.

It's Thursday now and we've been told that because of the Strike on Wednesday, we won't be paid until Friday so this letter will be posted then. The march was really great and I reckon between sixty and eighty thousand were there with banners, placards, sashes and bands. I took

18  Agit-prop in Frickley

# URGENT:
# Much more picketing

To all Frickley and Kirkby N.U.M. members:

If ever there was a  time we needed you its <u>NOW</u>.
Your  workmates need help <u>ON THE PICKET LINE</u>.
Phone this number for your strike headquarters:

## - 42213 -

the NUM needs you!

The way to stop arrests like this is to spread mass pickets as far as possible, and stretch the police operation

JOIN THIS FIGHT NOW !
Only a small percentage of men are picketing.
The police are having an easy time of arresting people for no reason. They
are being brutally effective in the role of strikebreakers.
DON'T SIT AT HOME AND LET THE MINORITY OF MINERS GET SMASHED. JOIN THE FIGHT
FOR THE RIGHT TO WORK AND A DECENT LIVING.

If the dispute is to be won it is VITAL:
• THAT MORE PICKETS ARE MOBILISED:
• THAT MASS PICKETING IS SPREAD TO STOP ALL MOVEMENT OF COAL:

FRICKLEY AND KIRKBY RANK AND FILE PICKETS.
SAY:
"IF THATCHER AND MACGREGOR GET UP YOUR NOSE,
PICKET "

lots of photographs but I couldn't stay for the later activities because it was Oslo Court's AGM so I had to get back to Colliers Wood.

When you write next Keith I hope you will have located a Frickley Colliery badge and let me know if you are back at work and if you are how you went back, in fact the whole experience.

That's all for now Keith. Give our love and best wishes to all of your family, friends and Community.

God bless you all
Allan and Bob


*SOUTH ELMSALL*
10.3.85

Dear Allan, Bob and family

Thank you for your letter. Also I will write to Siobhain and thank her for everything she's done for us. We watched TV for the march but we could not spot the Merton Banner but I hope it all went well for you all. Allan after four General Meetings, we decided to march to work on Wednesday with the colliery band and our banner at 9am. About 2,000 people marched through the village to the colliery. I felt very proud to lead the march but it was very emotional. Women and children stood clapping us with tears running down their faces. When we got to the pit gates there were two Kent pickets there and everyone was stunned and shocked because we had no idea there was going to be a picket on the gate so I called all my lads into the pit car park and told them that we were not prepared to cross a picket line and a mass meeting will be held on our football ground at 12 noon the next day.

So they all went home very upset about the Kent lads and we had the meeting and decided to return to work straightaway so we went to the pit and spoke to the Kent lads and asked them to withdraw. I told them the Coal Board nor the government had managed to split our village up so I am sure the lads don't want to either. After they heard me they shook my hand, they withdrew and we went into work but we don't know for how long the management have warned every man at the pit if you are heard calling anyone scab you will be sacked straightaway. So I told him he had better start with me as I shall always shout abuse at the B......s. Anyhow Allan and Bob thanks again for your gift, but I drew £24 back tax on Friday and I felt like a millionaire but when you sent your gift it was great.

Allan please find enclosed the badges long since promised. We have had our own badge made just for Frickley. When they come I will send you one straightaway.

God bless you all
Annie, Keith Proverbs

*SOUTH ELMSALL*
17.3.85

Dear Allan, Bob and family

Allan, now we are back at work the management have come down very heavy on us all. If you mention scab or shout anything at all, it's instant dismissal but the lads put a hangman's noose at the pit head and it terrified the scabs. They have got their own bodyguards and they are frightened to walk about. Just what they asked for Allan.

The gaffer put me on night shift for the first time since 1967 but it never bothered me. I went to work smiling but the pit life will never be the same again with the hatred that's around.

*9 OSLO COURT*
21.3.85

Dear Annie, Keith and family

Thanks for your letter. I'm sorry to hear things don't seem to be very good at present.

I see from your letter management intends to harass the activists in the dispute and you must be top of the list unfortunately. But your strength of character will carry you through as it will with Mike, Chick and all the others. It's sad that authorities can't recognise that people who can remain on strike for a year and suffer the way you all have will not be bowed by petty alterations and restrictions.

Going back to petty harassment, I get quite a bit of that myself. I think management at the depot see me as some sort of threat and so are always thinking of ways to get at me. During the Strike they shunned and did their best to ridicule my poster and paper selling and were particularly annoyed with the collection for the 'Gray Shop'.

I'm writing this on the tube going back to Colliers Wood after getting paid. When I was back at the depot a shop steward 'pulled me' in the yard over the latest little ploy of management to get at me, and just would not listen to what I had to say because he too sees me as a threat because I have previously noted at Branch (Camberwell NUPE) that the men did not like the way in which stewards were not elected by the general work-force but by a minority at the Branch. Anyway, after a while he made me wild and I started shouting back at him. Next thing he rushes me and there's a fight. It finished up with him being pinned over a car bonnet with a bloody face and two other dustmen pulling me off. All that happened to me was that he broke one of my badges, not the Frickley or Yorks Area NUM. So now because the Union reps in Southwark are like a small mafia, I've got to wait and see what develops tomorrow morning. Well on that happy note (Ha Ha) I'll sign off.

God bless you both
Allan and Bob

*SOUTH ELMSALL*
25.3.85

Dear Allan, Bob and family

Thank you for your letter. I let Chick read it and he was really chuffed at what you said about the character we have got anyhow Allan, we are having it rough at the present but as you said it does not bother any of us. We shall get through, Allan.

Allan, when we read your letter Annie and me was very worried that you have got the sack after that trouble with the shop steward. He seems to me to be an arrogant so and so and I am pleased you put him in his place but we hope you are back at work again.

Allan, thank you for your gift but now we are drawing my wages again we can now manage but I wish to God there was some other way of saying thank you to you and Bob.

I hope you understand we have had enough off you over the past few weeks.

I hope you can understand the contents of my letter. We feel so humble but grateful.

God bless you all
Annie and Keith

*9 OSLO COURT*
27.3.85

Dear Annie, Keith and family

That other bit of trouble I had is over now. There was a big court of enquiry Friday morning so I played it really cool and as I am a Branch Chair in a different area, all the parties involved behaved similarly. Anyhow, certain points were noted, certain assurances given and that was that. I won't bore you with all the details cos it goes back a long time and is very complicated, it would take a chapter of a book to explain, but one thing that does happen now is that the steward always comes over to me in the canteen and tells me what he's going to talk to the men about and he's being very conciliatory. His face don't look too bad now either.

I was glad to hear you will keep in touch Keith, and we don't need any other thanks than that. I know I speak for men and women all over London who became involved in The Miners' Historic Struggle and that is they consider it an honour to do what they could. All of us only wish we could have mobilised the whole of the trade union and Labour movement behind you all and saved every mining community and got investment for more. The idiots who can't see that their turn is coming are beyond helping themselves, let alone helping anyone else. There's none so blind as them that will not see!

When you wrote you never said whether Davy Jones worked at Frickley or South Kirkby, Keith, and I was also wondering if any Frickley lads are in prison or are still facing charges that may result in 'nick'.

Many people down here are asking me why the lads effectively disowned their mates over the 50p levy. Are there any lads from Frickley that haven't been taken back? I don't believe most of the things we are hearing down here, tell me what it's like in South Elmsall.

. . . I'm going to close now but I just want to say one more thing and that is never let the lads forget the tremendous support the women have played in the struggle. The ladies in the Grog shop, Women's Support groups – still there – women like my mum, my ex-wife, my neighbour, one-parent families many of them, black, Asian – they all did their best and give the ladies at Frickley Grog shop a big thank you from Bob and me for our breakfasts.

God bless you all
Allan and Bob

*SOUTH ELMSALL*
30.3.85

Dear Allan, Bob and family

Thank you for your letter. We are pleased to read you have not lost your job and things have settled for you.

Allan, Davy Jones did not work at Frickley, he worked at Acton Colliery but he knew our Michael, the night he got killed he phoned our Michael asking him to ask me if he could come picketing with us, so I said 'yes' and he came with us just the once and he got killed that night. It upset us all but our Michael blamed himself for phoning him back telling him to come to the pit at 5pm that day.

Allan, as you saw on TV and in the press that 50p levy was turned down but this makes no difference to us as we are paying 50p per week. We have got six sacked, one of them got eight months in prison for hitting a policeman. We have not been able to talk to management yet regarding getting their jobs back but we are paying their wages every week and will continue to do so.

Allan, regarding the Women's Support Group we presented them all with a bouquet of flowers and we are giving them a party as soon as possible. They are all going to Russia on 5 April for two weeks.

Everything paid for by the Russians.
   I'll close for now, God bless you all.


*SOUTH ELMSALL*
10.4.85

Dear Allan, Bob and family
   Allan, yes the ladies was in Russia when your letter got to me and
they were looking forward to it as were also forty children from the
village who have gone to Italy for two weeks without their parents but
they will be well looked after.
   Allan, regarding your work with Southwark Council it seems very
dodgy for you all. This morning we had a meeting with the
management regarding the future of our colliery and they are knocking
about 400 men off the book with redundancy payments and I am one of
them and the management are gloating that they are getting rid of
some Branch officials. But as long as the terms are alright for me then I
don't mind even though I am only 54 years old. I shall be glad to get
away from it all.
   I'll close for now.

                    God bless you all


*9 OSLO COURT*
April 1985

Dear Keith and Annie and family
   Thanks for your letter Keith. So far I've tried three times to write a
reply so I hope this one says what I want to say. Everything you've
written to me since the return has confirmed what Arthur prophesied.
The government, the Coal Board and their management are hell bent on
emasculating the NUM and demoralising the work-force. It sounds to
me from your letter that the redundancies are compulsory, is that true
Keith?
   I suppose it was inevitable that Branch Officials and activists would
be on their hit list. They virtually eliminated all the Kent officials at a
blow when they sacked them for the occupation.
   Are all the 400 men going from Frickley? If they are, that must be in
the region of a quarter of the work-force and if that's not butchery I'd
like someone to tell me what is. What about Michael and Chick, are
they relatively safe?
   I read recently in the *Express*, a scab's wife in Kent was bleating
about the treatment her husband is getting at Betteshanger Colliery.
Blimey, what did she expect, he went back after three months not like
some of the others who didn't return until ten or eleven months. I don't

know how you feel Keith but I find it hard to call those men who were out for all that time scabs.

The other night my mum, Bob and myself were talking about it all and the nearest I could come to describing how I felt about it all was when my wife left me, I had a terrible void in my life which for a time became worse and worse, an empty feeling in my stomach coupled with despair. I've felt something like that since the return. My mum says I got too involved, maybe that's true but I don't think so, I didn't have to suffer. A lot of people pinned their hopes on you and you didn't let us down. It was others that could have helped and didn't. They let us all down and now I can see Thatcher and her jack-booted mounted cozzers riding rough-shod over all the working class and it won't matter whether you are a miner, dustman or teacher, that's the future as I see it.

I'll talk about down here now Keith because I can't think anything calmly to say about it all.

Bob flies to New York on Monday and will make his way down to Arizona and he said he will write to you and let you know how he's doing and what it's like. Annie's right Keith, Bob's a really good mate and I will miss him. It's funny how we became mates being a bit of a rough diamond myself and Bob being like a gentleman but life itself is strange I suppose.

My ex-wife recently tried to commit suicide where she lives in East London, things have been getting her down and she's run up big debts with the LEB so I asked her to come home. She says she's thinking about it and is seriously considering a trial period before giving up her flat. If it happens it will be great but we'll have to wait and see.

Well Keith I've gone on a bit again so I'd better draw to a close but I must say this, you and Mike, Chick and all the other men and women that fought in this struggle made me proud to be English.

God bless you all
Allan and Bob

PS Mum read your letter as does all the others and was glad to hear it arrived OK.

# 8 WOMEN'S GROUPS

## Women's support group at Maerdy

Barbara Bloomfield

### Maerdy, Rhondda Valley, South Wales, January 1985

As the narrow Rhondda Valley road snakes its way up to Maerdy, it gets narrower and more tortuous as the hills on either side close in, forcing the road to adapt to their contours. They're not called hills in the Rhondda but 'mountains', an ancient term, and perhaps they did seem like mountains to the young boys who pushed the slurry carts up the track in the old days and tipped them on to the man-made hills that came out of the ground. They are also mountains in the sense of the lack of communications between the valleys. A person from the Cynon Valley, just a handful of miles as the crow flies from Maerdy, lives 'over the mountains' and is an outsider.

To this outsider all the hills looked the same, meanly covered with grass, bare except for a few grazing sheep and some stubby trees. The miners, though, point out which of the shapes are in fact slurry tips, grassed over and fairly recently lopped and levelled in the wake of the Aberfan mining disaster.

Going north north west out of Pontypridd, a decent-sized town which is dominated by what looks in context like a skyscraper but which is really a five-storey building housing the area office of the NUM, the Rhondda proper divides into two, the Rhondda Fawr to the left and the Rhondda Fach to the right. The right-hand road leads to Maerdy, the last remaining pit in the Rhondda, a village with a formidable reputation as a stronghold of the Communist Party, a 'Little Moscow' of trade unionist history and a place where they don't even need to put a picket on the pit during the strike because there's no chance of anyone trying to return to work.

Although it is only a short ride, five or six miles, from Ponty to Maerdy, the changes are noticeable. In Ponty, the town has evolved, newer buildings are in evidence and there is the usual run of stores and civic buildings. But further up the valley, past

19 Megan Webster and Jean Bromage from Maerdy Pit Wives Group

the dinosaur pits like Lewis-Merthyr, which are closed and rusting now, and past the grassed-off bits of deserted parkland which were once pits (there used to be fifty-seven mines in the Rhondda alone), the housing becomes smaller and more uniform and the shops lose their name boards. 'Well, we know who runs them, don't we . . .' people say.

Near Ponty, the hillsides are dotted with grander homes. Some are old and used to be Coal Board property, homes for pit managers and agents. Now they are interspersed with modern, medium-sized bungalows and the village looks up at them. There is still a vague feeling of being spied on from above as you stand in the centre of the village. The hillside must have been the only place in the valley where the pit owners could build themselves a bit of distance from the workers.

The coal owners built the workers' homes too. They threw up the small uniform terraces after the first strikes of coal, to attract in workers from other parts of the country. When one miner said, 'My house is over 100 years old' it didn't connect for a moment until I looked it up and found that the first strike in Maerdy was in 1875.

Maerdy is the last village in the Rhondda, ringed with a semi-circle of hills to the north which forces the road to peter out as it approaches the pit, sitting alone in a bowl of hills, old, redbrick and squat.

The social centre of Maerdy is the Workmen's Institute, a square, unlovely, apparently semi-derelict, building with graffiti on the blackened outside walls, which started life in 1881 as a coffee tavern. Within twenty-five years it had become the Workmen's Institute and Hall, capable of fitting up 1,200 people and concealing within it labyrinthine corridors, a gymnasium, a swimming pool, a billiard room, a fine library and two reading rooms, one of them 'for the Ladies'.

It was an instant social centre for an instant village and it still fulfils that function today. The ladies room has been replaced by a room full of space invader machines and the library has become a bar, but the whole place buzzes with activity and argument, especially in the downstairs room where the walls are lined with sacks and catering packs of tinned food and in the strike centre room opposite where the male lodge officials organise and harangue and hold meetings and telephone.

During the strike it's been the men who spend much of their time around the Hall although they are not all miners by any means. There are plenty of teenage boys and older men in their fifties and sixties. They're mostly out of work like 32.4 per cent of men in the Rhondda (Rhondda Borough Council figures) and 84 per cent of men over 44 years old (NUM figures). This is a place for early death of 'the dust' as pneumoconiosis is called and it is a place for early retirement so that the younger ones can have a go and for golden handshakes that say a man is finished at the pit at 45 years of age.

Up the sea-green painted stairs of the Institute and through swing doors is the massive Hall with a sweeping balcony around the top of the room. The whole is decorated in a variety of styles. Around the proscenium arch of the stage is a solidly ornate Art Deco design in plaster from which the rest of the room takes its cue. But the Art Deco light fittings now have disco spots bolted over them and the wooden floor is half covered in orange lino.

Since the beginning of the strike the Big Hall has run up huge debts, not so much because striking families can't afford to go out, because money can always be found for the odd celebration but because of the tension between the miners and the NACODS deputies, called 'firemen', who both use the Hall for their Saturday evenings out.

The firemen didn't like it when the miners' wives started singing picketing songs and 'red' songs in the Hall and, as the evening wore on, some of the wives of deputies were seen sticking two fingers up at the other women. There was the possibility of a bit of trouble and some of the miners' wives said it wasn't worth the hassle of going up there.

Now the atmosphere is so bad at the Big Hall that the women

from Ferndale prefer to meet in the centre of their own village
(the next small cluster of houses down the valley from Maerdy) at
the little knot of clubs known as the Band, Con and Imps. To a
stranger these clubs appear to be one large building with a score
of different rooms, each one attracting a different clique but the
clientele staying the same. In fact they are three separate clubs,
each with its own rules and atmosphere. The Band is the Band
and Musical Instruments Club (the general impression among the
women is that the band doesn't exist any more but we found out
later that it does). Next door is the Con. or Conservative Club
which is run by Communists. The carpet-bagging Tory candidate
for the Rhondda in one election apparently arranged to hold a
meeting there to explain his policies but found himself barred
from entering by a picket line of staff and members. Dennis
Skinner MP, however, was suspicious when he visited Ferndale.
Even though the set-up was patiently explained to him, the story
goes that he sternly refused to walk through the doors of a
building which had Conservative Club written in large blue letters
outside.

Next door to the Con. is the Imps. or Imperial Club. As Gwen
Williams, who was the first woman member of the Con. explains,
in the Band, after twenty years of paying, you're entitled to
become a life member and get the perks . . . but not women. She
only gets some of the benefits, like beer tokens. In the Imps.
women pay the same and get the same benefits but you can't go
into the men-only rooms. Since these are populated by elderly,
coughing men in a fug of pipe smoke, this is seen as no great loss.

The butties, that is, the men from Ferndale who work together
in the pit at Maerdy and socialise together after their shift, tend
to meet in the back room of the Con. where there is a billiard
table and separate bar – men-only again. The women tend to
gather around a big table in the front bar although occasionally
their husbands will come through and join in the conversation or
reach into their wives' purses to get the money for another round
of drinks.

It is in these situations that the burning issues get discussed,
seated round in great sprawling groups of fifteen or twenty
people. The strike is number one of course, and feminism, and
Greenham Common and food, the Labour Party and fuel and
the family. There is not much that doesn't lead back to the strike
or relate to it. Old friendships have fallen away as the urgency
and momentum of the women's group has grown. New friends
are other activists in the group; it seems as if everything else has
faded away. Are these activists, women and men, unusual? They
seem so to me, always fighting angry with the government (at
least verbally), always living on the edge when I see them. I

retired to bed, head spinning, when the *World in Action* video about the miners was brought out to be played at one o'clock in the morning, and they've all seen it a dozen times before!

Everyone is very nice to me, coming from Ruskin College in Oxford to write my thesis. Very nice indeed. I feel that Ruskin has a charmed name from the days when serious-minded Welsh miners were among the students, despite the allegations that over the years the 'working-class trade unionists' college' has become deadly staid and 'establishment'.

Yes, people are friendly, but guarded too. They have befriended outsiders before and then found themselves named and quoted in all kinds of newspapers, right and left. 'Revolutionary Communists! I don't want to be associated with that,' they say. 'We're Labour here!' The women themselves never identify with the Communist Party which rules the NUM lodge but doesn't seem to have a hold outside the pit. The women are also guarded in the sense that they are newcomers to the power game and afraid of putting their feet in it with the NUM when they talk to reporters. (Later on, they didn't worry so much about what the men would think.)

They had been asked so many questions before and now they were repeating their answers to me. Once upon a time, questions about Greenham or about women's liberation would have caught them off guard but now everyone had a view which rolled easily off the tongue. There is, on these sorts of issues, a kind of corporate view, 'the women's group thinks', which seems to come out of a loyalty to each other. People instinctively seem to think it is necessary to stop the group splitting apart under the pressures caused by complicated relationships not only between the women and their husbands but between them and the non-strikers or the NUM or the support group in Oxford which was fund-raising for South Wales.

The prejudices that I took with me to Maerdy were perhaps typical of a single woman, a student too, with no home ties. I was definitely anti-home. I didn't want to write about housework and children, I told myself, it was the women's public face as 'workers' and 'activists' (both of which I knew them to be) that I wanted to study and here I was being thrown back to the fireside discussing fuel and meals and husbands. It didn't take long to realise that it was silly to try to pigeonhole the Maerdy women into some perfect socialist/feminist theory and that they were trying to find a way forward as a group which suited (rather than threatened) their existing way of life. At the same time there was a balance to be struck between home and 'activism'. I'd read countless books about mining life in which women hardly appeared at all except as the invisible labourers who propped up the whole filthy business of being a miner. Always I remembered the words of the author who claimed that the single most revolutionary act for women's liberation in Wales was the installing of pithead baths.

The image I hold in my mind when thinking of the Maerdy women is of a group of twelve or thirteen of them sweeping down the main street of the village toward the Maerdy Hall like the right phalanx of an Amazon brigade with Barbara Williams making the running out front in her chariot. The group's lynchpin, Barbara, lives just around the corner from the Hall and she waits for the others to come and help her negotiate the steep slope in her wheelchair.

Perhaps the first thing that binds them together as a group is that all the members I have spoken to were born in the Rhondda and have husbands who are or were miners. It seems that the most 'active' women also have husbands who are activists though the same is not true the other way round – not all the most 'visible' men have wives who belong to the support group

As a cross-section of Rhondda women, their life stories add up to a chronicle of hardship and early death and of the same ambivalence to the pit life that is felt by the men themselves.

Glynis Evans (34), who lives in Blaenllechau, has three children and is married to John 'Chuch' Evans. Her mother worked in the canteen at the pit and her father was a face worker at Nantgarw, 'the scabby pit', where he was killed by the cutter at the age of 29. A tiny stone flew off and hit him on the back of the head. 'I was brought up by my grandparents, more or less, and on my father's death certificate it says "Act of God". My mother got £100.' This is Glynis's second marriage after a difficult two years in which she was a one-parent family existing partly on social security and then, because of lack of money, found a job:

'I had to go back to the factory for one year, the EMI factory in Treorchy . . . and that was extremely difficult. I had to get the children up at 5.30, take them to the girl, and then work. I was in bed by 8.30. I was a spring setter which is making the dial on the back of the telephone, a difficult job. A long time ago I was a nurse but then I got pregnant. Also I was a taxi driver.'

On the other side of the valley slope lives Jean Bromage (27) who was born in Maerdy. Her husband is Verdun 'Nobby' Bromage, quiet, shy and quite the reverse of the sociable Jean. As a diabetic, Jean has been 'on the sick' and hasn't worked for several years. Before the strike she says she felt useless and hardly ever went out. The only paid work she has ever done is working at a Christmas trimmings factory in Tonypandy. She is one of those in the women's group who says the strike has changed her life. She now spends most of her time outside the home and there's been another change, she has lost eight stones in weight. She contrasts her life with that of her sister who is also married to a striking miner but doesn't approve of the strike:

'She hasn't got a clue what the strike is about, all she knows about it is what's on telly cos I do have argument after argument with her and a lot of people are like that, people who aren't involved in the strike . . . they think what's on television is right.'

Jean and Nobby decided to split up during the strike which left Jean with a confusion over her loyalties:

'Well . . . my marriage has been on the rocks for quite a while, right? These last two, three years we haven't really been getting on. . . . I would have left my husband six months ago but I won't leave him because of the strike. Not just because of what people will say, because people will talk and say "she pretends to be active in the strike and she couldn't give a damn." Well that's not true. That's not why I'm staying with him, I'm staying . . . the guy kept me for eight years and if I can't keep him during the strike I'm not much of a woman, right? But it has affected me in the way I seem to have gone ahead and he hasn't. He's stayed where he is and we don't have that much in common.'

Around the corner from Barbara Williams in Maerdy lives Gwenllian Chambers (45) with her husband Lyndon 'Chick' Chambers, just a few doors from the house where she was born and where her mother still lives. She says:

'Six people in my family are on strike. Me, because I work in the mine canteen, my husband, his brother and three nephews. I am one of five people who work in the canteen. I've been there fifteen years. I usually go to work from 5.30 to 2.30 in the afternoon. I belong to COSA . . . I don't know what it stands for. The feeling was there in the miners and at the beginning of the strike we'd go up to the picket line and then turn back. In the second week we voted that we wouldn't go to work.'

Unlike most of the other women in the group, Megan Webster (34) has a background in trade unionism from her work as a nurse in a hospital. She has been 'on the sick' with recurring problems for some time and while her husband Glan 'Corker' Webster was away in Oxford collecting money during the week, she found herself devoting a lot of time to the support group. Like other people, Megan has turned against the police, fuelled by their treatment of women on picket lines and also, perhaps, by the feeling that unlike the faceless NCB here, at least, is an enemy you can see:

'I was always brought up to respect the police but now . . . I was in
Treorchy with my mother in the car and I said, "Christ look at the
pigs". Well, she looked at me and I could see she was frightened by
me.'

Q  What about the local police in Ferndale?

'If they've got a uniform and a hat on, they're pigs. My mother saw
the Tonypandy riots and now she's frightened. She was 7. She
doesn't like talking about them. She's afraid to speak of it too much
cos of the bad memories from all those years ago. She says "will it
ever end?" She remembers the way the boys were treated then.'

This attitude, not exactly defeatist but certainly pessimistic is
prevalent among elderly parents in mining families. But when it
comes to support of their children, the grandparents have played
an important part.

Almost every striking family relies on the generation above for
fresh food like vegetables and fruit and for financial help to keep
them going. The grandparents have been the only people in the
village who can afford to spoil the children, trying to keep some
semblance of normality when it comes to treats like sweets and
toys. There seems to be more contact between families during the
strike. Doris Williams, the 76-year-old mother of Barbara, came
to help her out in the house when Barbara first became affected
by multiple sclerosis. Now Doris does almost all the cooking and
tea-providing when the support group meets at her daughter's
home. Doris, whose mother was a pitbrow lass (though not at
Maerdy where women were never employed in coal mining
work), was one of the generation of women who were driven out
of the Rhondda during the mining slump of the late 1920s and
1930s and went to become a domestic servant in England. She is
violently anti-Thatcher, referring to the Prime Minister at all
times as 'SHE'. Everyone in Maerdy knows who 'SHE' is. When
Doris made this remark: 'I think what SHE'd like to do with the
Rhondda is build a big wall around us', I couldn't help but think
of the Tory Minister who admitted that pit villages are 'Socially
useful if economically unviable.' After all, they embody so many
'virtues' which Tories would claim as much as socialists to be
their own: self-sufficiency, help-your-neighbour, family, tradition
and, above all, a pride in hard work.

Beneath the smooth, united surface of the Maerdy strikers,
there are many tensions between wife and husband caused by
partners stretching against the limits of 'acceptable behaviour'.
Around Christmas time, according to one woman:

'The men became concerned that the women were taking a more
stringent role in the striking . . . the women were reaching the
ordinary man and woman in the street more than the men with their

speaking about the day-to-day things of the strike. The men were a bit worried that we weren't going to be the same. Now things are on a more even keel. They can see we're not going to run off and split the families and demand equal rights for women.'

Women in Maerdy will say that they have sorted out the domestic duties with their husbands but really things are not so simple. There are rows about who's going out and who's going to babysit, who's going off on a speaking engagement and for how long. Women say that since the beginning of the dispute they share the cooking and cleaning but I have never seen a man do either in Maerdy. The burden is still on the woman to plan and organise the home although it is possible that men are taking on more than before.

It seems from talking to men that most of them draw a sharp line between the strike-based activity of the women, which they think of as good and useful, and other kinds of female militancy which they see as bad and unnatural. The point at which the women's group begins to affect the running of the house is the point at which many become frightened of 'the fems' and spend a lot of time talking about them. It almost goes without saying that it is an eye opener for them to meet, often, middle-class feminists with radically different lifestyles from their own.

Maerdy miners who were billeted with one woman in Oxford would come home at weekends with tales that she would 'rather build a wall in the garden than wash a cup'. The Oxford woman's argument was that she had spent enough years of her life serving men and that, when guests appear, she doesn't mind looking after the women but the men can pour their own tea. The miners claim to be deeply offended. It breaks every rule of Welsh hospitality they say, and the whole thing has turned into a usually jokey battle between the two sides with the miners trying to wind her up by singing songs like: 'Get into that kitchen and rattle those pots and pans . . .'

Jokeyness is a familiar weapon against the unknown and often I saw it lower the tension in tricky situations. For example, there was a noticeable policing operation going on between miners when they were away from home in the face of 'temptations of the flesh'. Sometimes the miners' pride, that swaggering, self-assured macho, which Beatrix Campbell so deplored in her book *Wigan Pier Revisited*, caused them to get into deep water in their dealings with women. Once at a benefit in Birmingham I was with three miners who were 'chatting up' three young women and persuading them to invite us all back to their flat. I was peeved with them for using the fact that they were 'striking miners' to take advantage of the situation. Within five minutes of arriving at the flat and opening the beer, the situation presented itself in a different light. The three women were from the Socialist Workers' Party and were using the opportunity to have a chat and possibly sell some papers and pamphlets. Talk about deflated egos! I laughed at them later and told them they deserved it.

At the same time as the strike has caused a wealth of new experiences and unfamiliar situations for women and men in Maerdy, there is a rear-guard action which wants to keep out change at all costs. It is voiced by the phrase, often used, 'We want to keep what we've got.'

One evening, sitting in a family's living room talking with them about tradition and feminism and how the two could possibly work in tandem, the husband suddenly looked up from his armchair and said emphatically:

'Write this down. We have got the finest way of life in the world. Look at me. I am sitting in my own chair, by my own fire, and my wife and my dog are sitting here at my feet [a great lion-sized Alsatian the dog was]. We've got our own home and enough money to live on. Now what more could you want for? Take that back to your friends in Oxford and tell them we've got the finest way of life in the world.'

The more politically sophisticated men in Maerdy make a distinction between themselves and what they call the 'collar and stud boys' on the question of women. Collar and stud means the traditionalists, the old-fashioned, 'gentlemen' miners who don't think women should go on picket lines in case they get hurt. The younger men recognise that this does not match the aspirations of the women, hence this cautious, jokey battle with 'the fems'. As Mike Richards, one of the latter group, told a group of schoolchildren: 'In 1972 and 1974, we called them "the sandwich girls". The women started this dispute behind us, they came up alongside us and now they're in front of us.'

It is one of the ironies of the strike that the resistance movement, which has kept, according to Hywel Francis, about half a million people going in the Welsh valleys during the strike, has worked up such a head of steam that the women feel it could go on forever. For all the images of fiery Welsh Communists which history provides, it was the South Wales miners who quietly suggested to the rest of the NUM that there should be a return to work without a settlement. . . . When this plan became public knowledge, the women were shocked. They had taken over the voice of militancy and were still using phrases like 'I've never let myself think for a moment that we're not going to win. . . .' But while the women, around Christmas time, were organising pickets and planning the occupation of the Furnacite

Plant at Abercumboi, the majority of Communist miners at Maerdy pit were talking about 'broad alliances' and about the possibility of an orderly return to work with 'dignity and honour'.

It seems from the look of Maerdy as a village that things have changed. Of course, the Communist Party itself has changed as has the politics of the NUM lodge. From its pro-Moscow days in which the comrades posed for village photographs underneath a blown-up picture of Lenin and the red and gold banner made by the working women of Krasnaya Presna and brought back from Russia in triumph by the miners' leader, A.J. Cook, the Maerdy Lodge has now become generally 'Eurocommunist' in style.

But, in its heyday, old photos show Maerdy as a bustling little town with a 'frontier spirit', full of miners with money in their pockets. Now the reality is subdued: a few quiet pints at the club, Saturday night out, home improvements – like an indoor bathroom – if you can afford it, and beneath it all the gnawing fact: this village has no future without the pit.

But what happened to the Ladies Reading Room at the Hall? These days it's a bar full of unemployed youths and space invader machines. And this is what happened to the books in the library according to Brian Davis, a former miner, now unemployed:

> 'We had a big skip and just chucked them in the skip. Lots of leather books were slung too. It was right in the media of TV, TV was at its peak. We had to open a licensed bar or go down and they wanted to alter this . . . and get the bar going. All craftsmen-built bookshelves and the finest set of bibles and theological books in South Wales. Slung out.'

It is noticeable, too, how few books are to be seen in the miners' houses. These days there is more likely to be a pseudo-bookshelf full of videos of the strike, taped off the television although, hidden away in a drawer, there may well be a history of Welsh miners which is brought out with care, the spine cracked open and the pages leafed through, pointing out with pride the faces of friends and relations now old or dead.

Looking through these history books it feels as if the whole tone of protesting has changed. There has been hardship in Maerdy during the strike but it is of a different calibre to the days of the bailiff's evictions in the 1930s when women and men surrounded a house where the bailiffs were trying to take away all the family's furniture for non-payment of money. The modern equivalent of that situation is for the miners to make use of whatever credit they can to keep the TV and video and the car and the telephone, even if it means storing up huge bills until the end of the strike. The creditors are seen by the village as being 'responsible' during the strike over the question of payments but then, they'll get their money in the end, somehow, won't they?

*Postcript* 5 March 1985. Thousands of Maerdy people and their supporters from Oxford, Birmingham and other places walked up the single road to the pit in the chilly dawn to see the miners go back to work in that 'dignified and orderly fashion'. As they neared the pit, the lights with the television cameras were switched on and, almost by instinct, it seemed, two dozen miners at the front of the procession, raised their fists into the air and shouted slogans like 'here we go' and 'we will win'. When the camera lights went out, they stopped immediately and soon filed into the pithead baths to start work. On the television, later that day, it looked a heroic ending to their strike. At the time it had seemed merely a sad one.

# 9 PROFILES

## Interviews at Armthorpe, December 1984

Mike Brogden

Roughly one in ten of Armthorpe's 14,000 population work at Markham Main Colliery. It is a relatively new development, only sunk in the 1920s. Situated on the coalfield that stretches from Sheffield to the East Coast, of the nine pits in the Doncaster area it was the only one to make a substantial profit prior to the strike. It was not directly threatened by the pit closure programme.

Throughout the strike year, Armthorpe was deeply committed. One of the first NUM Branches to vote wholeheartedly for the strike, it was one of the last pits to resume production. Situated on the border with Nottinghamshire and adjacent to the North-South motorway corridor, it was a pivot for picketing in the Midlands area. It had suffered its own share of police depredations (especially the punitive assault on the village on 22 August – see *Guardian*, 3 December 1984). After twelve months of extreme hardship, there were still only twenty-two scabs being thrust through the picket line by the police convoy.

Some of the following accounts of life in Armthorpe during the strike were recorded in the homes and shops of local people. Not all views expressed on tape were those of the mining community itself. Despite its apparent unity, Armthorpe had other preoccupations than the strike. With substantial local unemployment, not every personal concern was with the fate of the miners' particular struggle. For others, including many local teachers who commuted into the village, Armthorpe was a 9-4 problem that needn't be carried home.

### Woman factory worker, married to miner

It's not that I've had a difference with the Women's Action Group. I just didn't like how they were going about some things. So I've gone out and done things on my own. What happened was that someone offered to put a party on for 200 kids in a place

he had. For the size of the place, that's all he could
accommodate. He asked the Women's Support Group if they
could run it and they said that 200's not enough – 'Give us money
for our party instead.' He refused – that wasn't on. He were
upset about it and were telling my husband. My husband said,
'hang on. I'll go and ask my wife and see if she can put the
party on for you'. I said 'I'll do it on one condition – that the
Women's Support Group have nowt to do with it.' I'm doing it
on my own for 250 kids – it snowballed from 200. I've had all the
toys given.

I helped send the kids on holiday. Do you remember the *Daily
Mirror* sending them all to Blackpool? I organised that one. And
I organised thirty-two children and eight grown-ups for a week at
Cleethorpes in a holiday camp.

I have a slot meter so I pay for my electricity before I use it.
They're letting others pay £1 a week. I haven't heard of anyone
being cut off. The only ones they're hassling are those who didn't
pay the £1 when they should.

We were six months in advance with our mortgage so we were
all right for six months into the strike. Then I rung them up and
they said: 'Just pay what you can, when you can.' No problems
there. Bank asked me if I would like an overdraft, which I
refused. We had wages paid direct into the bank – so we were
good customers.

The local shops are helpful, very helpful. There's one on the
corner – Howard – he's a miner's son. He'd only just taken shop
over when strike started – hadn't had time to get on his feet. He
has been – well, I just can't put it into words what he's been
because he's been – fantastic. You'd think it was impossible to do
what he does. Every day he sends bread cakes over for the lads
going picketing. He gets up at 5 o'clock and bakes them before
he does his own shop work. He will give the lads anything they
want. Yesterday, for example, I wanted a Father Christmas outfit
for the party. He got it for me eventually. It took him about two
hours, he phoned all over. He's a fantastic man and he deserves a
medal. The only trouble with the shops is that one was thought to
be serving the police on the day of the riots and it had its
windows put in. That's been the only trouble.

I've lived in Armthorpe all my life. My father was a miner and
my grandfather. When we were children, this was a small, close-
knit village. As years passed – I suppose this has happened all
over – people got a bit better off, bought their own houses and
community spirit was disappearing. But this has brought it all
back. It's like it was years ago. People banding together, helping
one another, sharing and shopping.

It has happened that people have had to sell things or return things to the shops, especially those with children – not as much as you might have expected though.

The electric shop in the village where I got my video has been good. I went to school with him. I went to take it back. He said 'Keep it'. I said 'I can't pay'. He said 'Pay me when you go back'. He's done that with three parts of the whole village. He said 'If I take all the videos back, I'm out of business.'

Personally, I think what the women are doing, being involved in the strike, is bothering the men more than it is the women. There's a few that has gone overboard, and they're frowned on – there's a lot of bad feeling over that. But I've never heard one woman say that she wants her husband to go back to work, while you get some men complaining that their wives should be taking care of the house instead of working down at the Welfare or going on picket lines.

I've no sympathy for those miners that have gone back to work. To me they've got the wrong principle in worrying about their family going without. Because them families have got to suffer for a long time after.


### Bob Jackson, faceworker, married, two children

Financially, I'm one of the lucky ones cos I've got my wife working full time. I don't know what I'd have done without this. I know a lot of single lads who aren't getting a penny and how their spirits are so high, I don't really know. Myself, well, when strike first started, all my bills, I wrote them a letter. I told them I was on strike and there's not a thing I can do about it. They've all been in touch with me, and, I've got to be honest, I think they've all been fair. I had a few problems with electricity bill but, that was my own fault. I had an agreement and I lapsed on the agreement and missed a couple of weeks' payments, and they said they were going to cut me off. I went to see them and said I'd pay them £5 instead of £3, and they accepted that. But, I blame myself for that. I've been to bank a couple of weeks ago, and they told me I owed them about 600 quid. I asked them what they were going to do about this money, when strike was over, and they told me when strike's over, they're going to open bank at night time, just for miners, and given them either an extended overdraft or put everything you owe in one, and give one big loan to pay it all off. I think that's quite fair really. Then there's mortgage company. I've got to admit they've surprised me. I thought they'd be treading on us toes, getting a bit more heavy than they are. I think I owe them about one and a half grand. They send me a letter every three months just saying, I see there's no change, we'll get in touch again in three months. I just hope they won't expect to call for all that money at once. I hope they'll just extend my mortgage, but I don't really know. I'm a bit worried, the hardship is obviously going to carry on after the strike's over, but, if you listen to press, and watch TV they say everyone's against us, but there's a hell of a lot of people doing a lot for us.

The financial pressure has put a great strain on my wife. When the strike had been on for about twelve weeks, me and my wife split up, for a couple of weeks. She could not get the things she was used to getting, and she was seeing the kids not getting what they were used to, and she couldn't take it. Also I think a lot to do with it was, with being on the committee, I was practically living here. I was never seeing my wife. Sometimes, at beginning, we never went home. I remember one time, I'd been here for three continuous days. In picket room there's a table, and I was fast asleep on this table and I lifted my head up and saw my wife in doorway, and I just shouted 'Don't get me up yet, it's not time'. And I fell back to sleep. That's how it's affected us. But, we got back together again after a few weeks and for some reason it's totally different, she's more involved now, she's helping me.

We've got a daily routine more sorted out now. I get up and go picketing in the morning, then go home and get the kids to school, then I come in here. I stay here till kids come home from school cos there's that much to do here. We've all got to muck in and get stuck in, there's so many jobs to do. Going to collect food parcels, going out collecting, going to electricity board to sort out people's fuel bills, etc. There's a desk in the room for all the day's correspondence, we all like to hang about and help, so there's not too much pressure on the same one or two people.

I've been involved in all aspects of the strike, picketing, collecting and even speaking. I'm amazed how, with being involved with the strike, you do things you never thought you could do before. Before this, there's no way I could have stood up on a platform and spoke. I would have been absolutely terrified. Now, I've been called to speak at union meetings and factory gatherings and sometimes I even enjoy it. I think it's important that rank-and-file do this speaking, cos you can say I know what it's like, I'm there every day and I think that helps your cause.

I've also been amazed at how much support we've got from other places like Birmingham and London from the other unions. From union members I mean not their leaders, people like steelworkers, printers and electricians in Fleet Street. We've found that work-place collections, asking people to their face, raises more money than say a levy of a pound. If you go round with a bucket people will put in fivers or £10 notes.

In Armthorpe itself, other sections of the community have rallied to help. In the women's action group, I think there are even women whose husbands aren't miners. The majority of shopkeepers have been great. For example, there's a guy over the road who sells bread, and every day he sends over four or five dozen bread cakes for pickets. He never takes money for them. We've been over and tried to pay him, cos we know what's happening to his business, but he will not take the money.

The community, now, is closer than it's ever been. The strike has brought us all closer together, especially now, around Christmas, it's knitted us closer together. I have to reiterate the part played by the young lads. The young lads have just been fantastic. I remember some old miners down pit saying that young lads would let this industry down, but I think those lads can hold their head up high now, in front of these old guys, which I'm right pleased for. I take my hat off to single lads, cos I think they've done great during this strike.

### John Mahony, pit development worker, married, three children

When the strike started my wife's first reaction was 'how will we manage'? I said 'We'll manage, you always manage.' My wife works part time in the club here. It doesn't really keep our heads above water. We've not paid any debts, only the water rates. If it weren't for the soup kitchen here we'd never get a decent meal. We have a good dinner here, then when we go home at night we just have a sandwich. The main thing is the kids aren't really bothered, though we've had to make a lot of sacrifices. We've sent the video back, but the television company have been very good to us. We asked them to take the television back, it's rented and our licence had run out, but they paid it for us so we could keep the set. We don't really have any other big bills as we have a meter for the electricity and for the television. I do the soup kitchen and get paid for that, so we're not too bad but there isn't enough money to buy the kids the clothes they need, or for me to get out at weekends, or my wife.

Apart from financial difficulties the family has suffered other disruptions. Earlier in the strike my wife left me for three weeks. I think it was just the strain, she just wanted to get away from me and the kids. After those three weeks she came back and has supported me 100 per cent since then. It's been really great. I've been luckier than most, there's some of them getting divorced over this strike. I can't really understand why, because it's their families' future they're fighting for. It's mainly the young ones, their wives can't stand the strain, they've never been in the last

20  Members of Windhill and Woolley soup kitchens, South Yorks
    and Ann Burrell of Rhodesia Women's Action Group at home with
    sons Richard and Ross, Rhodesia, Notts

two strikes in 1972 and 1974/75. I was in those strikes and we managed on a lot less in those two. Then we only got £6 a week and that was it, my wife was not working and there was no picketing. The children were only eight, six and four then and she had to feed, clothe and run a house on £6.

Friends and relatives have helped us. Those who are working buy us drinks or maybe send us some food over. It's very good, it's getting back now to an old community, where you can go next door and borrow a cup of sugar or tea from a neighbour. It's great, it's made us really close, miner or not, whereas at one time you wouldn't talk to one another. That's in the old village of Armthorpe, in the south field, where some of the younger ones live, they don't want to know. In fact, in the beginning, when some of the wives went round there asking for donations, or help in the soup kitchens, they had doors slammed in their faces. If this pit shuts then this village dies, and their houses will be very hard to sell, yet they've offered no help. It's more pensioners who've helped us. Some pensioners come in every week with some bits of food in their bag. They're great, so we try to help them by keeping security up by the coal yard, because coal is getting pinched left, right and centre up there, and keep their coal coming in.

My best memories of the strike will be of the women and what they've done here. They've organised holidays for the kids. I went with a couple of other adults and took the kids to Cleethorpes for a week. I don't know how they've survived, how they keep this place going. They're out all the time, they won't finish here till 6 o'clock tonight, then some of them will go to Haworth at half seven. Haworth is in South Yorkshire but it's a Nottinghamshire pit, the men on strike there have been denied help at every turn. They've no union facilities, no welfare, no help from the council, whereas here the council has given us everything we want. One of my best memories is of a charity concert we organised for them. We gave them a real good night and raised some money for them. Things are much more difficult there. It's like a holiday camp here compared to there.

My main contribution to the strike has been picketing. I've travelled around, I stayed a week in Coventry, everything was first class, we wanted for nothing. We've had no problems here organising or maintaining transport, we've our own breakdown lorry, a bloke that repairs all the cars, we've never had to hire a transit van to picket, blokes have always turned up in their own cars. We've been lucky, we've been one of the branches that's been lucky.

## Keith, 37-year-old methane borer, five children

Armthorpe is one of the most solid pits. People they've got back
working at the colliery now don't come from Armthorpe – one's
only just moved to this pit a fortnight before strike, a couple of
lads from way around who've only been there a couple of years.
Out of the twenty-three going into the pit, only two were
underground workers, the rest were mainly office staff.

All my friends are miners and we all go picketing together. We
all muck in together, get wood, travel around together, help one
another. My wife works part time, twelve hours a week – it's not
a lot of money but we manage to get by. I've had no trouble with
Social Security and so on. With having four kiddies at home, I
haven't stopped paying my mortgage because Family Allowance
is £27 a week which pays for my mortgage. Kids don't go without
– I know it's their money. We don't go out much. I brew some
beer at home and things like that. It's been a bit hard – we go out
virtually once a fortnight. It's not like it used to be – as compared
with twice, three times a week. Used to play pool on a Thursday,
used to go out on my own on Friday, take wife out on Saturday
or a Sunday.

Strike hasn't affected relations with my wife because she's been
really good about it. She goes picketing in morning with me, the
money which we get for picketing, she saves hers to buy some
coal. She turned round to me and said 'If you go back to work
scabbing, I'm leaving you.' Not like some of them saying that 'If
you don't go back . . .'. I've definitely got a lot of support from
my wife.

The only effect strike's had on my wife was last week when I
was sent a letter by colliery telling me that I'd got to see the
manager within three days otherwise I'd get the sack, for being
caught pinching coal. And I wasn't within twenty-five mile of
Armthorpe at time. Thing was, somebody gave my name,
address, number, everything. I went to see him with Union
representing me and all they could turn round and say was
'You're on report.' And I said 'I don't care about being on
report, It weren't me' And it's been proven that it weren't me
now.

Kiddies have been alright. The three big ones know what it is
all about. They know they're not going to get everything for
Christmas and things like that. Little one's only 4 year old and
finds it a bit hard to understand. I tell him he's not going to get
this, that and the other – I tell him I'll make it up to him when we
go back to work (if we ever go back). The big ones, 15, 12 and 11
– they know what it is about.

Community's been affected because they used to have a good

relationship with police in this village . . . it will take a long time to get it back again. I had a friend who were in police force and I still talk to him now and again, but the relationship's not what it used to be.

My lifestyle's definitely changed. Daily routine is still much the same though – eat and go out as if to work like I normally do except that I'm going picketing, not to work. I go picketing every morning, wherever they send us – we go all over. If somebody's going in at half past four, we'll leave Welfare at half past three. Only difference there is that I've got a little more time on my hands to bibs-and-bobs.

Shopkeepers are pretty good because a lot of them have put notices up on their windows saying 'No Police'. That was after they had a bit of trouble up at top of village with Waltons serving police. I think that was just a few of the lads getting a bit overheated, that got a bit out of hand.

They got a lad to go in here scabbing – Chicken George – and he's been working since beginning and he's just been sacked for stealing a telephone. Just shows what Coal Board are. They get you to scab and then they sack you for taking a telephone. Why didn't they just tell him to take telephone back?

### Irene Fretwell, 31 years old, miner's wife, four children

I first became involved in helping with the strike through coming here for assistance myself. I'd had my son in hospital and he had to have a hot bath, every day, for medical reasons. I just came here to see if I could get some help with some coal. My neighbour came with me, and, at that time, we'd thought about getting a busload of women together and going rallying, saying we backed us husbands in this strike. So, we just came to see union and asked if there was anything we could do to help. Well, they said best place to help would be down here, it was just more or less making sandwiches at that time. So, anyway, we decided to call a meeting for women that wanted to join, and it started from there really. There weren't a right lot at first, I think about fifteen of us, but we called another meeting to get more organised and we raised enough money to get a kitchen going properly.

I'm secretary of our group. I don't do any cooking. I do most of the writing, organising, making sure we've got enough food in for the kitchen and for the food parcels. I stay here and deal with all the correspondence and ordering food, etc. I went to London once, collecting, but now, with being involved with the day-to-day running of the kitchen, other activities have fell through. We had lots of things go wrong at first, I mean we've learnt by our mistakes. We've had snags and problems, running out of gravy mix and things like that, but we've got more established now and we know how many we're cooking for, so normally it's running pretty smooth. With Christmas coming we're trying to do a bit more. I've never done anything like this before, I've only ever done a party for my own kids, with about ten coming. Now, I'm organising for 200, 300 or even about 400 people coming in for their dinners. It makes you wonder how you do it.

My youngest has started school during the strike, so I can spend a lot more time down here. Still, I always think I don't give my kids as much attention as I should though. I feed them and make sure they've got clean clothes, but I don't give them the same attention they used to get. But, I think they understand, I think it's made them more independent, it's made them realise they can do a lot more things for themselves. And me, I think I mothered them a bit too much. I've found out that my kids are a lot more independent and can do a lot more than I thought they could. I do the cooking for them, but half the time, I can go home, give them something to eat, then get called out again down here, but if they want a snack they can get it themselves. The boys are old enough to be left anyway.

My husband and I have had some problems. I mean we do argue, it does put pressure on you. We argue about who wants to go on picket line, I mean I want to have a go and with having children it causes problems. If it's late night picketing you have to have someone there, we don't like leaving them in the house all night by themselves. My housework has dropped behind and sometimes my husband gets fed up. Sometimes I get fed up, but normally we pull together.

Financially, we are struggling, but, we've learnt to economise on a lot of things, and we've had a lot of help from his parents. All my family is in mining, so they can't really help. They're in the same position as us. They help as much as they can, with us having four children. I've made a lot of friends down here, but they're all in the same boat as well, so we've just had to learn. I mean we don't throw anything away, when dustmen come to empty our bin it's empty now, where before it were piled high with rubbish.

The strike has changed me, my life has changed a lot. I used to be tied to the kitchen sink all the time, washing nappies and all that, and I don't think I could ever go back to it now. I want to get involved in a lot of things round here now, it's opened my eyes to a lot of things. I'd like to be more of a welfare or social worker, I'd love anything like that, you know, to see everybody sorted out and happy and content.

I've grown up in this village, but there's a lot of people I didn't know until now. Now I can't walk down street without people shouting hello, so, we've made a lot of new friends in this and I hope we keep it up. I just hope community keeps together like it is now.

## John Jacques, transport manager, 54-year-old widower, two sons

I was born in a small village just outside here. My wife died on Good Friday. I have two sons living at home with me. I am a Secretary Manager and a Transport Manager. That means I am in charge of distributing all retired miners' fuel and workers' fuel. I do all the secretarial work, it's really a hard job.

This work has continued throughout the strike. When it started we had a meeting, the NUM and myself, with the management about distributing retired miners' fuel and a few sick notes for working miners. This worked quite well for a few months; we carried on as before. Then in August we had some clashes with the police at pit gates and they stopped us going in for about two months. We had to travel about eighteen miles to Manders Main for the fuel then, which was very expensive plus they only let us have five bags instead of the usual twenty bags allocation. After a while manager relented and opened up again so we could carry on as before. At another time he stopped us distributing the one or two bags to sick miners, of course we had trouble, but he relented again and let us carry on as normal. These decisions will affect relations at pit when the strike is over, manager did mention this to me one day, it does concern him. I said to him 'Well boss, these things do come – and they do go. Time's a great healer.'

One of the things that stands out in my memory of the strike was, somehow or other, one of our lorries was taken to the pit gates and turned over, by whom I don't know. When I got to know about it I went to the colliery entrance to see about it. I've never seen anything like it in my life. Hundreds of police with riot gear and shields. I walked up, by myself. It was really horrifying. I explained who I was and that I'd come to see about the lorry. They gave me permission to have it turned up and drive it away, which we did, but that was one of the most horrifying times of my whole life, walking through all those police, and I'm a hard man usually. Other than that, as regards transport in this village I've had a good relationship with local police. I mean I've had nothing else to do with these riot police, the ones they bring in from other areas. I do have to go up to the colliery every day, for coal notes and sick notes, and I've had no trouble getting through, I must say that. There's always different policemen on and I go up five days a week. They're not local men, they're from all over. I hear Liverpool accents, London accents, I don't know them, but I've had no problems.

On a personal level, I've been in a very funny position over the last nine months. My wife died on Good Friday. My two sons living at home are single, and I'm classed as single, so we've had no income whatsoever, none at all. I've lived on my savings, that's practically all gone now. Of course we've been helped out with food parcels, and by my sisters and my married daughter and other relatives. We've applied for some assistance to the Metropolitan Borough Council, but we've heard nothing yet. So, we've just had to live on charity really, and all my savings. Well, we've managed, but things are going to get worse, when the savings run out. I've carried on doing my job, but it's all voluntary now, and it means I have no time to go picketing or do any other jobs, so I've no money coming in at all.

I think the people in this community are marvellous. The way they've carried on, it's wonderful. I was involved in the 1972 strike, but we had no problems then, compared to now. There was no trouble with the police, none of these riot squads, and if I remember rightly, there were no scabs either. We had good relations with the management then too, they let us take out all pensioners' coal, we had no troubles at all. Well, now, these young miners who've never been involved with strikes before, they've been marvellous. Us older miners always said if they hit hard times, these young'uns, they'd never stick it. But, by gum, they've really surpassed it! They really have stood up to it. They must be a tougher generation than ours was, I must say that.

The strike's not only affected miners. There's a slight cloud over this village. Business people have really been hit, and some of those people are ex-miners. Harry Taylor, up top end of village, he has a newspaper business, and he told me things are really bad for them. It's hit all business in Armthorpe, but most of business people have helped, they all contribute in some way or another. It's marvellous.

**Christine Mahoney, housewife, three children, born Doncaster, 39 years old**

I've assisted the strike in every way. Collecting, picketing, fund raising, dinners. I've been on everything that's going, all of it. You're that busy you don't really think about what stands out most. I've been one of about six women who've organised the food in the kitchen, getting it ready, putting it out, then you've got all the washing up and clearing up to do. It's not easy, you're doing more, a hell of a lot more, than before the strike, in fact I don't know what we're going to do when it's all over. It's going to be very quiet compared to what it is now.

When the strike first started I was chief fund raiser, so I got a raffle going every week. I've seen me be out till 11 o'clock at night, it's been one or two in morning before I got to bed. I got a group of women and we'd do the whole village. As long as I saw money coming in I didn't mind. My daughter does her whack and my eldest son's done his bit, young'un gives papers out, everyone's involved, the whole family, we're all in this.

Why am I doing it? It's not just for mine, we're all in this together, it's not like you've just got one husband, you look after everybody, and that's how it should be in a village. In a mining village everybody sticks together. I've found it has made a difference to the community in Armthorpe. I can remember when I was little, it was a mining village, then all of a sudden you got your hoity-toitys coming in and it sort of split. Well now everybody's back where they should be, there's no fences in village now. In my view that's some good that's come out of the strike, that's the only thing I'm really pleased about, everybody's back together the way they should be. Now, I've hundreds of friends round here, five of us may share one bag of flour, they're friends, but I've lost all previous so-called friends through strike. I've got no one to thank when this is over. My husband's family, not one's come forward to help, only my own mother, but she's worse off than us, my stepfather's a miner, they're on their own, so they get nothing. But best memory I'll have is way strike's brought everyone together and new friends I've made in the community.

Sacrifices, God, there's more than I can say. No coal for a start, no clothes, no shoes. I've got a whacking great big dog, he's on half food but I won't get rid of him, I've done without. There's been a lot of sacrifices, the kids doing without, my lad's got no shoes on his feet just now. I've had problems with his school, I sent a letter asking could he go to school in trainers, they said yes, till Friday, then he must have shoes. Well I can't afford shoes, I've had to keep him home, I can't get shoes now till after Christmas. They should realise this. They've been good in some ways, at beginning of strike everybody got a new pair of shoes, but he's worn them out now and their attitude makes no allowances for the financial hardships we're suffering.

In my view, when all this is over, many attitudes will have been changed. I've been on picket lines with the other women and those women are never going to go back to the way they used to be. A lot of the men don't like it, and think a woman's place is in the home but most of the women who had that old-fashioned attitude have changed now. Also, I think it's going to take a lot of years to get over the experiences we've had with the police. When all's said and done, they've got to live in this village and I don't think it will ever be the same again. My son was arrested a fortnight ago, he's not a miner but he's been helping out, and police came for him. I nearly got taken away with him. My worst memory of the strike will be when they fetched riot squad into village in August.

Sometimes we get fed up with the strike, but we're all in the same boat, we have to help each other out of the depressions. We sit down and talk it over with someone else. It's gone on a long time and it does cause tensions at home. We split up three weeks ago, but only for a few days, we've had twenty-one years and it's not first strike I've had. I mean we've argued before.

It's Christmas in a few days and the kids know it won't be the same. I can only get them one present each, they realise that, but as big as they are it still hurts. Still, we'll have our Christmas when they go back, they know that. They're not bothered, they haven't done bad. We'll have some'at on table to eat.

### Dress shop sales lady

If this pit closed down, the whole village would close down because of the number of men working there. This shop and a lot of other shops would have to close down. A lot of the customers aren't miners but it's affected a lot of people who aren't miners. My husband's not a miner but he's on short-time because of the strike so it's affected a lot more than those on strike. Sales just haven't been what they should be at Christmas which is unfortunate really.

Even the big businesses are having a bad time. You can tell in the market, the clothing stalls are just standing. It's only food that's selling. Shops still have to pay rent and rates and they may not have sold a garment all day.

You get one or two customers come in and ask for something you haven't got, and you try and explain that you don't carry a lot of stock, and they're irate because their husbands don't work at the mine. They've still got the money coming in but you can't explain that you haven't got the turnover, so you as the shopkeeper can't spend out the money you would do normally, so you get one or two who voice their opinions strongly.

There's a lot of people affected by the strike who aren't miners but no one thinks about them – a lot of people have gone bankrupt because of it and no one thinks of them.

I haven't got very involved with the strike myself, to be honest. I'll agree with anybody who comes into the shop to keep the peace – I'll agree black is white and white is black, because I just don't want any trouble. You've all got your own opinions but some are more willing to air it than others.

I think that the mining community has stuck together, rightly or wrongly – they're closing ranks. But it's causing a lot of trouble for the miners who want to work because I think a lot of them do now, because they're so hard up – they'll never get the money back that they've lost. The ones who want to go back are simply afraid of what will happen to them.

For example, during the Armistice parade, there was one gentleman in the parade in uniform and he was jeered all the way up to Church, and on Armistice Day I think that sort of thing should have been forgotten. If that happens on Armistice Day you can imagine what might happen to them down the pit.

Shops – in the village, they're not serving police who aren't local policemen which I think's a shame because they've only been brought in to do their job. Shops that have served them have had their windows put in. So they've got to pick and choose who they serve.

I feel sorry for the older men who're coming up to 40 and 50, they've used up their savings and never get any more. They'll be as poor as Church mice. The wives and children are suffering. They've no fires and it's dreadfully cold now. I heard of one man and he put the washer on to heat the water for a bath and then the washer broke down, and he's going to have an enormous electric bill.

There was a strike when my lad was little, my husband went to Social Security and they didn't want to know him. We had to make do with what little bit we'd got but it didn't last two minutes. But the miners never got anything from the Union. My father was in the 1926 strike. He didn't get a penny. They went to what we call Relief but they had to pay it back over the years. He was still paying it back when we came to live here and that were ten years later.

Whatever the miners stick out for, it's the wives who have to bear the brunt of it. One lady says she absolutely balks at chips – they have chips and bread, chips and bread. They must be at their wits' end. A loaf of bread, almost 50p, doesn't go anywhere, and a jar of jam – you go through it in a day. There's no substance in it.

I know of one lad going down to the Welfare when they were supposed to have some money, and they didn't want to know him and yet another man who was out of work next to him, he got something and he didn't work at the pit. It seems as if they're only catering for those who're willing to go on the picket lines not the ones who're on strike because they've got to be on strike. If you're on picket duty, you can get your free meals, and food parcels, and the pick of the toys and clothing – but it's only if you've been on picket duty – which is unfair. If you're unmarried and you work in the pit, you should be still entitled to something. I know a young man who lives by himself – he's got his electricity to pay for, he's got his fuel to get, he's got his food to buy and he gets nothing.

## Schoolteacher

The main thing we've noticed is an increase in violent attitudes amongst the children. That's in the last three or four weeks. They always push each other around in the yards – children do and they're average children. But I've noticed in the last few weeks that when they push or hit each other, they really mean to hurt. They watch the picture on television more than they actually watch the picket lines here and they think it's much more amusing to throw stones and pebbles through windows. We've always had broken windows from stones but it's much more now than before. I think it's part of the violence thing.

We have particularly noticed children not staying away from school. I think their parents are glad for them to come to school. The attendance rates are as good as they ever were.

Some problems with clothing because money is so tight. We have a uniform but we've eased the rules – people wear trainers instead of real shoes. But on the whole I think the parents are coping incredibly well. What I have noticed amongst families where the father is on strike, we are beginning to see some of the signs of classic, incipient malnutrition – cold sores around the mouth, hair looking all lack-lustre – little hints you get. Coal is incredibly difficult to come by and so people are washing in cold water, families that haven't spare fuel for heating water for weeks and weeks and weeks. These are all little miseries that people are living with.

Only about a third of the children here are from mining families. We've had one or two hints of trouble and we did see the beginning of trouble but it settled down. For example, two boys – one whose father is an ordinary miner on strike and the other whose father is on a safety team and has been down the pit. There were remarks like 'Scab' but they didn't push it. I don't think there is much conflict in the school. We never did pull entirely from mining families and the days that there were actually jobs round here, people were working at British Rail, ICI Fibres – but now in a great many of the families, father has been made redundant, so the family patterns have changed with father staying at home – not so many jobs for women round here. About a third of the families with one active parent rather than two which must have an effect. What people should realise is that the strike here is an extra burden, not a separate one. It's not just that there are lots of striking miners' children at the school, there are a lot of children from unemployed families as well, and sometimes it's hard to distinguish between the two.

Unity in Armthorpe – sitting here I am neutral because there are a lot of families with children at this school from all political persuasions. We draw from this end of Armthorpe – which is the old pit housing and it's not bad housing. Built before the War this was good quality pit housing. This was a late pit to be sunk. Barnsley seams were sunk late eighteenth century and possibly early nineteenth century. They were quite near the surface. And the further east you travel, the seam gets deeper and deeper. Rossington next door is 2,000 feet, we're deeper still, Hatfield is the last one along the line and it's the deepest of all. Rossington was 1920? so this will be early 1920s and if you look at the size and shape of the housing, these are really big houses with big gardens. This isn't your archetypical back-to-back housing. In fact, when the Coal Board sells them off it gets quite a good price. Now there's also the new housing which means this end of the village has become quite a mixed area.

Lots of stories around about the police that you can't prove – like people who've done their time in Northern Ireland – parcels of unnumbered police clothing on the back doorstep – but perhaps they've been sworn in as specials – I just don't know.

I think that the family men who've got hire purchase out on cars, a lot of commitments, they'll just get on with the business of living when the strike's over. They simply won't have time to bear grudges against the police and the Coal Board. However, the kids who haven't got any prospect of a job and who will probably be the long-term unemployed have got a taste for the other side of the law – it's one of the few excitements in life. When I think of the characters in school, it's only a few kids who are into trouble and who are involved in the activities on the picket lines with the police.

The familes are hungry, one of the ladies who comes in to do small jobs in this school, I know her diet's been spuds and baked beans and she's looking underfed, she's got all the signs of it. Her bronchitis won't go away and things like that. The wives aren't getting the food from the Miners' Welfare like the men are.

The community spirit's always been here – it's not new during the strike. What's sad is that when it's all over, the unspoken trust that the miners have underground – they have to – that won't be so good in relation to the strike-breakers. However, the few that are going to work here may have problems in a dark corner of the pit when it's all over.

Maybe there are communities elsewhere which are totally in support of the strike. But that isn't true of Armthorpe – it's much more representative of the overall social cake. It's not like Rossington where at the end of a long bus route the community is much more isolated – that isn't the case here. There may not be as many people against the strike as there are for it. But in some of the new housing, and even perhaps amongst the unemployed for various reasons (after all the miners have got a job, haven't they) there's some opposition. But a lot of people, mining families and non-mining families, just want to sit it out – trying to make it affect their lives as little as possible.

Keeping the school warm has been an incredible problem – we're getting open-cast coal at the moment by some agreement – hospitals first, and then schools at the end of the line – it's rubbish really and so one by-product of this strike is that our caretakers are having to work exactly twice as long as possible because of the ash – there's fumes, there's sulphur dioxide, coal-dust emissions. This depresses people here because you're always up against dirt and smells and fumes. But the caretakers have kept us warm. The Authority laid in hundreds and hundreds of Calor-gas heaters in case but we don't think that's a safe means of heating. There's all these odd little niggles that go with the strike.

Matron looks ready for sick leave because she's dealing with organisation of the meals for the miners' children because that's doubled the numbers taking dinners in school. And at the same time, she's dealing with the rising level of injuries because of the strike, she has an appalling time. She's an SRN but she's having a very difficult time coping with all the many different little things that have been affecting the school through the strike – all sorts of little things.

I think that there's an element of intimidation around for anyone who tries to go to work. You can gauge the power of the feeling against the scabs when everyone is hungry when nobody has hot water, when Christmas is a lean time – the loan sharks going round the picket lines offering loans at 33 per cent interest to get them through Christmas and you've got to be very strong-minded to recognise that that's going to lumber you for ever. All the swap shops around this part of the world can hardly buy anything any more because they've bought up household goods, all the nice stuff. I saw a cricket bat in a swap shop, signed with the Yorkshire and Lancashire sides – one of those special bats – all the treasures are going.

It's very easy to regard miners as they were in the eighteenth century – as inarticulate grunting beasts – which is how many Southern people in the Home Counties view them here.

## Miner's wife, grandmother

I've had to give up everything. We're near enough to starving alone. I'm not proud who knows. We get £7.33 a week. I have to pay the council £1.33 a week for a garage, 50p a week for water rates and about £2.50 to £3 a week for the light. So you know what we're living on. We eat bread and marg.

This last week I've been coming to Welfare Centre. Before I was too proud to come. We just sat in the house. We had nothing to eat for three days, just water. I have a friend, an old lady, who gives me bits. She buys me ½lb liver, a carton of milk and ¼lb tea every week and the occasional loaf of bread. Else we would have been starving.

I've gone to Nottingham. I've a sister-in-law in Leighton Abbey. My niece came and took me for a fortnight. I'd gone that ill I was ready to commit suicide and they knew it. She's a widow, she took me there to give me some food and light.

I've got an urgent call note off the doctor. My electric's been cut off. We're sitting now with no fire. I was on a quarter bill and I couldn't meet it, they cut me off. Now I've got a 50p meter.

We don't pay any rent, it's rebated. It's a Labour council.

My husband likes a cigarette. So my daughter-in-law and her friend save their cigarette stumps and he breaks them up and re-rolls them.

My son has two little kiddies, his money is only £11 a week. So there's nowt that lad can give you.

The strike has brought people together. I've only been in this village eleven years, so I don't know anybody this end of the village. But these women this end, I've only been coming a week, I think they're marvellous, they do a wonderful job.

Most of my neighbours my end of the village are not miners. I've not had a lot of help. One lad has by us. That lad's on dole with three kids, but he's given us dinners and the odd cigarette.

When you get to my age you get to habit. Things have to be done whether you work or not. I feel sorry for the young ones. I haven't got the heart in things I do normally. When you come to our age and you can't afford toilet rolls. My little grandson, he's 8, he come and said Nana I walked home from school, here's 2p. Put it on one side each day and then you can buy some toilet rolls. It's things like that that are heartbreaking. And when they're eating an orange and they'll see you and say, here are Nan have a suck, have a suck. Do you want a bit of this cake? I'll give you a bit. It touches.

We've got a television and I've never failed me licence, never in me life. So we said well we can't have telly. So we took the plug off, rolled the wire round it and put it in another room. The men came from the Post Office, not the detector van because we never had it on. So he explained to him that we were off for three months before we were on strike. So they summonsed us for £77 because we didn't have a licence. But we wasn't using the telly. So now he's been to court and he's got to go back in January.

The only good memories I've got is coming here to the Welfare Centre the last week. Mixing with other women and putting parties on for kids. I've enjoyed helping. I've helped to put up food parcels. I'm not spending hours at home sitting worrying.

We make up carrier bags of food. There's a tin of beans, tin of spaghetti, four eggs, two bits of boiled ham. It was for single lads but now they're giving it to people like us who are destitute.

Strike has had a terrible effect on women. Depression hits some more than others. Strike had made women bitter and stronger. Men sitting and drinking and women looking after kids doesn't happen any more. It's brought husbands and wives closer together.

### Agnes Currie, miner's wife, activist

My husband were on sick when they come on strike. He come off the sick on Friday because the strike was to start on the Monday and he didn't believe in being off on sick when others were on strike. He didn't hesitate about coming out.

I've had a threatening phone call from scabs saying they're going to put me windows through. But it can't be from scabs because scabs don't know me. I definitely think it's the police. They know I'm on phone. I mean scabs don't know me. It's definitely police that's phoned me up. Wherever you go, say we went into Nottingham when we were going on picket lines, we couldn't get back out. They wouldn't let us home then. They thought we were going somewhere else. They just didn't believe you.

Me mother's 56 years old and my dad died during this strike in May. She likes to get involved. I took her on picket line and they were kicking hell out of my mother's legs. She was, we all was, there peacefully.

My dad had that pit disease, he lived on oxygen for fourteen years. He was 61 when he died but he retired from the pit when he were 40. That's why I'm behind the strike because I seen how my dad suffered.

Financially, it's been hard, really hard. My sister here she's been good. Me mum's been good, me mum and me dad cos he only died in May. I got me Sunday dinner each week sent up to me. I've got a 50p slot for me meter and they used to send money up for that. Me mam still does send the odd couple of 50ps and she buys me a chicken every week for Sunday dinner. For Christmas and me kids, it's me sister that's bought them some new clothes. I just couldn't afford it. Before the strike we got about £90 a week now it's £27. But that's just gone up cos me daughter turned eleven. I've only been getting £27 for this last three weeks.

We also had a shop but we've lost that during strike. It were a clothes shop and they were the first to go. So I'm paying a bank loan as well. The shops that have kept going were lucky. My shop depended a lot on pit vouchers. My family allowance pays the bank loan so I live on £27 a week.

We don't have meat, new clothes – my kids for first time have had to run around in second-hand shoes. Well that's my youngest one not me eldest one because she won't do it. Me family make sure she's OK. We've sacrificed a lot but we've not sacrificed respect. One of me friends bought a pub just before strike started and she's been good to me. We all muck together and share. We share what we've got.

It's going to take us about two years to get back on our feet. I've not paid the mortgage since February. I haven't paid my milkman since February. I haven't paid anybody since February. I haven't had any problems with people I owe money to. Except my telly firm, they were going to repossess my telly. I wrote and told them it was the only pleasure we had. They wrote and told me to write to them once a month to let them go on. But then they did take it. But them from Liverpool fetched me a telly this weekend. So I've got a telly again.

We've always had a solid marriage. But with strike coming on I were out very much. There's only a few of us who can go out and get money, others have got ties. I were getting away that much that me daughter was saying it were like having no mum. I were having a lot of rows with me husband until three weeks ago when he came down to miners' club for his dinner. He was a very proud man and he wouldn't come down for his dinner. I were in London and I phoned up club to ask for some details about strike centre. They said do you want to have a word to Pete. He came to the phone and told me he'd been coming down for last three days on the trot for his dinner. Since he's become more involved and has been coming down and helping it's been a lot better. He now knows what pressures are and what's got to be done. He used to think we were going out for the sake of going out but not now. He'd go out picketing but then come home and I'd be out and he'd be cooking and cleaning and seeing to kids and he resented that. He's always been handy but now he had more to do. It did cause a strain. Now he's more involved it's better for everybody.

Community's a lot closer. Before the strike everybody had money in their purse and went about their own business. Now we stop and talk for hours in street. Community's back together like it were years ago. Money is not important any more, friendship and community is.

Marie Ann is the local parish councillor, she's not even involved in the strike. She's ever so good. For a parish councillor to be involved with you, it's something. She's here every morning faithfully doing them pickets' sandwiches. She's a good lass. there's quite a few who I didn't think would be involved in strike but have. I wish even more were involved. We've tried all sorts, we've put letters in shops and called for help in 'rank-and-file' letter that goes out weekly to lads. We've tried everything.

There's a lot who need Welfare but won't come for help. I got to a few of them by taking the food parcels to them. I let them get used to it and then I'd say look I'm sorry I can't come round this week, nip down to the club and I'll be there, I'm busy. And they'd come down and then they'd start talking. They'd find other people were in the same boat as them and so now they'd come down. But there's still a lot you can't get through to.

There's only been a Women's Action Group since the strike. It started for me when a woman called Sheila Christian were out collecting round shops for miners and she popped into our shop and asked if we'd like to donate anything towards a raffle. I said yes but is there anything else I can do. She says there's a meeting tonight come down. So I did and I've been involved ever since. That was the second meeting they'd had.

I organise picket lines for women, rallies. For people to get put up when they go away collecting. Get them contacts where they can go and meetings where they can speak at. I was the first one in our group to speak at a public meeting. It were to two and a half thousand people. My legs were shaking, it were at Sheffield in the middle of the town. My first speech I asked someone to write it for me. He said he'd help me but not write it for me cause he didn't know what I thought. He said you can come down and I'll show you how to put it. And he did. But after that when you're telling truth you don't need a speech. So I never have a speech no more. That were only one I've ever had. None since. When you're telling truth and you know what's happened to you, you don't have to write it down.

The first place I went to collect were Liverpool. I went to Hardman Street in Liverpool to get a permit. I got in touch with Felicity Dowling, she was the first contact I got in touch with in Liverpool. She gave me a permit and house numbers where we could go and sleep at night. From then we went on and stood on street corners for eight hours. We were successful, Liverpool was

fantastic. They were first-class people in Liverpool. I mean
they've gone through it, haven't they. Fantastic response in
Liverpool. From there people would invite us to their union
meetings. We'd speak and say how we need food and clothes.
And that's how it all started.

Most food we have to buy at wholesalers. We buy it in bulk. It
costs us roughly £2,000 a week just to keep going.

I never bothered about politics but I do now. When it come to
voting I just used to put a cross against Labour and stick it in the
box and that were it. But now, I can't argue on a lot cause I'm
still not right clever about it, but I'm picking something up every
day. I get different books. It's changed my way of thinking. I
think we must have been ignorant miners' wives. We were all in
the same boat, just go down and vote and come home just as
mam and dad's done and their mam and dad's done. Politics
never come into our house and it never came into my own house
with my own kids. But now my kids are getting politics and it's
going to make them more aware than I ever was.

The strike's changed a lot of attitudes in the community. I
mean there's lads in this club who'd say 'I'm not peeling taties or
washing them pots', but not now, I mean we all muck in
together. On Sunday there were lads working in kitchen
alongside us, cooking dinner and making tea, they wouldn't have
done that a year ago, they'd have said that's women's job, I'm
not doing it, but not now. I think men and women are more
equal in this village now.

## Alan Bailey

Strike started here as far back as Grunwick. It's always been a
militant branch. What you put into a branch is what you get out
of it. When rest of Doncaster Area was putting together to fill a
bus between them and Grunwick, we managed to fill a bus just
from our pit. We've always put everything that comes up in
Committee out to the general meeting and keep lads informed.
Plus we've a secretary who's really politically aware. He was
prophesising they was coming for us. So our branch was more or
less prepared. But when Yorkshire Area called a strike action
from the Monday that to our branch was the first mistake because
they gave a week's notice so they shipped all the coal out of the
yard stocks before the strike started. If they'd have said you're on
strike from now it would have been better. They wouldn't have
had so many stocks at power stations. Ours is really high grade
coal and they moved it in the first week. We couldn't picket 'cos
there was no strike.

We ceased work on the Friday, on the Sunday we called a mass meeting. They approved of what Yorkshire had done. There were about two abstentions and two votes against in the 1200 men present.

Straightaway we made plans to picket Nottingham as per normal. Our branch, as soon as we cease work over anything, we've always picketed the other pits. That's the only way we know how to strike – picketing. Pull as many out as you can as quick as possible.

On the Monday morning we all went to Haworth pit, it's only just over the border into Nottingham. We went in, the lads picketed the day shift out. Very few went through on the day shift. About midday I was back here at the strike centre. That first day I was in control of strike centre. Yorkshire Area rung and told us to pull us men out of Nottingham. I said I'm not pulling them out. So I got in touch with the branch President and Secretary and they said straightaway no we're not pulling them out. But Yorkshire then sent the Doncaster Area agent into Nottingham to Haworth and he went to our picket line and told the lads to break it off and come home. But he promised that the Yorkshire Area officials would come and speak to us on the Monday night.

By this time Hatfield and Rossington, they'd had no instructions. They'd been sat at home. So they were on the phone saying where are you going. So we'd said, well our lads are at Haworth. They said if you're still there tomorrow we're coming.

Everything hinged on the meeting that night.

The Vice-President of Yorkshire who's an ex-delegate from this pit came. He says give them a week to have their ballot in Nottingham and let them decide to join us or not. Well, exactly as I told you about the week they shifted all our stocks, well the same thing was going to happen in Nottingham plus they'd have another week's production. So our Branch President said if there wasn't picketing then we was going back to work and Yorkshire Area would have to come and picket us out. If we come on strike the only way was to come on strike to win. So rest of the meeting backed what the President had said to carry on picketing.

Although Yorkshire Area officials argued for half an hour about policy of union, the Area, stick with area loyalties and everything like that, we said if we're out on strike we're out to win. So because he failed then to persuade us he then had to move his executive meeting forward from the Wednesday to the Tuesday morning. But on Tuesday morning we was picketing in Nottingham anyway.

Rest of Doncaster Area pits had phoned up and asked us where we was going and they'd go with us. Well Area Executive was then rushed into action and then all Yorkshire went

picketing. Because they couldn't pull us out they decided all
Yorkshire better go picketing. So that's really when it started in
Armthorpe.

The Area Executive was reluctant to take that step because
apart from one or two they've had no experience about strikes.
Jack Taylor was never involved in any grass-root action. No rank-
and-file action at all. Arthur Scargill has experience of rank-and-
file action. In 1972 Scargill was leader of the Barnsley panel and
Bristow was leader of the Doncaster panel. Yorkshire Area
wasn't very happy on picketing but Scargill and Bristow pulled it
through. But Scargill moved on to Yorkshire area with experience
of rank-and-file action which Taylor has never had to this day.

The militant tradition in Armthorpe goes back to more or less
when the pit opened. It's always believed in picketing the
Doncaster Area Panel out there and then if it's involved in an
issue.

A good example is when we'd been picketing up in North
Yorkshire over the Rescue Men's strike in 1978. We got very
poor results. It's always been the right wing of Yorkshire Area.
But then in 1981 the pressure came on to shut so-called
uneconomic pits then in North Yorkshire. They came to picket us
and within half an hour we were all out and taking them all over
Doncaster Area pits. We joined the picket with them. The
people who were involved in that from North Yorkshire moved
to Selby and it's paid off in Selby.

Like I said it's what you put into a branch is what you get out.
At our branch meeting any literature that comes in is read.
Wherever it comes from and whether committee agree or
disagree with it. For example, at one miners' meeting we once
spoke for half an hour on abortion. It was when anti-abortion act
was going through and we had a good interesting argument for
half an hour.

We're always having interesting meetings and discussions in
our Union. Another example was when there was a resolution
about the hunger strikers in Ireland. It came up in the meeting
but a few days before there was the bomb explosion at Old
Bailey or Oxford Street in London. So when resolution was read
out the current opinion was words like 'hang the bastards' and
everything like this. About five of us stood up and put arguments
as to why there was a hunger strike. And about the issues in
Northern Ireland. Finally the resolution of support for hunger
strikers was passed by about 80 per cent of meeting. There were
about eighty or ninety at meeting. We normally get ninety to a
hundred at meetings because they are interesting. You must keep
your members informed.

I've found this when I'm going round collecting. You'll get to a

factory and say can I see the convenor. You'll meet him and he'll
say 'I don't think you'll get much support in this factory. When I
listen they're all anti-miner.' But when you get to speak to them
they don't know the issues. They've not been explained, they've
no information. The convenor is underestimating or underfeeding
his own members. When you talk about it being a total fight for
jobs not just pit jobs, then they begin to understand you. They
respond with money and gifts.

Many miners have come to our pit from others which have
closed in the past. That's why we've all sorts of nationalities
working at our pit. Racism is laughed at here. We've Ukranians,
Poles, West Indians, Indians, Welsh, Scots, Irish, every nationality
under the sun. We know we can work together and we do.

In the strike we're on a plateau now. Most people's adjusted to
it. It's not getting any worse or easier. We can exist and carry on.

My main memory of strike is young lads. I tended to see them
as a weak link. Thought older men who've been through it
before, they'll be all right and solid. But perhaps young lads
who'd had it easy and got it easy might be weak. But they've
been terrific the lads. They've taken some real beatings off police
and bounced back the next day.

My wife's working full time so I've been cushioned. But my
lad's out on strike and he's single and not a penny from
anywhere. In the branches there's a hot meal every day. It's not
just the young single men, it's the older ones as well. The
widowers. There's one old man who came in the other day and
said I hope this strike never ends. It's the best he's fed for years.
Proper hot meals and terrific company. He can chew over old
times and at weekends he's a food parcel to go with it. Before the
strike he'd lived a lonely sort of life. It's brought people together.

With working three shifts, each miner stuck with his shift and
followed it round. He wouldn't see other shifts. Since strike,
miners, especially from outlying districts, have met other miners
from their own pit that they didn't know existed cos they weren't
on their shift.

As soon as the strike started all the clubs cut the price of beer.
You can get a pint now for 55p when normally it's 65p.

The strike has welded people together. We've got community
cooking, community woodyard, people are working together for
a common cause. They realise that they can live without help
from the state.

It's costing round about £7,000 per week to run this village.
That's without the costs of picketing. We've adopted about 200
miners from Haworth in Nottinghamshire. We've a spill-over
area to the east where there's about 400 men and we supply them
with cash.

It's a struggle but we exist. I wish Scargill would stop going on telly and saying everything's rosy, it's not, it's a struggle. I mean you can be sat in the strike centre like today and have to decide whether to give a woman a fiver to stop her electric from being cut off. We try not to make it a means but resources are slim. Some women are good managers and some are bloody awful – same as the blokes. So we try to make it a means test and just shove the money where help's needed. The families are under a lot of pressure. The fight should be stepped up.

The women's movement has jumped forward fifteen years during the strike. In 1972 and 1974 they were content to stay at home and scrimp and save. They're not now. Look around Miners' Club today, there's men sweeping up, washing dishes, cooking and there's also women on the picket lines. If they'd have told me last year that after every weekly union committee meeting we'd then have a meeting straightaway with a Women's Support Group, I wouldn't have believed it. I think there's everything in this strike for the rest of the workers.

### Miner's wife, born Armthorpe, 30 years old, two children

At the beginning of the strike, I didn't really think it would last this long, so I didn't think much about how we would manage financially. But we've got two very good neighbours and though my mum and dad are pensioners, they've helped us, so really we haven't gone short.

We get about £41 per week. I have to pay £3 per week electricity, the mortgage interest has to be paid and I've tried to keep up paying my insurance. I've just paid my telephone bill, it's mainly the mortgage that I haven't kept up and house insurance I've had to leave. My husband and I haven't had any new clothes during the strike, we've had to buy the little one some warmer clothes, just little bits. Foodwise, we don't buy proper joints anymore, things like that, we've gone to sausages and mince, belly pork, cheaper meats. We don't buy biscuits, cakes or sweets for the children anymore.

We haven't found it too difficult to manage, because we've had such a lot of help from me neighbours and my parents really. They've sort of got us through it. The neighbours are not miners, they pass food over, even money. I felt a bit degraded when they first offered to help. Instead of putting into collections outside supermarkets, knowing that we were miners, they said they'd just give it to us. We said 'you haven't got to, it's not your responsibility to have to look after us' but they said if they didn't want us to have it, they wouldn't offer it. My husband's mum also helps, she's divorced but she sends us what she can, a cabbage or a cauli, any little bit that she can she'll send and she gives children 10p for sweets at night. We have been lucky. We go to my mum's every Sunday and have a good Sunday dinner and some days in week as well, that saves our electricity as well, so we don't do too bad.

The thing that gets to me most is sitting without a fire, now it's the winter. I mean over the months we've got used to going without luxuries, not going out, not buying clothes, but it's mainly the cold now that gets you down. We can sit wrapped up but we have to put Leanne in our bed. She's only eighteen months and it's too cold to put her on her own. And getting baths, we've got an immersion heater but we try not to use it to save electric, so we have to get bathed at me mum's. Sometimes we have to put it on, but even so, unless we can get some bits of wood for a fire, it's too cold to bath her and bring her down afterwards. I think if we had heating we could stick it out a lot longer. Of course, there have been other sacrifices too, no holidays, no birthday presents for the children, not being able to send hardly any Christmas cards or buy any Christmas presents for the family.

We are not really actively involved in the strike. It's a bit awkward with Leanne. She's a very clingy child and I can't often leave her with anyone else, so I can't go off collecting or anything. I've never been on a picket line. I'd be too frightened to stand on a picket line, my husband was on picket line when there was trouble at Armthorpe and he was right shook up when he got home. I don't think people outside realise how upsetting it is. Like when the police came into the village, me mum had got me little girl in a pushchair and she was on the opposite side of the road from where she lived and she couldn't get across for all the police vans that was coming in and she broke down and was crying, it really frightened me mum. Where we live, for some weeks at one period, there was a patrol came in at about quarter to four every morning and the lights and the noise used to wake the children up every morning. No, I wouldn't dare stand on a picket line.

Our daily routine is not very different, I still have to get up and see my elder daughter off to school then me and Leanne sit wrapped up in blankets and watch TV for a while, then shiver and get dressed. If we get really bored we go to me mam's and get warm and something to eat. My husband does a lot more round the house now, he does some housework and cooking. Sometimes he helps one of his friends delivering miners' coal. He doesn't get out much for a drink any more. Sometimes some good friends will take him out for an hour but he can't afford to go out himself.

We're not going to be too bad at Christmas, again me mum's been very good and lent us some money to buy the children a new dress each and we'll be going there for our Christmas dinner. I've also managed to keep up my payments on a Christmas hamper through year, so we'll have that, so we'll do pretty good really.

We've always been a close family and I feel we've been getting a lot of support from them but we were never close to the neighbours before, it's brought us a lot closer to them. I think we will continue this new friendship after the strike's over, because we can never repay them in money for what they've done for us. They've sort of got us through it.

### Young miner

What's happened is that we've all come closer together. When you've been harassed by the police just because you're a Yorkshire miner – telling you to move on when you're not doing anything – that's the real key memory of the last few months. That what's brought the lads together. The community was splitting up before the strike, with all the lads leaving the village, buying houses outside, getting mortgages, and getting families. But now the police action seems to have brought everyone back together.

Everybody's in it together. Supposing you went to another village before the strike, there'd be a bit of animosity between the lads in one place. It was a lot of pit lads against another. You'd be lucky to get out alive. But now you go to any pit village – I've been to Goldthorpe for the night out, Rossy (Rossington) come up here, you can go anywhere now. 'You a miner?' 'Yeah, yeah' – you get on really well with everyone now. It's not just one village. It's all pit villages have come together. You're getting all the women pulling together – making snap for the lads and stuff like that. There's a good feeling now. You haven't got much money but it's much better than it was.

I've not done very well as far as cash is concerned but got by better than I thought I would. You just seem to survive on whatever you can get. I get a pound a day picketing and me mam might slip us a couple of quid on Friday night so it gets us out for the night. Me mates have been really good to us. I've not done too bad really. I've sacrificed two holidays, getting rid of car, sold me push-bike, cashing in the insurance. I was going to buy a house but that's gone out of the window. It's mainly the financial sacrifices of the strike that trouble you – that's all it is.

The bank's been very good. We've had a problem with insurance. I tried to cash in an insurance policy and they won't

21  Confrontations between miners and police on the streets of
    Armthorpe, 21 and 22 August 1984

give me any back – they've been awkward. But the bank's been all right. I'm overdrawn but they put no charges on. My dad paid off a bank loan for me, but I could have got that frozen. A few of the lads have got it frozen.

Relationships have got better with my mum and dad. They've been great with me. My dad used to be a miner and they've been fine with us . . . slip you what they can, when they can. . . . My brother's a copper and we didn't speak for four or five months despite living in the same house. We're speaking a bit now – to keep the peace with my mam, but you still feel the tension.

My view of the police has gone straight down the line. Before the strike, if I'd seen a copper in trouble in Armthorpe, and my brother being one, I'd have gone in to help. If I saw one now, I'd walk straight past. I'd leave him . . . no chance, after what they've done to our lads on the picket line. You can't forget what they've done to us.

There's one law for one and one for the other now. If you're a miner, that's it, you're a criminal. There's going to be a lot of repercussions after this lot of police have all gone back and these local cops are left here. The feeling of the lads now, they feel that badly done to, there's bound to be some what go off because of what they have done to us . . . not just ones from outside but these local cops have been as bad . . . trying to make out they've all been as nice as pie, but they haven't.

Most of the shops in the village are pretty good with you if you're a miner. There's a video shop round the corner from us. It gives videos for half price to try to help us any way they can. There's one near here, and he's got two shops, one near the pit and when they had all trouble at pit at Armthorpe, he was actually serving the police and nobody ever goes in there now. . . . But you get a lot of them that have a sign in the windows 'Any Police on Picket Duty Can't Come In' – they're not getting served in there. A lot turned them away. Fish shop did as well. Said 'we're not having you in here . . . we've got to live here after you've gone, like'. And there's my mate who lives in this big garage here – its one of the biggest garages around Donny – they've got three or four. Well, they used to do police cars, service them and all the lot. Well, they told them 'No more . . . it's not worth it . . . we've got to live here, you haven't' and they've stopped taking police cars. My mate's been asked to drive coaches of scabs and he said 'No chance – I'm not going in with them'. Most of the people and the shops in Armthorpe are pretty good there's only a few exceptions.

Problem now is passing time. You get into a sort of routine – it's just like going to work in a way. You're up about 4 in the morning, picketing, meeting at the Welfare and driving to some

local pit. Then we'll come back to the Welfare for our own pit
gates at 7 o'clock. Then we'll probably stay here at Welfare up to
1pm for dinner – usually, I hang about, we have a game of cards,
snooker, any of lads want running in to town, something like that
I'd do that, anything like that. We'll hang around here till they
throw us out about 3 o'clock to clean the place up, then perhaps
back home for television, a bit of snap, and then back here in the
evening cos it's warm and you can probably scrounge a drink
while you're playing cards.

Before the strike I hadn't liked the Union. I wasn't interested
in politics – didn't understand what Union leaders and politicians
were on about. Thought Union leaders at Armthorpe were a set
of shit-stirrers but once the strike came along, I thought I might
as well find out for myself what's going on. I've changed right
about now. I realise that we are fighting for something worth
fighting for. If this had been over money, I wouldn't have come
out. I wouldn't have agreed with it because it's something
everybody agrees with, it's great. You learn a lot about politics
too. It makes you realise what the Conservatives stand for, and
what Labour stands for – the SDP, they're the biggest set of shits
walking. They're probably worse than the Conservatives. Before
the strike, I thought they were probably all right but since the
strike was on, it's changed my views on politics entirely . . . going
to join Labour Party afterwards – apart from Kinnock (I don't
like him), but people like Kaufmann, they're not so bad.

Some of the older miners are some of the best really. They tell
you about the 1974 strike, and you get on better with a lot of
them. Now they try and guide you about and, if there's a bit of
trouble, then 'Come with us' – lads in their fifties, if there's any
coppers about, they'll look after you.

**Malcolm McAdam, electrician, underground, with a wife and child, born
Askern (Doncaster), Union Committee member**

I started strike by picketing pit gates but soon after I was taken ill
and rushed into hospital, so for two months I was inactive. Since
then for five or six months I've been sorting problems out with
hardship and fines, things like that.

I had a new car in January. I gave me other in part exchange
which was only eighteen months old and got a bank loan to cover
the difference. As soon as the strike started, I went down to the
bank and asked them to freeze it. My mortgage is very low, so I
don't have to worry about it and Building Society has frozen that.
Sunday dinners have gone bye – we can't afford them now.
We've been living on curries, they're cheap and easy to prepare
so that covers Sunday dinners up.

I have my meal a day down at the Welfare here. My daughter
gets free school meals. My wife comes down maybe two or three
times a week. So we've really no outgoings. I get picket money
and they put me a bit of money for petrol down here at the
Welfare for running about for the Union but that's all I do get.
I've taken over as paymaster because of Branch Paymaster being
in jail so I can afford to run car. I've got good relations. We're
getting all expenses paid down to Somerset – my wife's sister's
husband's a strong trade unionist down there, Labour Party
member and that and he got a job as a County Organiser for the
Agricultural Workers . . . so now we get free and cheap holidays
in Somerset. They asked us what we were doing for Christmas and
we explained. They've been up here two or three time and seen
all the carry-on and they said 'Get yourself down. Pack a case.
Scrounge some petrol money to get down and don't worry about
owt else.'

Apart from that, my wife – I won't call her a scrooge – she's
very economical and the Family Allowance money, we take a £1
out of it every week for the TV money for the stamps and £5 goes
straight into her purse, back of her purse, ready for paying off
bills like telephone and electric. If we did get into difficulties, the
Union would attempt to pay some of it. They offered to pay my
telephone bill because I'm doing a lot of Union work so I think
we're slightly better off than a lot of people. We're managing to
survive but that's all it is – survival.

Armthorpe's always been a strong community. There isn't one
man from Armthorpe that's actually going to our pit. We have
got some going to other pits. It's proved to be a strong village
during the strike. Every one of the five clubs have dropped their
beer prices to cater for customers – they know the miners can't
afford it so they bring the beer prices down.

There's no doubt it's put a strain on my marriage. It's only just
recently. Being down here at the Welfare, you're among the
Women's Action Group. My wife hasn't come down here until
recently. She's been worried and it's taken a long time to get over
it – there's been a lot of talk and people have accused me of
having affairs with this woman and that. The wife's a bit
understanding but it gets a bit much when she hears it from
different people. There's certain lasses hanging around me but
there's nothing to it. But you try telling her that. So that's put a
bit of a strain on me. But I don't think that's been the main
problem. The main strain has been me not going to work, being
around at peculiar hours. We've had to adjust and it's taken me a
long time to adjust. She's gradually come to terms with it and
now she says 'There's no way you are going to go back to work
now, until it is settled.'

There's no boredom – eight hours' sleep and sixteen hours' strike – If I'm not working down here at Welfare, I'd be listening to the news, finding out what's happening elsewhere. There's plenty of life down here – concerts and things. Then we go to different places – there's a few of us going out tonight. We've been invited to Haworth. They've only got seventy-two members on strike. We adopted them. Every so often we go over there for a social. Tonight we're going over for a chinwag and a bit of a drink.

My job is to take care of common fund, to pay pickets out, to write begging letters and to write thank you letters as well.

I've not done any collecting on the street. At present I don't think I've got the guts to do it. It takes a certain type. Personally I don't like begging for money and I don't think I'm that type of person.

I'm not a good speaker. I've never spoken in public. Once you've spoken once, it becomes easy. But until you've had a bit of experience, it's difficult. I'm supposed to give a talk tonight, at our Ward Labour Party – they want a talk on the miners' strike – there's three of us from this branch who are from same ward as me. So what I was going to talk about was the events leading up to the strike – the Ridley Report and so on. But unless I had notes in front of me I'd be lost. But I've had to cancel that now because we'll be over at Haworth instead.

My daughter'll be glad when it's over. She doesn't get pocket money now. She gets ribbed at school a hell of a lot – a lot of the kids where we are, just outside Armthorpe, come from farms and from RAF families. So the miners' kids are a minority there and they're getting a hell of a lot of hassle from them – kids can be the nastiest people on earth, back-stabbing and that. It gives us a lot of trouble at home. There's times when she's come from school in tears because the other kids have been picking on her. I've been accused of being a scab from school – they see my car going out every morning and they see it come back late in the afternoon and a lot of local kids just jump to the conclusion that I'm going to work. A few of the kids call me a scab. My daughter knows I'm not but you try telling it to a classroom of kids that I'm not a scab. It's a hell of a lot to ask. But she's pulling through. And the Christmas is going to affect her more than us. She wanted a home computer but she'll have to make do with the dictionary!

## Steve Ciebow, faceworker

My dad was in a Polish mining strike in 1936 and he can see the cause his sons are fighting for now. When he was in Poland, martial law came into it – like martial law has come into this. Where I live, there's a majority on the dole but even those lads are helping us out with bits-and-bobs.

With me being on a picket line from March right up to now, I admit from my point of view that I've done my bit of violence but the violence I've seen is from the police.

I've got a friend working at this pit right now. I can't go to his house and ask him what's his problems because police would arrest me. My mate I've found out is in a lot of debt. But he'd never been in picketing, he'd never been in to union to find out what help he could get. He's not my friend any more.

I am in financial debt with my first wife and now with my girlfriend that I live with now. What I did when strike started was to go to all the firms that I owe money to. I said 'I'm earning no money. I'll pay all my debts when I return to work.' I've had two come-backs – from YEB with electric bill but my union is helping us out with that and I'm paying a pound a week on it. They've taken me to court on my water rates – but that bill is now suspended to end of strike. Only money I get is the pound a day picketing money. My wife gets family allowance for our 4-year-old daughter – she gets £7.40 off SS and £5.80 plus Family Allowance and my ex-wife – I live with another lass now, she's got a little lass, also 4 year old. But my wife's a one-parent family because I left her at beginning of strike. We have troubles before strike started, with bills and debts and that sort of thing. Before strike I had debts – everybody has debts if they're working, that's only way you can live. If you want to buy some furniture, you've got to go into debt for it and pay so much a week.

Bought myself a motorbike to get myself to work before strike. I lived twelve miles away from pit. I paid so much down on it and I still owed a lot of money on it, when it got pinched while I was on strike. I told police but I've heard nowt since. I don't get any insurance money back on it because I could only afford third-party cover. So I've lost bike and I still owe quite a bit of money on it. I'm in a state and it'll take me a long time to sort it out when I get back.

HP company was very good. I thought they'd respond with 'Well if you don't go back to work we'll take you to court. We'll get it off you somehow'. But instead they said 'Don't worry about it. Pay us when you return back to work'. That was nine month ago. Now debts are adding up and adding up and when I return back to work I'll have to pay what I can. See, I owe on my washer, I owe on my furniture as well as bike – this is all from my first wife. Now I'm separated but I've still got them bills to pay because they're in my name plus I'm living with Brenda now, and I try and help her as much as I can. Only way I can help her is to keep her warm and to give her the £5 a week from the picketing and she's satisfied with that. She's not working herself because of young'un. She comes and helps in strike centre and gets her bits-and-bobs that way. And we're happy because we know what we're fighting for.

Strike's affected Brenda a lot. She's broke up with her marriage and I've broke up with mine, divorce and that. But she's happy and I'm happy and we just have our ups-and-downs. Every day we have an argument about something because I know she wants something. It's coming up to Christmas now and I say 'We've got to manage'. She knows we've got to manage but she says 'I'm sick of begging. I'm sick of coming down here to the Welfare'. But after nine months of this you're used to rows and arguments doesn't last long because everybody else is in the same position.

The shops in the village have not been bad during the strike. Say I get £1 picketing money and I know that the cheapest twenty cigarettes are £1.6p. I go into shop and I say 'I've only got a pound picketing money. Can you give me twenty cigs?' Or if I want some firelighters. They just give you what they can and help you out. People in general are all right – if I'm invited out and we sit down in Welfare, there's a lot of people not involved in strike and they help us out because they know situation we're in, and they'll buy us a pint. You know who your friends are now.

I think that this strike in this village has brought all people together – community of Armthorpe is all mucking in. If anybody's got any problems, Union will sort it out or other people like your neighbours, will come in.

I've got several mates who are in police force. Since I've been on strike, I've seen them on picket line and now they'll not talk to me at all because I'm a striking miner.

But there's problems like your kids are suffering a lot. Even the kids are coming to the stage now when they see Maggie Thatcher on television and Ian MacGregor – they're calling them names. They know even when they're 4 years old what's going on. It's an education for them – they know I'm earning nothing and they're accepting it. As long as they're warm, as long as they've got something to eat – and if they want a toy or something, I'll say 'Father Christmas is on strike' – soon as we go back to work we'll be sure to give them a better Christmas next year. Christmas is next Thursday, and we've got nothing yet. It's first Christmas I've dreaded coming for kids' sake but I know this time next year, when we're all back at work, we'll have a Christmas to make up for it. Union has put on parties and kids have really enjoyed it.

Both the 4-year-olds know the situation. In fact, I went up to see my daughter the other day, and she gave me a pound out of her money box to get myself some cigarettes. I thought it was great. I told her to put it back and it would go towards Christmas tree because that's all she'll get.

# Interviews at Grimethorpe, June 1985

Guy Boanas

### Family economy
Gail Hancock, Ken Hancock, Margaret Keneally, and Audrey Clark

We got by on second-hand clothes. I was walking about – I had a pair of trainers that I used rain or shine. And as soon as strike started I brought my pit boots home and wore them and the going down to meetings and standing there in a pair of trainers you felt such a prat. For a time I didn't even have a pair of trousers.

As daft as it sounds, he put weight on during strike, but then again we were eating all the wrong sort of stuff. Another thing – when they were going up for these special diet things to claim this money they were saying you need a special protein diet and you know what one woman got told? 'Baked beans. Full of protein, baked beans.' I can't live on baked beans. 'Eat baked beans, they're only 17p a tin.' If I'd had been there they'd have put me in prison. I would have ripped her head off.

They had juice for scrumpying. They never scrumpied their own – it were always on the way back from Nottingham or somewhere like that. And one day Mick come home and he'd got all these turnips and cabbages. And we had a set to there. And he stood there right proud of them, these two sacks – 'look what I got'. And I said – because I'm lousy in the mornings, terrible, keep your distance – well, he stood there so bloody proud – 'That's disgusting, that.' He says – 'what do you mean that's disgusting?' I said 'that's bloody disgusting. All right, fair enough you know, one or two, but why did you go for this many?' He says – 'look, if I'm getting caught for taking four, I'm getting caught for taking forty. He'll do as much damage to me for taking four as forty.' So I said – 'Well what the bloody hell are we going to do with a sack of cabbages and a sack of turnips?' He says – 'You selfish bitch!' I said 'what?' He says – 'Don't be so bloody selfish. Don't Mary want one? Wouldn't she want one next door? Couldn't they use one across there with four kids?' And that were at the beginning of the strike and that's how things went on. It were back to the bartering system – 'I'll swap you a cabbage for two lettuce.' And we helped each other but there were a lot of selfish people. We had a deputy's wife put her name down for a parcel! A bloody deputy's wife came and expected to get a parcel off us!

We got caught though, didn't we, with the television licence. Yeah, we did.

My brother sent mine, from away. I thought, 'Thank God for that'. I went up the street trying to tell everybody, 'Detector van's round!'

But it didn't work. We'd got our set unplugged. A lot of people got away with it you see, because it were their own sets. And with this van, it went around, and kids were racing round on bikes, right left and centre: 'Me mam says "unplug the telly! The van's on its way."' And what they did was, they shifted them into the bedroom. But they know that you've got one anyway. They've only got to check down the list of who's got hire sets. . . . So they caught us redhanded. So they come in and Ken didn't half give it to them – 'Are you in a union? Do you feel . . .' And it upset me. . . . And my son went, and he got his little money box, with half pences and owt he could find, and he came, and he knew, I were ashen, I thought, this is it, we have to expect the worst, £200 fine and all. And Matthew tipped his money box out and said to the misters, 'Don't take the telly away. I've got some money here.' And it's little things like that hurt the most.

And when they came for our video. The first day of the strike I knew straightaway that we couldn't keep it on, so I rang and said come and fetch it back. They said – no, keep it on and when it's over we'll sort something out. I says no because – you may think I'm crazy but I class television as an essential when you've got kids in house but video, no. And they came and Matthew were watching *Play School* on tape. And he sat up and said – where you going with that? So man says – it's broke but I'll take it and mend it and when it's mended I'll give it you back. And lad says – it isn't broke, I've been watching that, it's been working. So in the end I said to Matthew – look, you're Dad's not going to work. He says why? And I said – because they wouldn't let him into work to get pennies to pay for this. So they've got to take it away cos we ain't got no money to give them. Soon as we get some we'll have one back. I explained it all to him. So he waited until Ken come in and then he run on to street and Ken's coming down and says – 'Dad, a mister's come and taken our video away because you won't go to work and get us no money.'

## The village shops

Your first help along with the NUM were some of the
shopkeepers and amongst them all were Gary Lee – a butcher on
Top Street. He must have lost thousands during the strike,
thousands of pounds. He's only a little family firm – he's only his
wife, his mother, his sister and husband who's in the shop, he just
employs his own family. And they were coming in on their days
off and baking pies for the NUM doing it for nowt with cheap
meat, things like that you know.

Other butcher [refused to help]. One of the butchers, in fact he
made a public statement he doesn't need the miners, he's got a
big enough freezer trade. And subsequently he were the first one
to put shutters and boards up at the windows. Still got them on,
he hasn't dared to come off now, hasn't dared. Because he knows
what'll happen. We've told him – you'll be out of business. But
that's another thing about where they forgot. I've seen miners go
in there and I think – Well look, there's a lad twenty yard up the
road did everything, gave support to us and this one did nothing.
It were the same in the 1974 strike. He's a man that has shown
nowt that he's for the miner. It's not as though he's from a
farming family, he were apprenticed there and he's worked his
way up to own the shop.

There weren't so many refused though. Electrical shop
couldn't, I mean people weren't having television sets repaired or
one thing and another. They couldn't give and when I went in
and asked them for our kitchen, we asked them to give a weekly,
not just a one off, we said 'Can you donate, no matter how small,
on a weekly basis?' just to make sure that this kitchen can open
and run, as small as 50p a week, and they did over seven or eight
month. The paper shop got kicked in the head – nobody wanted
the papers. They helped, small amounts. The shop next door to
that we left alone because the parcel group were getting their
stuff off them so we couldn't abuse them and have two lots. Then
even the small sweet shop where she'd suffered of course because
kids weren't having the cash to spend and cigs weren't being
bought, she donated weekly. Veg shop couldn't give us money
but they gave us a sack or two of taters – whatever – every week.
Butcher gave us £10 a week, and like Ken said, he's been getting
it all over and giving to the men as well. He were doing
everything. Bread shop, they couldn't give us cash but they gave
us bread. So, you know, it all came. And then we'd got such as
the Co-op who couldn't help because it were a big concern, it
weren't up to the local manager – although he did put me on to
the manager at Barnsley but that were a waste of time. We
asked, on behalf of the group, could we have damaged tins at a

22  Elsie Walker – whose father, husband (now dead) and sons were all
    miners – outside Grimethorpe Colliery

reduced price and he turned round – he'd got the gall to turn
round and say 'Oh no, damaged tins can't be sold. It's a risk,
selling damaged tins – could be salmonella or whatever – can't let
you have them.' They sell them in the bloody Co-op now, you

can walk round there now, there's damaged tins on the thing and
there's damaged tins in the basket reduced. But they couldn't let
us have them. And like, it sounds daft but I only patronise the
Co-op a little bit and that's only due to the fact that if everybody
stopped going in there and thought 'well we'll shop at the G' that
would mean at least six people from our village would be put out
of work. So I just patronise them when I have to, for my
convenience.

It [the butcher's] were donating £10 a week into our kitchen.
Plus every time I went in and it were for 30lb of mince it were
rock bottom, as low as he could make it. And it were a case of
when you went in for your own meat he just used to say – here,
there's one on the slicer – and stuff like that. And he were doing
it for the men's kitchen as well as us, so he must have been
suffering. We repaid him back as much as we could. Like if we'd
got meat vouchers it were 'from Gary's' and stuff like that.
Before I never shopped in Grimethorpe, I always found it too
expensive. I come from Barnsley, and because I go and visit my
mum I do my shopping in Barnsley. I don't now. I always get my
meat from him, regularly every week. I get as much veg as I can
afford to in Grimey. Like I go down to Mrs Evans and I
patronise her whereas I wouldn't normally. But when it comes to
fruit I always buy it in Barnsley, because whereas I can buy a
pound of apples for 30 pence off her, I can get two pounds from
Barnsley at 36p. So I've got to. I think to myself, 'Well I'll buy
my beans and potatoes off her, and my fruit from Barnsley.' And
that's what I'm trying to do. I'm trying to go into the shops that
has helped us, and patronise them. Before the strike, everything
came from Barnsley, didn't it.

## The Women's Support Group

The group began when men started picketing pit office's main
headquarters and we learnt of the verbal abuse they were getting
off women – how women were abusing them verbally and how
when they retaliated they were getting their collars felt and their
earholes thumped by the police. We decided then that because
there were a few COSA women in village who we thought –
canteen women and such like – should go down and do it. When
I say 'we' – Ken were coming home and telling me what were
happening and I were getting incensed about it. So one night I
decided I'd go round to who I thought would come with me and
we'd go down and firstly take coffee and sandwiches to pickets
cos of cold weather and then after that we talked about forming a
group. And I come across this advertisement in *Barnsley
Chronicle*. So I went looking for this house – only I'd forgot the

address and I went up and down Blenheim Road to find this house – to see what these women were doing and to find out what – how they planned to do things.

And by that time we'd gathered a few women. There were Margaret, Christine, myself, my mother-in-law and a couple more who I heard their views and believed that they'd come in with us. And I went to Barnsley and I found this house and attended one of the first few meetings they had at Barnsley and I got lay-out from them. Well, I says, well how am I going to go about it? I've got a rough idea, I've been round to those whom I believe to be militant in village. How are we going to go about it? So they give me a rough idea – so we then leafleted village and got club packed out and we organised a couple of women from Barnsley who were used to speaking – college students and people who'd been in various organisations – to come through – and a welfare rights person and that's what dragged women in.

We played it crafty – we advertised welfare rights to get 'em there and to get 'em interested. We got some leaflets printed and got kids to go round with these leaflets shoving them through people's doors. We put 'Ladies: Do you know everything you are entitled to? We will be having a public meeting to discuss the effects of strike on us and there will be a welfare rights worker there who will advise you on whether you're getting what you should be getting.' Because there were only a fixed number of weeks for you to appeal, if you didn't – that were it.

And they were surprised when they came. We must have had 200 women down at old club and they were really surprised how many we'd collected. And we had to use tactics to get 'em there at first because, you know, it's a funny thing being in a village like this. And once we got 'em there the idea were to keep 'em interested, keep 'em coming. And a lot of women who'd come solely to find out what they were due to have and how to get things sorted out stuck with us because they learnt along with us. We weren't the most organised group in country but we got by – we catered for village, which were what we were about. To be honest with you, sole idea when we set off was to take care of our village. That's your first aim – to make sure that the village where you're living is sorted out, then you spread on to helping others. I mean, it's natural like that I believe. I think anybody would have thought – 'get it sorted out at home first'. And it just sort of sprung from there.

We did a sandwich run, early days of strike. We picketed head offices [NCB offices at Grimethorpe]. We said – 'we're not having them cows come in our shops, standing there while we're stood here with kids crying their eyes out. We're not having them floating past buying their mars bars in our shops, they don't even come from the village, and we're stood here with kids and their combing it in and our husbands are going down the pit breathing the muck in? So we went and stood on top of the street, just daring them to come into the shops. We'd stand there abusing them. If they were a bit on the thick side – 'you fat cow, you could do with your jaws wiring. Do you mind going in there for your sandwiches?' All this. And little bags of soot to throw at the sandwiches if we could.

So we had a bash at everything. So what surprised me was that, first day we picketed, we stood outside this shop. My mother-in-law were that aggressive! As soon as they came out she used to shout 'Cow!' across the street. And people used to come out and look at us on the top of the street. And this man – I thought he'd come out to say to us 'look, move away, I've no trade' – but he didn't. He came out – 'here you are love, I know it must be hard' – bottle of washing-up liquid, packet of biscuits. At first I thought he were trying to bribe us, but it wouldn't have worked anyway. So half the village didn't know how to react to it, they were surprised. I mean, it were early days of the strike.

We started with door to door collections. We went round all the village and we collected tinned stuff. And . . . .

Early days though, it were just what we could scrounge from door to door. And then what bit of cash we'd got we'd use to go to the shops then and get things like – first it were just taties and meat, and then as things went on, men started dropping strong hints, like 'We could do with some soap', or 'We're running short' [of newspapers] – they'd stopped the papers, so they didn't even have newspaper to use as toilet paper. 'It's getting a bit rough now, even newspapers are scarce', dropping us subtle hints.

And washing-up liquid, because they could wash their hair with that.

But we must admit, they used to have some weird concoctions in the early days. We used to sit for ages doing stupid things like saying, 'Well, if he's going to have to have that tin of bloody curry stuff, we'll give him that as well, that'll make do for that.' We were up to us earholes in beans and soup. And we all said, when we got back to work, we'd never again purchase beans or soup.

We were knocking on some people's doors and they were saying, 'I've got three sons on strike as well as me husband'. And we used to say 'Ok . . .' and the women used to say 'Hang on though, I've got some blancmange, I've had it ages', and we used to say 'It don't matter' . . . .

Originally though when we set up with sales, it weren't our funds that set them sales going. It were – like, Ken did NUM

kitchen . . . and he'd loan us on the sly £20 and he would fetch
£20 worth of stuff down out of NUM funds of veg into the club.
We'd sell it and put a penny or two on, give him his £20 back,
and we might make £2. . . . This went on for near on six months.

## The police raid on Grimethorpe

*Kevin Eland*    That morning there were lorries on the coaltips
which were loading coal what we thought were going to power
stations. And a lot of lads – they'd been attacked and molested
for stealing coal to keep their families warm – didn't like the idea
of what we've worked for being taken away and dispensed to
power stations or for industrial use. From what I can gather,
these lorries were stoned to get them off the tips and two or three
riot vans were called for and they chased these people off
through the woods. After about half an hour the police called for
reinforcements and there were about five-six vans which came in
full riot gear and chased people, including women, all over the
woods and tips again. From what I can recall, about half a dozen
people in their anger went to the local police station – which
wasn't a full-time police station but only used every now and
again for paper work or people who have a rest during shift
times. And two or three windows got broken.
   An hour later, word had come that police in riot gear and their
vans were waiting to make an assault and by this time 200-300
people had congregated on top of the coaltips – which included
women, children in pushchairs and prams, young girls –
everybody, whether they were associated with the industry or
not. They were there out of public interest. It's a close-knit
community and they like to see what's actually going on if the
village comes under siege by outside riot police. People made
their way down to the police station where bricks were thrown,
not knowing anyone were inside. There were two vehicles there –
there was a car from Cudworth which were measuring up to
replace the broken windows – a contractor – and there were a
police car there. The windows got smashed, and the police car
got smashed – all the windows put through, spotlights, headlights
and the car got turned over onto its roof. People then decided to
go to the back of the building to stone it there. It was more or
less an act of vandalism towards what had happened in the
community – they took it out on a deserted police station. When
the people went around the back they saw a policeman halfway
down the playing field with a policewoman fifty yards behind
him. I'd heard that this policewoman had been brought down
with a rugby tackle and took one kick – which isn't what were put
out on national press and television. She says she was savagely

beaten but that weren't the case. Feelings were still running high. We let the police and the woman go. A lot of people were sick after they'd seen a policewoman brought down in this fashion but it was not more than they deserved. That were the feeling of the people.

About half an hour later, a convoy of about a dozen riot police came storming into Grimethorpe – people scattering everywhere. Women and children, not wanting to be involved in what could have happened, they ran away. People ran away and some people just stood there waiting for them coming. The police came and those that were in charge were trying to find out what had gone wrong – but in the meantime they decided to guard this deserted and empty police station, for what reason I don't know. There's no windows in the place, nobody used it much and there were 200 police guarding it. So that night, Monday night, children of about ten, eleven, twelve year old who had got involved in being attacked by police – been involved in seeing the community being stoned by police and their fathers who were miners . . . they'd seen what had gone off on television had nothing to do with mining industry, and they had the same feelings as what their parents did – apparently they started stoning the police at night time. They were only young kids and police made several baton charges and there stood one or two youths and they were very roughly treated. And obviously the people who live in Grimethorpe, when they'd had a few pints of beer and heard about this . . . after some hours the people came from all over Grimethorpe. Police made baton charges unprovoked and it led to stoning and riot and fighting. Outside police were brought in. They were beating innocent people, arresting innocent people, running people all over Grimethorpe. There were shop windows got smashed, telephone kiosks got smashed and it were a complete riot. And it were unnecessary – for the sake of a deserted police station to lay siege to Grimethorpe with 200 or 300 riot cops were absolutely terrible.

*Kevin Hancock*   There were some bastards on our side. No doubt about it, some lads on barricades – there's some rotten bastards. They did things that they'd never ought to have done and a lot of times it caused trouble when we never ought to have had this sort of trouble. But all the same, you don't expect it of people who've got uniforms on – they're supposed to be there to keep law and order – and it were new to people around here. They've seen it in other cities – big cities you see it – but a mining community? They seemed like Gestapo troops parading through. As I said there were men who'd been on strike ten and a half month and you've got some sick bastard [policeman] with a teddy bear there [standing at the picket line] at Christmas. And you stood there looking at him. What else can you do but despise him?

Before the strike – I've never been a big lover of police – but I could see we needed some kind of police force. But not what it is now. They're not accountable to nobody, only themselves. Before the strike I wouldn't have gone out and done any harm to police, if a policeman had been in trouble I would have assisted him. But if a policeman were outside this house now and ten men jumped him and kicked him, I would go outside and my only concern would be – have they kicked him hard enough? And it's a terrible state of affairs.

I've got a 4-year-old son and his mind's that mixed up with what's been going off that if he sees a police car when we're on bus he says 'scab'. He don't know what a scab is, he don't know how we feel about police. But he's got a connection. He knows that somehow – police, scab – that there's something there. How can you ask him to respect law and order, to say 'well, if you're in trouble lad, go there'? I've had my brother with eighteen stitches in his head, they arrested my mother on picket line at bottom of village – and I were there then. When they arrested her they said 'now what do we do?' . . . 'Treat her like a fucking man'. The exact words – and that weren't no rank-and-file bobby, that were the inspector, the big man.

## Politics

*Margaret Keneally*   They have aproached us [the Women's Group] to join the Labour Party. We had a woman come along and talk to us and that but – I couldn't join the Labour Party because they're so slow in getting things done. I says, 'Right, say you want to do something for the village, what would you have to do?' She says, 'Well I've got to get in touch with somebody, then they get in touch with somebody higher up . . .' and it goes up the ladder like that. Well, we're used to just going and doing it, and I says, 'No, I'm not interested in joining the Labour Party. They're not for me'. And then they wanted us to join en bloc as a group and just have one or two spokeswomen. And then in next breath she [the Labour Party representative] says 'But then you wouldn't get a vote'. So what point were [there] in us joining if we didn't get a vote? We've got to have a say in what we were doing, because we're used to doing it anyway. And then this other fella come. He used to be a Labour man . . . and he were saying, 'You women are doing brilliant, you've got things done in this village. Don't let all these Labour Party women or the Socialist Worker Parties or anybody get you into their parties.' It were as though he wanted us to form us own party you know!

*Gail Hancock*   We were used by Labour Party at the beginning of the strike. We were used to vote court at our meetings. We had one of the councillors come down, 'Can we address your meetings?' this, that and the other. 'You women are doing a splendid job . . . Labour Party needs you. If we could get women like you to join the Labour Party we would get things done. Blah blah blah. Vote for me, vote for me and I will set you free.' All this business. And [he said] he'd made a donation to the women's group. The donation never came to the women's group. It didn't, it went to NUM. It would have got there anyway but the thing were, we earned that £50 that they donated by letting them come and vote catch, listening to him. We considered we'd earned that. Women were coming to our meetings waiting to see that £50 appear on our books and it never did. And what happened were this certain member of the NUM who were in the Labour Party took it and handed it over to NUM, so it were 'Good old so-and-so got £50 from the Labour Party for us' and it weren't.

Listen – this man who were going to be voted Mayor of Grimethorpe, put idea through for Grimethorpe to have [modern swimming baths] because there's nowt in this village for kids. And what happened were Labour Party in Grimethorpe messed about so much and didn't get down and fight for it for our village and it went to Barnsley and it got passed for M. to have it. They were going to make [this man] Mayor and on the night when they were voting him on as mayor he stood up and says 'No thank you very much, you're not in it to help people and to help village, you're in it to say "I'm Councillor So-and-so", or "Look at me, I'm a Councillor!" And he said, 'that's not why I'm in it, I'm in it to get things going for this village'. And he says to me, 'Don't join Labour Party love, take my advice, go in, listen to what they've got to say, say your piece and get out sharp because you'll find they'll corrupt you to their level.'

*Ken Hancock*   People have got more radical than what they've ever been in their lives. My wife's talking about joining the Labour Party. I said – 'Well, they're piss weak. Why do you want to join the Labour Party? What are they going to do for you?' She says – 'Well, there's nowt else I can do. There's no other party worth joining at present and I feel I must have a say in what they're going to do to keep this community.'

This is the thing – *Socialist Worker*, *Militant*, one or two of your newspaper sellers, they're all there. You could be fighting in the heat at Orgreave, you could have bobbies chasing you – you could be running across Orgreave field, there's 500 bobbies chasing you with riot gear on – and there'll be some prat trying to sell you *Newsline* or *Socialist Worker*. But you never come out of

pit at 4 o'clock in the morning and see someone selling you a
paper then.

## Trade unions

*Ken Hancock*   It's a different attitude on unions. See, they'll
consider themselves 100 per cent union men, I'll consider myself
100 per cent union man. But I'm not, I don't honestly believe
that unions nowadays, unions which they're representing – the
trade unions which they're representing – men 45-50 year old, is
the same union that I want to be a part of. I believe that unions
have gone away from representing membership, rank-and-file.
They're prepared to be more a style of management, they're
managing the work-force. And they're not there for that. The
bloody lads are underground, the lads on pit top, the rank-and-
file tell them what to do – they don't tell them what to do. And
they get a job – I've just been given this delegate's job. Now I'm
prepared to stop on three shifts on my own job, stop on coal
face, and still be with lads and still do delegate's job. It can be
done, there's no argument against it. These have had four or five
year where they've been on pit top. Before strike there were four
of them in office and there were only really branch secretary
doing any active work. Other three were just spending their time
in one union box – passing the shit stuff, dilly-dallying and I
always said then it wouldn't hurt you three to put your pit clothes
on and go and visit different parts of mine or different parts of
surface, get amongst work-force even it it's only going around
and saying 'any problems lads?' You're coming away from work-
force. And I like to think I'm speaking for work-force, or a
majority, a party of work-force at least and putting work-force's
views over. I'm still a workman, I'm still a coal face worker. So I
haven't left that, I'm no better than the rest of bloody lads. They
put me up – they can soon put me down.
   That's what the problem is – there's too much, too much of it.
And times are coming for a change. Young lads, well the average
of union's dropped as membership of NUM has dropped to 20-
21, so they're looking for younger men to lead, they want a
younger leadership, they don't believe the older end have got owt
to offer 'em, because all they've said is hold yourself back. Don't
bother. But we don't want to wait five or ten years, we want it
now. Next year, year after, is no good to us because by the time
it gets to that we're going to be like them and we've gotten
bugger all out of it. We want it now, and if not now we'll have it
sooner but we're certainly not waiting a while later. Someone
stated earlier that they've opened a hornet's nest up with these
redundancies cos all they're doing is whittling it down to the

militant few – and the NCB know that. This ain't over by a long chalk. It ain't dead, it ain't forgotten. And we will dish out to Coal Board what Coal Board dish out to us.

## Aftermath

*Ken Hancock*  When we first got back to work there were blokes who'd come knocking at the door for their bills and I'd say – 'no fear old pal, not for you, not for first five week'. First five week that's hers and mine and the lad's – that's ours. First thing we did was we took him up to town and dressed lad up – that was the first thing we bought for him since the strike.

During the past twelve month people round here didn't pay no rent. They also had central heating bills. With these houses we get electricity from pit so we pay electricity bill to pit. Now I normally pay £6 a week electricity and £5 a week for my central heating – that's £11 – and I don't have a rent problem. But there's some they're paying £15 rent, they're paying £6 electricity, they're paying £5 central heating, 20-odd quid in one week. Now what the Board's doing – being very benevolent – they've agreed to stop and double – every week they're paying double rent which is 30 quid, double central heating which is 10 quid and double electricity which is 12 quid, we're talking 50-60 quid a week. The blokes just don't have it.

I'm not ashamed now, that's my pay slip for a week – that's taken out and that's what I draw. I work on coal face, I'm on coal cutting machine – you can't earn higher than what I'm earning, it's impossible – and that's my fetch home pay for five days: £90. But yet there's people in country that keeps talking about £200 a week miners. You know, I wished I'd find one, cos they owe me some bleeding back money.

Well, out of my £90 we have the central heating – £10. I've got me electricity – £12. So double that – £22. I've got me mortgage, about £8 – £10 a week, and there's the rates and the water rates and the insurance – cos you must have insurance. By the time we've done, we're talking about £50 out of my £90 wages just to pay the bills. Before we start eating. We don't even eat. So out of my £90 we've got £40 which we give to her and then we start eating. And to eat these days isn't that cheap; to buy a bag of sugar and a loaf is a pound or something. I've been out for a drink this afternoon but that's the last time I'll probably be out for a fortnight. She ain't been out.

*Gail Hancock*  When strike ended we all went out and we didn't give a bugger. We all went out, we had a night out. And there's still people who say 'bugger this, I've had enough after twelve month of stopping in'. Ken has to go out once a week. I insist, I

wouldn't live with him if he didn't. There'd be no living with him
unless he got a break. But there's still women who's doing more
than one part-time job as well as their husbands working full
time. Taking sewing in, supervising kids up at school and working
four hours at local factory. They're all hunting for jobs and it's
going to take some getting over, it's going to take some getting
back to normal.

We [Women's Support Group] didn't know what to do with
money left over. And so we threw it up – What do you suggest?
We got a few pointers. Someone said throw a party for old folks.
Well, a majority of them decided it would be best if this money
went to schools – that were the only way to get it to the kids, to
help them. And it were a majority vote that it went into the
schools because we couldn't think of any other way to channel it.
I mean, we've got four sacked miners – now then, it's a dicey
situation. I mean you could share that money but thing is, if we'd
shared that cash between them four it only takes one person to
hear about it who's got a grudge or who thinks that they've
suffered enough and they ain't got nowt but to ring up the SS. So
that were defeating the object. So it was said – how can we do it,
you know, to the benefit of the community? Well, idea was to
start something for kids, as kids had suffered a lot. But we
couldn't decide how to do it and how to go about it. To start
something off in terms of building a new club and that – it would
have meant a flow of cash and we couldn't envisage people giving
us money to keep it going and all this. So we decided the best
thing to do were to share it out and let schools buy equipment or,
you know, sommat of value to schools – because I mean they're
getting clobbered, they're trying to reduce the number of staff in
the schools and when they do that they'll reduce classes and in
the nurseries and such like. So that's what we're doing – it's
getting divided up between five schools – we'll class two nurseries
as one school – and we hope it's going to be sommat. The idea at
first was, if we'd got enough cash, to get them a computer – we
thought that'd help kids cos everything's computerised these
days. So if one of our schools has got a computer we're helping
kids from our village be aware of computers before they set off.
So it was decided that that would be the most beneficial.

We had a hell of a lot of kids in this village who did without
and to throw a party or something daft like that ain't beneficial.
It's all, you know, a few cake and buns, a bit of pop – it's gone.
We've given them parties.

# 10 PRISON

## Letters

Ray Patton

In replying to this letter, please write on the envelope:
Number 1121047      Name Patton
1.5.85

Dear Dave

Thanks for your letter and the papers and mags. Sorry it has taken me so long in replying to you, but I suppose you know the score here with the letters.

Well Dave, not much changes in here. Me and Willy are still in the kitchen. I don't see much of the 'Jap' or Mick, and I have seen even less of Gary, but I know he's still about somewhere.

Willy and Gary went to London yesterday for their appeal. I believe they found lodgings in Brixton Hotel. Willy came back speaking West Indian and has started to like reggae music, I'm sorry to say, but they both got a knock back on it. Apparently the lads from Shirebrook were down there for their appeal also, and according to Willy they were both up at the same time. All the Shirebrook lads and Will and Gary, so their barrister from Shirebrook kept saying that our offence in Stoke was more serious than theirs, so the judge said that Willy and Gary were fortunate to get only a couple of years, and said the sentence stopped as it is. Then he knocked six months off the sentences for the Shirebrook lads. Anyway I was sorry for Willy and Gary, but still, good luck on the other lads.

I heard that you gave a good speech at the meeting in Liverpool. Will said his missus was there. He got a letter off somebody who was there and it said that he would come and visit Willy when his wife comes up next time.

I had a letter off Mark Fisher. He said that he would be visiting me this month sometime, also Terry Fields, from Liverpool, wrote a nice letter to me, so I have written back and asked him to come up and visit me also. Well at least some of the MPs haven't forgotten us. When I get my next v.o. which should be in the next two weeks, let me know if you will be able to come on the visit, and I will put your name on it, then you can come up with Debbie, so let me know Dave as I would like to see you and have a bit of a chat.

I was glad to hear . . . lost out in the elections. Serves the shithouse right. Is he still on the workers' committee? I know where he should be. Also fancy that bastard . . . getting on the union. He doesn't know the meaning of trade unionism. The only thing he is good for is strike breaking and creeping for overtime. I should have belted him when I had the chance that night in the Trent. Anyway Dave, let me know the latest news, if any, on the situation at the pit, and in general.

There's still no sign of us moving up to Cumbria yet! Also we haven't started on our parole reports either. I wish they would start something then at least we would know if we are stopping here for a while or moving up north.

I haven't heard from anybody at the pit, not one letter, sorry all except one from Jimmy Colgan, saying that we wasn't forgotten and that was it. Mind Roy Evans has been in touch with my lady, but none of the lads have written. It's a couple of months since I heard from Rob Anderson. He was going to come up but he didn't so Deb came up on the train by herself. I think its a case of out of sight out of mind, but still, I know we have some good mates.

Well Dave, that's it for now. I hope all is well with you and that the family are keeping well. Give my regards to all that know me and I look forward to hearing from you soon.

Ray

PS Sorry about the writing, but I think my pen's about fucked.


H21045 Stephen Lowe
Sunday 24-3-85

Dear Dave

First of all, thanks for the letters that you have sent. This letter comes to you via Dawn. As I only get two letters a week to send out and one of those I have to buy out of my wages. In your last letter you said that you didn't write to Mick as you haven't got his number, well his number is 'H21048', as a matter of fact we are both in the same cell so he reads the letters that you send to me. I notice you haven't changed much. You put 13p stamps on your letters. Mick says 'Did you hear the shocking news about Thompsons, I myself couldn't sleep all night.' He says 'Due to the lack of buses, they've lost the contract with the NCB.' We were 95 per cent sure nothing would happen like that (but you know what 95 per cent sure means). Anyway back to me. How is the Mansfield Riot case going on? Have you been to court again yet? Ray says to ask you what has happened about that 'times' levy they were going to have? Is it still on? Willy and Ray are working in the kitchen and seem to be doing all right. We see them at least twice a week, so if you want me to pass any messages on, just let me know. Keep the letters coming in Dave, as it keeps us in touch with what is going on in the world of the Union. What do you think the chances of us getting our jobs back are? If this levy for 50p goes through, how are the Union going to collect it, if *they* won't stop it out of the wages? If you get in touch with Dawn, you could visit me on one of your free Sundays. Mick says he hopes you are getting plenty of practice in on the snooker table at Ruskin, as last time you played he thinks you conceded with the colours still on and don't try to blame it on your poor partner, Willy, as his partner had never played before. He says he will be anxious to have a good session with you when he gets out.

I saw my probation officer a couple of weeks ago and he said that he was pretty certain that we would get parole, which is in September, so we will all have to keep our fingers crossed. Dawn is busy trying to find a cheap house for us to live in, as I will have to have somewhere to live before I get parole. The Union were supposed to have got me somewhere to live, but they haven't mentioned it again, so I don't know what has gone wrong. Maybe you can find out and then let me know. Also tell the Union to give money, etc. to Dawn as we will be married when I get out anyway. I'll sign off now, keep in touch, all the lads send their best.

yours fraternally
Stephen

PS We keep getting papers sent to us called *Fight Imperialism*, *Fight Racialism* and another called *Workers' Power*. Did you send them? Also I've had some letters off different members of Militant.

PPS Thank the Union for everything they have done so far. I think all the lads echo this sentiment. Keep up the fight.

## Diary
Steve Lowe

### The inner thoughts of an innocent miner

A quick summary of first week
On being taken to Stoke police station I was questioned all day Sunday and told that I wouldn't be able to get a solicitor on a Sunday even though Mr Day's colleague tried to get to see us over eleven times. Ray told me that he had been held for two days without being allowed to see his solicitor. I was locked in

23  6.30am picket duty, Tilbury Power Station. Bill Martin from
    Betteshanger Colliery, Kent

the detention centre and slept on the floor on a mattress with one
blanket. We were all taken to court on Monday and all remanded
to Risley for a week, except Dave who was remanded to Stoke
for further questioning. On arrival at Risley we were searched,
bathed, given prison clothing and fed with some disgusting offal
which was supposed to be food. I was put in a cell with a lad
named Ian Butcher who was a miner from Doncaster. We had a
good chat and he told me some of the things that were happening
in the Yorkshire area. He told me of the police ambush on a
convoy of a hundred miners pickets' cars. He said how the police
had got a road block set up and vanloads of riot police came from
out of the bushes and proceeded to drag drivers, etc. out of their
cars and smashed window screens, door panels, etc. with long
staves. Obviously intending to damage the cars so much that the
pickets wouldn't be able to go anywhere after that. Ian also told
me of riot squads bursting into miners' homes without warrants,
and breaking furniture, etc. One day of the week we joined the
library, Gary who was in the y.p. section of Risley told us how
after he had a visitor, six scousers went in and took his sweets,
etc. off him and told him to keep his mouth closed or he would
get 'filled in'. The first day we went for a medical, expecting a

good and thorough check, on entering the check up room the doctor asked if there was anything wrong with me. In answering 'no', he said 'Okay that's all, next'. I was expecting at least a listen to my chest, etc.

Friday 24 August

Got up at 5am, had a wash and then went downstairs with Ray. Mick and Willy waited by the office; whilst waiting Ray put down his bedding and had a drink of water from a rushing drinking fountain. When he picked up his bedding a cockroach had crawled under his bedding. The smell of urine wafted in from the exercise yard where the inmates urinate at night through the windows, if you look in the corners you can see rotting food and cockroachs sitting in the shadows. A warden took us through to the reception and we got back our own clothes, we were then given breakfast which consisted of one boiled egg and two rounds of bread. We were then put in the 'sweatbox' for about an hour with our breakfast and a cup of tea and filthy mug which you have to get from a bin at the side of the tea urn. I decided not to have a cup of tea when I saw the state of the mug. After an hour in the sweatbox, we were shouted by a warden and me and Ray were handcuffed together and taken to a coach, we arrived at Henton court at about 9.15am where we waited until our solicitor arrived. He told us that the police were still making enquiries and advised us to wait until next Friday to apply for bail. A lot of lads were disappointed but we all could see the sense of what the solicitor said. There were a lot of friends from the pit plus wives, girlfriends, etc. who we could see were visibly upset about us being remanded for another week. We were all transported to Stoke police station where we were locked up in individual cells. Me and Gary were put in the women's section of the cells and the rest of the lads were put the other side. Some of the lads asked if they could go into the exercise yard to have a smoke as there is no smoking allowed in the cells. They were told to wait for ten minutes then they could be allowed to have a smoke. After half an hour, the policeman came back and said he would come back in another ten minutes. This continued for two or three hours. Then they said they couldn't go out as the van to take us to Risley would be here in ten minutes. They waited a further hour then the lads rung the buzzers in the cells to ask where the van was, the only answer they got was that the policeman shut all the shutters on the door and switched off the buzzers so that they could not communicate. We were allowed visitors earlier for about five or ten minutes. On getting back to Risley after an hour's run, we were allowed a bath after being searched and having daily newspapers and the local union paper confiscated.

You are not allowed to bring in shampoo, soap, etc. as you have to *buy* it from Risley. We were given prison clothes and a meal consisting of cold beans, one sausage and some potatoes, and then shoved into the sweatbox for half an hour whilst they tried to fix us up with a pad. We were told it was full today and some of the new inmates might have to sleep over the hospital complex. Dave was sent to A Block and Gary to the young prisoner's section. The rest of us were put in B Block. Me and Ray were put in a recently painted cell and found that there was no freshwater jug, or bucket for overnight use. We made our beds and sat talking about the strike, etc. and then went to sleep when the lights were turned off at 10pm to the sound of chirping crickets.

Saturday 25 August
Woken up about 8am by the wardens and go to have a wash. Me and Ray have to lend some soap off Mick as our canteen order hasn't arrived yet. The fly-infested toilets are crowded with inmates all trying to get a wash and trying to empty the slops. The stench is enough to make you throw up and there never seem to be any disinfectant available. It's a wonder there are no fatal diseases floating about. After our wash we go to fetch our breakfast which has got to be seen to be believed. It consisted of half of a tomato and a piece of bacon (or was it fat) about two inches in diameter. I refused the porridge which looked like wallpaper paste (some of the lads use it to stick up pictures in their pads). We were then locked up for a couple of hours so after discussing what to do we decided to go to sleep as there is nothing else to do. We then went to exercise for an hour which consists of walking round in circles in a yard which stinks of urine. We talked to a couple of the inmates who said we hadn't ought to be in here. The majority of them are behind the miners and encouraged us to keep it up and don't let them get us down. We are locked up for the rest of the day so the hour exercise is the highlight of the day. We go back to the cell and go to sleep. I am woken up as I've got a visitor. It's my girlfriend, Dawn. We have to talk through a sheet of plate glass and have to virtually shout to hear one another. It's nice to get a visit in this hell hole as it gets you out of the cell for at least half an hour. Ray also gets a visit from his brother and sister which gives him a lift. They tried to find out if it was all right to visit Ray by phoning Stoke. The police were their usually helpful selves and told them to phone the operator before they would look it up in their books. We fetched lunch next which consisted of a piece of fish, a few roast potatoes, spoon of peas. And a lump of rice pudding and a cup of pea and gristle (ham) soup, which has done amazing things

to my digestive system. This was given to us before we had
visitors. We had salad for tea which consisted of: one piece of
lettuce, one tomato, two pieces of cucumber, one piece of
luncheon meat, one spring onion (uncut and unwashed), one
piece of rancid cheese, and a cup of tea (which contains sugar).
You either have sugar in your tea or you get no tea at all. It's a
good job the visitors bring food in else I will be able to crawl
under a snake with a hat on before the end of the week. Ray's
visitors brought him a chocolate cake which we'll have tomorrow
for his birthday. It's slightly worse for wear after being opened
and searched for strange filling, objects, etc. We are now sitting
here waiting to be let out to go toilet. We can't decide whether to
go up the noggins head for a drink or to the local disco, after a
discussion we decided to stay in and read instead.

Ray's birthday
Woken up to the sound of banging doors and jangling keys. Ray
got out of his bed and went to have a wash in the flypit
(washroom cum toilets) closely followed by me. On entering the
washroom, I thought the tide had come in. The flypit was three
inches deep in water, whilst having a crap and watching the
inmates over the small door of the toilet, I was hit by an
incoming wave of dirty water, which proceeded to fill up my
shoes and soak my trousers which were around my ankles. On
entering my pad, Ray was uttering obscenities and saying that he
wished whoever has swiped his 'snout' would catch cancer and
die choking. Somebody had entered our pad and pinched his ½oz
of tobacco. A nice start to his birthday. Billy came in and told us
a few things about his cell mate. We then went down for
breakfast which was: one sausage (half cooked) and rounds of
bread, one cup of tea (bromide?). We are then locked up till
chapel which me and Ray declined to go to. A lot of lads go to
chapel to get out of their pads. The pad is opened and we go to
Mick's pad for a chat and hear a rumour that some of the inmates
are to be moved to Strangeways. Some of them aren't very
pleased to hear this and talk of barricading themselves in their
pads before they would go there. Dinner is called so we ask a
warden to open our pad (which we locked after the last
experience). On coming out he starts singing 'Only you' and
saying 'fancy having a record at No.1 and then ending up in
here.' I decided he's just a pisstaking bastard and ignore him.
Dinner was the usual 'Cordon Bleu': cabbage, slice of gone-off
ham and coconut pudding with custard, a cup of funny tasting
orange. I was enjoying the pudding and custard until I found
some big chunks of yellow unmixed custard. Me and Ray decide
to have a party tonight for his birthday and eat his cake and drink

the can of lager which me beloved brought in for me yesterday. We also discussed getting pissed on the winegum that he has got, maybe have a couple of rum ones and a port one to top them off. At about half one we go for association and have to sit there for two hours bored to our craniums. We get to read today's newspaper, even if it is a Tory rag. That must have been today's highlight of the day. Went down to fetch my can of lager which is dutifully poured into my plastic mug. Just in case I slash my wrists with the empty can. I get to my pad and share it out with Mick, Ray, Willy, Antony, about two sips each. After we get tea which was beef?, chips and carrots also, lo and behold, we got a lump of orange stuff which I was told was melon (actually it was quite nice) and declined to have tea and instead had lemon crush. Ray's been rolling his own fags for over a week now and they still look like pieces of rag hanging out of his mouth. After a couple of hours' sleep it's slopping out time so I wash my hair in expensive shampoo (Head and Shoulders which cost a fortune in here), after that we are locked up for the rest of the night. Me and Ray decided to have a feast and get stuck into two harvest crunch bars and a bar of original nutty crunch. I think Dawn has decided I should become a health food nut. It says on the nutty crunch bar that it is low on cholesterol, so if we survive the food in this place we aren't likely to die of a heart attack. Had some shortcake with currants in and a cup of tea for supper.

# THE RETURN TO WORK

## Pit delegate's report at Hatfield Main, March 1985

Dave Douglass

(This report by Dave Douglass is on the Doncaster Panel meeting of 7 March 1985.)

Mostly it was concerned with a review of what was happening in the area and what we had just been through.

We were told there was no co-ordinating committee report and no executive committee report since there had been no meetings.

I asked about the widely reported statement that the Yorkshire Executive had called the Kent pickets illegal, and was told . . . so far as the Executive was concerned they had said no such thing, it was only a rumour . . . some said Sammy Thompson had said it but there was no confirmation of this one way or the other.

The next matter was a criticism of the panel branches who had not attended the Camden Rally. Armthorpe thought this a big insult to the people who had done so much work for us over the last year. Only Armthorpe, Hatfield and Frickley had attended. The others said they could not get anyone because they were not going to get paid.

Our proposed rally for the 11th was discussed and I informed the panel that we had adjourned it, until we had a certain date for Arthur coming to speak at it. It was still our intention to try and organise a day strike on that date.

The question of coal to the area was discussed and we were told we were trying all sources to get more. Workers would have to work 2 weeks before fuel could be ordered.

The NUJ had sent up a number of vouchers for food and we agreed to have a draw. . . .

ASTMS said they still wished to adopt a miner's branch, we suggested their fund raising now be directed towards helping to build an association of victimised miners to help comrades in gaol.

There next followed an inquest on the ragged return following the Yorkshire area's decision to go back.

Goldthorpe said they had spoken at the Area Council to stop out but nobody else had done so, so they went back as instructed when the decision went against them.

This has not been correct, I had seconded the resolution to stop out, but Taylor would not allow any debate on it, saying the vote would be either for the recommendation to go back or against. At the end of the meeting the Doncaster delegates got together and I canvassed support for Doncaster stopping out, they all said it would not be possible. Inky Thompson confirmed that this had happened.

Armthorpe said they had been betrayed by the panel, their pickets abused, insulted and in some cases assaulted. They would never have put pickets on but for the fact every branch in Doncaster had stated their branch policy was no return without amnesty. The Doncaster panel's position was no return without amnesty and here had been Armthorpe carrying out our official panel policy and being treated like dogs.

In the process of very bitter polemic against the other branches, Armthorpe said they had heard at Hatfield's meeting on Monday night the Delegate had recommended a return to work but the floor overturned it. This is, of course, untrue and our branch ought to write to the Armthorpe branch to set the record straight.

The Hatfield Delegate reported that he had spoken for and voted for Yorkshire to vote to stop out at the special Delegate Conference in London. This had been carried, and Yorkshire had voted to stop out but lost. At the recalled Yorkshire Council Meeting, Hatfield voted for Yorkshire to stop out (along with 7 other branches), we lost. At the end of the meeting Hatfield had tried to get other Doncaster branches to organise for Doncaster to stop out, and was told it would not be an achievable aim. At the mass Hatfield meeting the situation was reported truthfully, no recommendation was given, only that if they wanted to fight on, we would fight on. A vote from the floor that we stop out was taken, the Delegate publically voting in favour and this was carried.

By Tuesday midday, the sight of most other pits marching back to work together, and the feeling of isolation felt by even the most determined pickets, had changed the resolve of the men and the branch meeting was reconvened. At this meeting a recommendation to return *was* put, although it was noted the position of our branch remained we did not cross picket lines.

On Wednesday we marched back and were met by a solitary Armthorpe picket. The Delegate urged the men not to cross the picket line, although a group of about 100 men did so. Later 5 pickets from the Kent area made themselves known. Amid heart rending scenes of Hatfield pickets and loyal members of the women's support group abusing each other and tearing each other apart, the branch and the COSA branch asked in the name of a unified struggle for the future, and so as not to destroy the loyalty to our branch, if the pickets would withdraw. Seeing the situation, the pickets withdrew, after which the rest of the men went to work, although some men went back with the Armthorpe picket, despite his request that they should not do so.

That was the situation, the Hatfield branch having loyally carried out its duty to the strike and the Union. Many of us deeply wished to stand to the end with Armthorpe having fought side by side with them throughout the strike, we wanted to march back to both our collieries together – but this had not been possible. Our people had given all they had left to give, although the majority still respected the picket line, even when they felt the picket line was counter-productive at that stage.

Which brings us to the question of picket lines and clarification of the Hatfield position.

As a branch we have a long-standing policy that we do not cross picket lines. This has been endorsed time and time again with only the very tiniest minority voting against it. It has been endorsed during the NUPE dispute, the Lawrence Scott dispute, the Dodsworth Colliery dispute, the Lewis Merthyr dispute and again and again during this dispute.

Without respect of the picket line, the whole trade union movement would die, it is the *only* way workers can call upon their mates to help them. Workers must have the help of other workers if they are in trouble. The picket line is the line uniting our class, it is an act of faith in one another. It is a line with principle on one side and slavery on the other. We sometimes do not like the picket line, we sometimes might disagree with its reason for being there, but we stand this side of it and have our disagreements there.

The Kent *area* was on strike, it was officially on strike, the pickets were genuine, the Kent picket line meant *we do not cross*.

The Armthorpe *branch* was on strike. It is the right of any branch on strike over any issue to take its case to another branch, form a picket line and ask for support. That right has been respected since time immemorial, and obviously the Armthorpe branch had a right to picket, the same as Dodsworth did, and we as branch by branch rule accept and respect that right.

Returning to the report proper.

We then had a review of what was happening in the area. Up until that time Hatfield had not been touched, ours came the next day.

What emerged from all branches was that the Board wished only to deal with secretaries, they were prepared to pay them five days a week for union duties when previously they had only paid three or four days. This would be paid for by not paying the Delegate, Treasurer or President on days they had done previously.

The idea seems to be to build up a 'cosy' relationship with the secretaries (whether they want one or not) obviously seeing the Delegate and Presidents as 'political' aspects of the branch and the Treasurer as a bone of contention on contract and incentive issues.

Likewise the safety committees have been disbanded or put into mothballs. Safety inspections will not take place and no meetings of the committee are scheduled.

This turn affects NACODS equally with ourselves and marks an outright assault on union rights and obligations. In human terms, its aim is obviously to disregard the bones and blood of the miners in exchange for production. As President Nixon once said: 'It might be illegal but that don't stop me doing it.'

At *Brodsworth*, members of the NUM Committee and officials were told unless given specific authority they will not be allowed on Board property (i.e. to be at the pit in the union office) unless going to work, even if they are in their own time.

At Brode and Bentley branch officials using the term 'scab' were warned it would be entered on their records, and if repeated again that would be the final warning before the official was sacked.

At Askern in announcing the end to their local agreements for early riding for eye baths (working in excessive dust) and early riding through working in excessive water, the manager boldly announced 'You have called me bastard right through your strike, now you're going to discover just how right you were.'

At Edlington the attack was on the rights under section 1.2.3. of the Mines and Quarries Act, i.e. our right to organise inspection underground paid by ourselves. The right we have had for over 100 years.

At Rossington the manager instructed us that 'things will not be going back to normal, things will go where I want them to go'. Among other gems which appears to be area policy, is that 'Undermanagers will be the mens representatives' it seems workers must go to them and not their union reps. The scabs at Ross come to work by appointment it seems, they simply phone in and say when they'l be coming and if they wish to knock off early well thats O.K. they can ride virtually when they feel like it, and in the presence of the Ross's officials the personel manager addressed them by their first names and organised their shifts, half shifts or whatever, like he was arranging a game of golf with an old mate.

Hickleton of course has come in for the thick end of the wedge, it is no longer a pit, it has only 'development status' only 200 men are required (for how long we dont know) the other men would be transfered to 'Long life pits' five Doncaster pits were cited . . . it is noteworthy Hatfield wasnt among them.

Highgate, the lodge led its men back to work, only to be told this pit closed on the 13th March, all men compulsarily redeployed to Goldthorpe, and thus Inky Thompsons career as a long life branch official came to an abrupt end.

ONE THING WHICH CAME ACCROSS LOUD AND CLEAR WAS THAT BRANCHES WHICH PRODUCE, OR PITS AT WHICH THERE ARE PRODUCED, PUBLICATIONS AND PAMPHLETS THE BOARD IS GOING AFTER THEM JUST LIKE EARLIER GAFFERS DID TO DEREK ROBINSON WHEN HE PRODUCED A DOCUMENT CHALLENGING THEIR RIGHT TO MANAGE. IN THE DONCASTER COALFIELD CERTAIN PIT PUBLICATIONS ARE WELL KNOWN AND HATED BY THE BOARD, THE PRODUCERS OF THESE TRACTS ARE UP FOR TARGETING BY THE BOARD. ANOTHER THING WHICH IS VERY EVIDENT, IS THAT DONCASTER HAS BEEN SINGLED OUT IN YORKSHIRE FOR SPECIAL TREATMENT.

The reason is simple, we didnt have enough scabs, too many people stuck to the union, the authority of the NUM in Doncaster is too high, we need more boot. Remember Doncaster ended up as the most strong coalfield in Britain with less than 2% working, as opposed to North Yorkshire which the Board see as the Nottingham of the coalfield, which had above 5,000 scabs and minimal picketing.

They have a great deal more to learn about Doncaster if they think the present wave of repression is going to break the men from their union or break their hearts, actually Mr Tuke, if you had been at Orgreave and seen our lads perform you'd know why you are a little woolly lamb by comparison.


Pit Report

The next report involves our meeting with Deeming and his new razor sharp deputy manager . . . a man who has been sent in 'to deal with us'.

This meeting took place in the one time 'Special Branch Surveillance Room' which had just been cleared of its spy cameras and snatch squad devices. Incidently we accidently came across this equipment earlier and its power was far greater than we had thought. From the pit its trajectory was 360° in all directions (including up and down) the most chilling thing however was its magnification. From the pit it could focus on every street on Broadway, individual houses, it could pick up clear details in back gardens in Hatfield and of course Stainforth had complete coverage. The snatch squad raids on individuals in the pit lane were obviously co-ordinated from here, as were the police attacks up certain streets and the filth laying in waiting on Broadway.

While waiting on the managers pleasure to meet us, we peered through the window of the Special Conference Room (which was locked) this room had been used as the police briefing room and obviously a place for joint meetings between the filth and the local gaffers. On the blackboard was a huge map of the villages, with certain 'targets' marked off with arrows, The Welfare, The Broadway Hotel, and 'Key Streets' but we couldnt read why they were 'Key' streets except that they seemed to house a lot of active pickets. On the neighbouring blackboard was written in chalk a fairwell message from the Chief of Police to Mr Deeming . . . it read

'Thank you Mr Deeming and Staff, get some coal out soon.
Best of luck, for Democracy, you will win.'

So now you know, incidently it was the deputy manager office which was 'the colliery detention centre' i.e. jail, and into which our lads, and miners wives were dragged, detained, bleeding and brutalised, questioned, photographed and charged, iron bars on the windows. The Ross' manager was right, *things will never be the same again*, the whole colliery with the willing compliance of management was a police fortress a spy centre against the ordinary folk of this village and a jail.

When we got to the meeting proper it was a question of sit down shut up heres what your gonna have.

1  Coal manipulators, arent manipulating coal, therefore will work 8 hours instead of 7½.
2  All agreements between the union and the management at branch level are null and void. i.e. no concilliation proceedure, i.e. no water notes, the Yorkshire Water Note Agreement agreed at Area level is no more. i.e. the agreements on late busses is finished the agreement on carrying stretchers is finished. THERE ARE *NO* AGREEMENTS.
3  All Developments, some salvages (and according to our new Deputy Dog) maybe the whole pit, will work a four shift cycle.
4  Craftsmen, they will fill in reports without payment or they will not be craftsmen.
5  Men will be paid the rate for the job they are signed to. This of

course means almost every man at the pit will suffer a reduction, it further puts in question our protection of earnings when not on our own jobs.

6   Chock fitters, after two decades of existance will be no more . . . they will be redirected to face work . . . NOTE IF FACE WORK IS NOT AVAILABLE CHOCK FITTERS WILL BE GIVEN ANOTHER JOB, AT *THAT* RATE OF PAY.

7   The fitters will do the chock fitters work PLUS THEIR OWN AT NO EXTRA PAYMENT.

8   Safety, the same as the others . . . none.

9   Disputes, 'we will not tolerate people walking out of the pit' (make your own mind up what that means).

10   The canteen will close between 11pm and 5am (all Doncaster the same) 'We arent sure if this means a reduction of staff i.e. NUM members, or their earnings'.

11   Checks out by 10 minutes before shift start, people sleeping in must seek special permission to come on the following FULL shift.

12   People found in the pit bottom early will be subject to dismissal proceedings.

AFTER getting ours I called in at the NACODs office to find out what they had been given, a similar plan was afoot for them.

Week-end rotas to get the pit ready for Mondays, the gaffer will [say] who and how many, previously obviously NACODS did this themselves. The length of time taken to inspect places will be determined by the Undermanager (who previously didnt inspect at all but just walked in and out). Places worthy of checking will not be NACODs job but given by what the manager thinks is important.

NACODs men will work 8 hours not the usual six.

Safety committee and inspections, same as ours, there is none. But best in the pack. Overmen are to be phased out 'we have found during the strike we can do without them', their jobs will be done by heads of depts and undermanagers.

Now then, the link between the NACODs and the management is broken, they should stop looking for it, their link is with us . . . whatever we do or they do in the future the message is clear, the NCB lump you with us, why not get formally with us and start a fight back, we werent joking when we said it was your jobs too, now MgGreggor has told you so.

People are now discovering the price of insubordination & insurection – & boy are we going to make it stick

(*Guardian*, 11 March)

# Lost rights at Hatfield Main, November 1985

Dave Douglass

D   Now for example, at the end of the strike, we've had all the local agreements taken off us. Now we've renegotiated the question of craftsmen's signing. The craftsman has to fill in a report which he's required to do by the mines inspectors. Before the strike, you got paid half an hour's overtime for filling it in, which came from the days when you used to have to sit in the bottom of the pit and write it out. What they do now is they write it on the way up. . . . And they took that off us. As things started to get a little bit back to normal we got that back for the underground men but not for the surface men. So we put on the agenda of the last Panel meeting the question of surface and signing in, which is a sore point. And the area agent will not negotiate that question with the area Coal Board on the question of whether Doncaster can get its signing money for its surface men. Now the Panel is committed to supporting some form of action on that question. They have to report back if they don't get satisfaction on that and ask the members what sort of action they want to take. I don't think that we'll come to a strike on that one issue because it's too small an issue. But it may be that an area overtime ban would start for example. Or that the area craftsmen – no craftsmen would work on a particular day. And they would take selective action like that. And the Panel would plan that without going to the Area. Because probably no one else in the Yorkshire area gets signing money anyway. It's a local thing. Now the priority system is another one. They've stopped the operation of the priority system at Rossington. Now that pit came and asked what support could it get from the Doncaster Panel. Now we agenda-ed it, at all branches. We had a mass meeting. It was just after the strike and my pit voted unanimously that we would take strike action if the Coal Board didn't give them back their priority system, because we can't envisage working in a pit without a priority. The priority system is that we run it, the Union who goes where . . . and we're not leaving it to the management to fix. Now we reported back, and it was the decision of the Panel that we would take action if Rossington called for it. So that gives Rossington one hefty bullet up the spout when it goes into negotiations again, because it now knows that if it couldn't get it back there, then it could come to any one of the pits. And it would depend how much the Coal Board want that system or whether they want the coal.

Q   *What's happening about water notes?*

D   No chance of getting them back at all. At my pit we had one of the best agreements in Yorkshire. We could arrive an hour early if you were getting bodily wet for a substantial part of the shift. Now we can't get them at all. And the only place that's got them, there's four men who are working in that shaft and they're working over a sump that's thirty feet deep. Well it's a battle for survival at the moment in terms of coal production, and it knocks an hour off the production. I'm trying to get it back but I know that there's not a lot of enthusiasm. You see not all the men get them, only the face men. So we've never actually been able to get the edge to stop the pit on it. It's not a widespread enough issue or a principled enough issue.

*Q    What about safety checks?*
*D*   Those things have come back. The Safety Committee is back in operation, the visits are back in operation. They had been cut right down. In Eddington they didn't hold one for about two months. But we got that back in co-ordination with the Deputies Union. . . .

## A resignation at Bentinck Colliery, Notts

Todd Clark

Alfreton
Derbyshire
4 November, 1985

Dear Barbara,
Just a few lines to let you know the outcome of the Monday after the ballot. I resigned my post as President of Bentinck UDM. I couldn't betray myself, my wife and my kids. I was made caretaker Branch secretary NUM but stood down because I need time for my children as they are my only priority now. I've taken a quiet little job as training instructor, out of the lime light, and I'm going to fade away and take care of the kids. I told the wife when she rang and she said I'm silly, but I have a duty to the kids, although my life was the union and I may have gone far, I can't be selfish. Everyone has been very understanding and wished me well. I haven't lost face I didn't sell out But I've lost my two loves my wife and my union. When I look back at what I've done I've still two little monsters who are proud of their dad and think I'm the best, and I'm sure it's the right decision, the only one.
                    Yours
                       RAC
                    (Todd Clark)

# Letters from South Wales, April, October 1985

Barbara Walters

Glyncorrwg
*Tuesday April 2nd*

Dear Babs

Sorry I wasn't clear on that tape. Not used to those answering machines. My father-in-law died suddenly that morning when we were preparing to come. It knocked us all sixes and sevens, therefore the delay in answering your letter that gave information of the weekend.

I see no Welsh addresses on your list. I also had a letter from a Dr Angela V. John, *you know*, asking if I was interested in Welsh History. I am, but I don't think I'll be able to join the Society for lots of reasons – mostly though – that living here without a car, travelling is not just dreadful, it's impossible. We have my son's car, fortunately, but not always available for the moment. Time is being taken up with May Elections. Believe it or not we have problems – two Independent Labour and two Labour. Each candidate claiming to be the true socialist. Support group will help in this election, although must admit already many are dropping away.

Losing the strike means the closing of the only pit that's part of their village. The fifty-six miners in this village will be halved by the end. There's much bitterness and depression, the factory recently opened at Cymmer – 2½ miles from Glyncorrwg is a German one making black plastic bags, conditions deplorable, NO UNION, eight hours' work, ten-minute break, £50 for seven days. If that's the kind of work we'll be accepting you can guess the feeling.

I think cooperatives are the answer. We have many gifted artistic people in these villages. Those women in the support group could turn their hand to anything from cooking to craft and to entertaining. They showed they could work as a team. If only all these energies could be used to sustain some kind of livelihood before the rot really sets in. There are rows of houses to be rebuilt. Our men and sons are good at turning their hand to anything they are survivors, after all, damn, why should money be the answer to everything. Sorry, but I just came back from a meeting now, they're accepting, not fighting.

I'm sending you our Christmas poster of St John's pit head and Nantyffyllon, children of one of the sacked men, Phillip Wirte, who gave his all as Welfare Officer on this strike. I can't speak too highly of him, not many like him about, he was always there 24 hours of every day.

Some poems – from Donna, Blaengwnfi Support Group Leader, another who deserves a bloody medal, the Harts at Glyncorrwg who ingeniously found a way of getting £8,000 through the post from every corner of the world, well nearly. We were a good band who deserved to win. There's a bitterness at losing here in South Wales but in villages

like ours we can look back on comradeship and the three men who
went back a week before they all went back, they call them super
scabs – why – well truly what are super men, a big joke.

This is it then – finish – I'll send you something I tried to write in 1969
when they were dismantling our pit. It might help you to get some
insight into the past of the villages.

All the best with the book. As you say history is about people. It
seems though in its path people don't care.

Babs Walters


Glyncorrwg
Tuesday October 1985

Dear Barbara and Raphael

Sorry for not keeping in touch with you. Sorry too that I have no
photograph, not in black and white and not on my own. Coloured
photograph in a group – I hope it's not very necessary.

Since my father-in-law has died, we are taking care of my mother-in-
law. She is 87 years old and unable to attend to herself so our time is
curtailed in where we go and what we do.

I'm tickled pink that both Donna (Jones) and I are in your book, *The
Enemy Within*. I'm glad you phoned, and I was able to tell you Donna
wrote the poem on parcel distribution. If you have those other pieces
please will you return them if you haven't, never to worry it doesn't
matter.

Looking back on that year's conflict, knowing now the axe has fallen
on St John's in spite of the sustained effort of the Lodge Officials,
those same good companions who gave so much of themselves to
sustain the strength of those around them during that year long
struggle. Those of us who helped during that period were wrapped in it,
we ate, drunk and slept it, for us nothing outside the good fight existed.

The time wasn't chosen (not by us anyway) for the conflict, it was
there as it was there in 1926. In 1984 we linked hands with our past.

We avoided the conflict in 1970 and let our own village pit and railway
slip away under our noses, without anything taking its place.

Just like after 1926 when there was the Thirties and there was
poverty, it sat amongst us. And here it is now, but you don't talk about
being poor, pride takes over and pretending plays a big part when one is
hard up. Just like in the Thirties there will be those living in the same
community whom it won't touch nor will we know how many it
touches but the divisions will be wider and far more.

Yesterday, a beautiful autumn afternoon, the mellow sun rays
coloured the earth as if it was its birthday. I walked over the sites of old
levels and pits knowing that under my feet were rich seams of coal
sufficient to last into the next century. Some day perhaps when it

pleases the world markets they'll come back for it, but at what cost then? While walking I met a young mother who had been taking a flask of tea to her young husband. He was picking coal where the striking miners had been picking in 1984, only he'd been filling his coal shed that way now for four years. 'It's lonely up here' she said, 'Yes' I answered. Yes, and its bloody lonely on the dole too, I thought.

This year we at Glyncorrwg celebrate the centenary of our school. Now my grandchildren go there, and my mother-in-law's great grandchildren. My great grandfather came to Glyncorrwg as a stone mason. He brought his skill with him to this village and helped to build the Viaducts tunnels for the railways. What skills will our children be able to pass on? What will their future be? There is nothing here for them now, losing the battle has meant just that. The fight had been worth fighting for, we paid our debt to the past, we have no shame as we face the future. There's no more I can say – I wish you well with the book. I'll certainly look out for it. Thank you for including a part of these Valleys in it.

Sincerely yours<br>Babs & David Walters

PS I'll keep the large envelope and when I get in contact with friends, I'll see what they have. Maybe after hearing today's news St John's won't close after all. If the review body has any teeth at all, saving those jobs could mean such a lot. The Welsh coalfield needs time to readjust itself.

# 12 AFTER-THOUGHTS

## Letter from Yorkshire, March 1986

Dave Douglass

16 Abbeyfield Road
Dunscroft
Doncaster

Dear Raphael

The strike has now been over one year, it seems incredible looking back that we went through such a struggle, ordinary people cannot believe it about themselves, let alone there would be no regrets. As a Hatfield winder said to me, 'I wouldn't swap that year for any other year of my life. I felt I stuck out for something really important, I was proud to have been a part of it.' I mention this winder because he never went on the picket line once during the whole dispute, didn't march, didn't shout, just stuck out for twelve months of hardship, and yet even without the stimulus of rallies and picketing solidarity he still managed, in his own mind, to know and feel what he was doing was right.

Lately, there have been a number of playback scenes on the TV of pieces of newsreel from the end of the strike, of course the one piece they've all picked up on is me coming out of the Yorkshire Council chamber after the return to work vote is announced, and screaming that there will be no coal turned in Yorkshire, the guerrilla war was on, etc. I've been ribbed something rotten over that because with Yorkshire breaking world coal production records it looks like a real turn around. Worse still, I've been urging strongly a strategy that the pit must become profitable enough to get out of the danger margin to stop it shutting. This necessarily has made it look like I've changed my point of view. The fact is that the clock has moved on; yesterday's slogan, like yesterday's top coat, does not necessarily suit today's climate. The fact is once the disastrous policy of a return without a settlement had gone through we were left with only the overtime ban and guerrilla resistance down the pit as our only strategy. It was only this latter that gave the proud march back to work any meaning; we were marching back to fight in another way. Of course Yorkshire had voted against the return, but we made the best of it telling the men the fight would go on

236

via a work to rule, etc. We might have guessed that the strategy of getting back to work was only the first step in what they would call 'a return to normal working'. It wasn't long before a special delegate conference was called and the final weapon thrown away; yet again Yorkshire voted and argued against it, but with only the Geordies and Kent by our sides it wasn't enough. Back in Yorkshire the Doncaster branches fought to keep the ban effective at least on a county level, but we lost that too. Having then went on to bring the money back from Europe and then go crawling to the judges to say sorry for what we had done, it looked like the last semblance of any organised retreat had been overtaken by a rush to the hills. Branches were thrown then very much into their own back yards to fight their own little corners as best they could. With some branches the back of the resistance was broken and disheartened and, war-weary, some places like Cortonwood just surrendered; others like Edlington, a modern pit with years of coal, ran themselves on to the rocks and let the pit flounder because they couldn't see any hope or direction in the Union and the industry. Well, I was determined to not let that happen at our branch. It was clear that unprofitable pits were closing, the Board weren't bluffing, our pit was highly, but highly, unprofitable and in the NCB's sights. For me we hadn't just fought a year to save other pits, just to roll over and die when our own loomed close to the rocks. I had to fight to get the branch, and the membership at large, to accept a strategy of trying to make the pit profitable, trying to turn coal, not for the Board's sake, but so that the great cause of the miners' union itself and our contribution to the rest of the working class wouldn't be lost. Some of our best pickets got stuck into those coal faces with as much determination as they had done earlier against the police lines. This has been fairly typical in Doncaster, with the Doncaster Area, once one of the most unprofitable coalfields, becoming a jewel in the crown. Mind you, that doesn't mean they have become class collaborationist or gaffers' men; as I've said this is something they are doing as part of the immediate struggle, and the proof of that pudding is seen in the record of industrial disputes since the strike ended. The ten pits in Doncaster, nine now, account for more disputes and lost production than the rest of ALL British coalfields put together. I compare it to Sinn Fein's Ballot Box and the Bullet strategy.

Of course, to the men standing at the gates, the sacked, victimised and worse, those who are still in jail and likely to stay in jail for some time, the mounting production figures look like a 'get lost' sign to them, like everyone has forgotten them. Well, it's understandable; we've tried recently to get a policy of guerrilla disruption at the most profitable pits, days of action, etc. over the issue of the sacked men, but when we took it to the Council chamber it was knocked on the head. Silverwood, a world production beater, struck for a week on their own over the sacked men and having proved they could and would do it, they brought a resolution to the Council asking for a campaign throughout Yorkshire on those lines, while sparing the unprofitable pit any loss, costing the Board through the teeth with actions at the multi-million tonne pits. Hatfield supported it, five or six others from Doncaster, but it was massively beaten, not just beaten; actually delegates expressed great dismay at the very idea of taking on any sort of action. Still, it's up to the members, and Rossington Colliery, also a top producer, took a day strike action last week on the anniversary of the start of the strike. We at Hatfield have drawn up petitions and letter-writing and wide use of the media in an effort to get our lads set back on; if it fails, we shall be Agenda-ing strike action for this pit also, although actually we still aren't profitable yet. I expect this sort of action to keep on spreading.

Mind you, it's an uphill fight all the way just now; the shift in political and industrial direction in the area leadership, at Branch and County level, is very marked and not necessarily because the respective representatives have changed. It's very hard to get any progressive resolution through and I feel that the left branches are rather isolated, if not from the membership itself, at least from their fellow branch officials in the rest of the coalfields. We were in a different situation, of course, with only 1 per cent of Doncaster's miners scabbing up until the last week of the strike, while places like Selby had nearly 80 per cent back: that changed the way things were handled at collieries. In Doncaster, virtually ALL the scabs have been driven out of the pits, either transferred or offered redundancy, or just plain left of their own accord (with a little persuasion, of course). The hostility towards the few who remain is still very bitter and even last week we had another shift ragging up because they wouldn't work with a scab. In other parts of the area, the NUM officials had to go back to a pit where anything from 50 per cent to 90 per cent of the men had scabbed. Where do you go from there? It stands to reason that what we respectively see as 'reality now' is very different. We, of course, have had to bow to their circumstances since we did lose the strike, and Doncaster's strength of solidarity was an exception. I actually attended a council meeting where one of the delegates scabbed! But then so did 80 per cent of the men at that pit; we've told them not to form any UDM branches, to stay with the NUM, etc. so having invited them to stay in the Union and fight in the Union it's hardly surprising they want to send representatives of their own. It's a hard pill to swallow but reality does dictate we have little choice. After all, if we want the Leicester Area in the NUM, and we have said loud and often we do, that means Leicester, which overwhelmingly scabbed, are going to send representatives to the National Conference, etc. It means treating them as full and bona fide members of the NUM, scabbing forbye. That is the reality, but try standing up at a meeting and telling it to people. One, a lad from our branch, he got arrested, sacked; his wife has left him as a result of the pressure, she's got the kids, he has no house, no job, nowt, and all because he tried to stop men scabbing; now we've got to sit in the Council meetng with them. The wonderfully brave thing is, that boy *accepts* that if the Union is to consolidate itself, we have to do strange things, things which a year and a half ago we wouldn't have dreamed possible.

Worst of all has been the attempt to shift the blame for all the misfortunes of the Union and the year-long strike to Arthur Scargill's shoulders. Some of his self-proclaimed comrades, aye and some in Yorkshire too, have been running to public platforms to stick the knife in. Mind, it's one we managed to repulse at least for the time being. The Hatfield branch moved a resolution of confidence in Arthur, the strike, the pickets, etc. in order to bring the back-stabbers out in the open, but they sat fast and the resolution was passed unanimously and should keep the critics in check at least in public places.

One good thing is that the Durham area and the Mechanics are emerging as the new political left-wing leadership in the Union; they have taken up a whole range of exciting initiatives and campaigns and are very firmly convinced as to the way to take the Union forward. Other areas have gone in the opposite direction, while Yorkshire, I feel, has no direction at all just now. We are fighting to put forward a systematic and constructive path, one that consolidates the Union, licks the wounds, but still leaps to its feet when the enemy thinks we are going to sleep. This is the way Hatfield and much of Donnie thinks. Time, I suppose, will tell if any new strategy emerges before the next big attack comes. It does look like a denationalisation attack might come in selected areas, not necessarily Selby, which although it collapsed in the end of the last strike, has been on strike two or three times since, and is proving to be not as compliant and malleable as the get-rich merchants would like. There would be a fight on that one, but with the funds depleted, with scabs still operating in the Notts coalfield, with cheap strike-breaking coal coming in from all over, with the convoys of lorries ready: in short with the same set piece as last time, only us far weaker, it must be asked what hope would we have of success? The future must lie in some alliance with power workers, perhaps the best elements, the most class-conscious and progressive. With even a minority of these in chain with us, we would regain some of our old power to go with the undiminished pride.

One thing I am absolutely certain of is the Union has not been defeated, the membership by and large is buoyant, and the womenfolk are still widely active in all manner of class actions and solidarity struggles. This generation of pit-folk – children, women and the miners themselves – have written another inspired page in the book of human resistance and one which will be read with pride by future generations.

# Interview with Iris Preston, April 1986

(the questioner is Raphael Samuel)

*RS   What is the feeling among your people?*

IP   The morale is low . . . for quite a lot . . . the morale is low because this year has cost them their homes . . . it's cost men prison, jobs, their homes, their wives, and what they've got in this next coming two years is work, more work and more work to cover that year. When I say to my son, 'Would you go on strike again?', he says, 'If it was a fight for our coalfields, a fight for the communities and a fight for a better standard, I would fight again and so would many others.' But it doesn't alter the fact that they've got now several years of just sheer hard work to try and repair, to make homes, bring themselves to any sort of living, so, the men are despondent and they're working their guts out to clear these debts that were incurred in the strike. Everybody in the pit villages, when you say, 'Why haven't you been to a meeting?', 'My husband's working over.' Do you know why he's working over? Because every woman has got debts. We don't parade them, we just know. 'Why hasn't Caroline come (for the sake of a name)?' 'Oh, my husband's working over.' You know why he's working over, not for the love of the pit and the love of the job, he's working over because the lad's got debts. Sometimes we're down to as low as eight – this is the Sheffield women's group – and why? because the women can't get out because the men are working over, and that isn't to put a holiday in their pocket, that is to cope with the debts, that is to cope with everyday living, that's the reason. . . . I know somebody who's been without a washer all through the strike – it broke down and her husband is having to work every Saturday because that Saturday just about really brings them to a decent wage.

During the strike my son Lance would come back and discuss Union meetings . . . but now, funnily enough, I don't think the men discuss the strike very much, they're too busy clearing up debts.

You hear about people having cars repossessed because they could no longer pay for them. What other things do we hear about? – insurances, of course, that have gone completely by the board. There's still big gas bills, particularly those that have been sacked. I know a guy, he's got five kids, and he got such a massive electric, gas bill – every bill – he took redundancy to shift the bills. He's 35, and that man was on trial at Orgreave for his freedom. He just couldn't cope. He went back into the pit after the strike and he couldn't see any way on the wages he was earning that there was any life for that man or his family at all.

*RS   What's he doing now?*

IP   Nothing, absolutely nothing. He's unemployed, but most of his redundancy money will have gone to pay bills, I mean he had an old car which he kept going during the strike mostly because people paid petrol money to help keep it up, and that's how he got picked up at Orgreave.

Some miners, there are writs in for eviction on their houses. At a Union meeting a bailiff came to me and he said he was appalled at the difference in the pit villages. He's going round debt collecting – collecting from the miners who incurred massive debts during the strike, some of them are small debts that are longstanding which have got really nothing to do with the strike, but most of them are what we call strike debts, and he said he was amazed at the debts. . . . The houses have had nothing that he could impound . . . and when he's asked the wife she says 'We've been on strike for a year and everything's been sold'. He said the bailiffs had all noticed the difference, visiting the people who've been on strike. Their spirit seems to have gone and that they were cowed . . . as if the strike had knocked the courage out of them.

My own son was lucky, he changed banks, but he still has got massive £300 bills to pay, which was the last bill he got in. He was lucky he changed from one bank to another. He changed to the TSB and they were prepared to clear off the mortgage and the back-mortgage that he owed and take him on again. Don't forget *my* lad was ahead of his mortgage payments, so can you imagine what it's like for the boys who are *not* ahead, who have just held their own. I've still got a massive overdraft really, for me.

*RS How much is that?*

*IP* It's £300, but that to me is a month's work and I just can't seem to clear it. I've cleared a lot, but I mean £300 to me is like a millstone round my neck and I never went in the red till the miners' strike. No never. All my life I've been pretty modest and I've been careful. I wouldn't owe nobody nowt. If I couldn't afford it I didn't have it, and that was that.

People say Notts men earn a lot of money – my brother comes home with £60 odd a week and he's a mechanic at Thoresby pit and I've seen that lad's wage slip, and he comes home with £69 to keep two kids on and a missus – that's my brother – I've got a brother in Notts who was on strike – that's Jeff. So anybody who says the miners should never have got into this mess, they were always in a mess, they never had the money to do anything else. . . . Each government coming in doesn't seem to give a damn for miners and their wages and their cost of living. The only person that really cared about them is their Union.

People are under the impression that a miner comes out with £200 – I've two sons who've worked in the pit and I don't remember any occasion when those boys did anything but come home with a wage and just a wage, and I asked my son what he got in the way of bonus when he worked at his pit and what he got, more often than not, 'blob blob blob', which means, 'nothing nothing nothing' – where the pounds and pence should be, was two blobs. The lowest he got is fifty pence the highest he got one week at Brookhouse – and remember he'd been there twelve years – was £50. But one £50 doesn't pay your Union bills, it doesn't pay for the rise in the cost of living. What would it do? £50 nothing. My son Lance, most weeks he'd come out with £70. I mean that's not a wage, that's a pittance. This is before the strike. In actual fact, per week I come out with £9 more than him, so some weeks I'd come out with £79 and he'd come out with £70.

*RS   During the strike, people said that everything would be changed afterwards, that the women in the villages would never be the same. Is that true?*

*IP*   For some aspects of it, it's not true, such as men involving the women in the Union. The women fought one whole long year alongside the men, but Union business is still a closed shop to the men. . . .

*RS   Give an example.*

*IP*   Oh when the Bevercotes came out on strike, Lance said to me, 'Bevercotes are out'. I said, 'Have you had a Union meeting?', 'Yes', 'What was said?', 'Oh, we're back up in the action.' 'Yeah, but how do you mean, do you mean strike action?' 'Well, mother, it's Union business.' I could ha' kicked him in the teeth. It's not only Union business, it's all our business. We made it our business. . . . Well, they *let* us make it our business when they accepted us on the picket lines, and accepted the help we were more than willing to give. If there was Union meetings during the strike, every word would come home and the wife would sit there and hang on every word, and discuss it, but now I think a lot of men are wanting their women back into the sink, no matter what lip service they give. I think a lot are afraid of their new women, as if they feel that we've metamorphosed too much.

A lot of the Women's Groups has folded. Some of them just collapsed when the strike collapsed. Some of the women wanted to go back to living normal . . . they wanted to forget the strike. For some of them it was very traumatic, and for others it was the greatest thing that happened to them. Brookhouse folded when the pit closed, but Carol Hallows still comes to the Sheffield Women Against the Closures. In fact, Carol Hallows, and myself, and Edith from Cortonwood are the regulars. When Sheffield Women said that they were only going to meet once a month, I fought desperately to keep it going weekly, because I had a feeling that once our group – which is more or less the mother base for the district – started only to have meetings once a fortnight, then the group would go down. And I've been proved right.

Also, the groups weren't coming for money any more. Do you understand? . . . It's got to be realistic. Sheffield Women supported seventeen pits, right, and two soup kitchens. Every week we raised money for each pit. Now what we did, if we got 800 in, eight pits would receive a hundred pounds. If we got more in, every pit would receive a fair amount. If we only got 500 in, five pits . . . any pit that wasn't desperate, on occasions Dinnington wasn't desperate, they were prepared to wait perhaps another week. Then it would go to a pit that was desperate.

*RS At the end of the strike how many women were coming to the Sheffield Women Against Pit Closures?*

*IP* We got the news on the Sunday, we marched back on the Tuesday which was the 5th, and the women's meeting was on the 6th. We brought wine and the only one who drank it was me. It was as though there had been a nuclear blast, and they were just remnants of women walking in. These proud women that I'd seen facing riot police, they were just shells that walked in that night. We did try the 'Don't let's have gloom and doom' but it didn't work. That night we had approximately fifteen out of forty to fifty. Then the following week we had even less and it just went downhill.

Kiveton, Brookhouse, Cortonwood, those are the three main pits that are still represented by women who still come to the Sheffield Women Against Pit Closures. Cath the chairperson has become involved in other issues – she's a community worker – but she does still run the group, she's still known as the chairperson. Janet Hudson, who works in an old people's home, she was the Treasurer, she's gone. So how many have we got? We have roughly about ten, out of all those women, and that's not every week. We only meet once a fortnight. I turn up come raid or shine, unless I'm away.

*RS And are there still local women's groups or not?*

*IP* Well, there's quite a few women in Kiveton. If you have a full quorum, they have at least ten. One of the strongest groups is the Rotherham Support Group. Now they have progressed. They've realised that there are sacked men who are hanging about with nothing to do, who are getting bored. Rotherham have opened their groups to the sacked men so consequently they encourage their wives to go. They take an active part in the running of the group. I've seen it in action and think it's very good. I like it personally. And so, of course, their group is now big. We have the South Yorkshire Liaison Group where women from all over the pits in South Yorkshire get together. Every women's group is represented but they do not exclude men from this either. The men can be a help. When we got our composite motion back from National Women Against Pit Closures, I knew it was wrong. But I'm not very good at putting things over, and I was really glad that Dave was there. I said to Dave 'Look, Dave, there's something I'm not happy with the composite. They've taken away the meaning'. And Dave, being he was the Chairman – he held an official job in the Lodge – he was able to put it over and explain what I was trying to say. So, consequently, we were able to send our delegates with a clear mandate. I think if I'd been on my own there, I would've been struggling a little to explain it to them. So the fact that the men have got the experience is a good thing in the women's group. This is quite a healthy group, the South Yorkshire Liaison. There are women from all over the pits, and anybody that can't come sends apologies. It's thriving in as much as we still support men who are sacked. We also have a Support Group for Sacked Miners and also my group which I was a founding member of – the South Yorkshire Defence Campaign. The men are in it as well. So we've nearly always got a quorum except when the weather's very bad. And it's very active, and I always enjoy it. It's very lively and this is where the women talk quite a bit about what's happening. And we've got the Morris's, a family from Wath, the whole family were sacked and they come and tell us how they're coping. They're still desperately in debt. (The family?) Oh yes. One charge was dropped on appeal but the main breadwinner, the man, Mr Morris, Ray Morris, he's sacked. No chance of being settled. His debts are not the trouble, it's his fines, you see. He's no wages, and I don't know whether the NUM are paying it.

When the strike ended a lot of the pits women that were coming to Sheffield Women stopped. Just like that. Which was a shame because we had planned a way forward to take up other issues, this is what we planned but it never seemed to get off the ground, Raphael. We seemed to go two steps forward and three back. . . . We were desperately short of money to follow some of the campaigns. The women cleaners at Chesterfield Hospital were on strike because they were privatising. Well, we wanted to go picketing but we didn't have the cash to get on the bus. We planned to support other women's struggles. And these fell through because we hadn't the money. We hadn't put aside any more for anything. All our money went to keeping the mining communities going. I personally regret that we didn't put some aside to be able to support other women's struggles. I felt that we were very shortsighted. I knew there was a desperate need in the coalfields but I also felt as a group to continue we should not just take NUM issues. There are other issues for us to take up and this was voted down and I accepted this as being democratic. I ground my teeth about it, I'll be honest. . . .

I felt that we could have easily supported other women and taken up more issues. It was a case of looking forward beyond the strike. We were going to campaign, like health campaigns, campaign for the mining men to be screened, or men that worked in chemicals, and women who had got children to campaign for more health vans to visit the villages. Education for the women. This was something that I campaigned for, and also brought up in the South Yorkshire Liaison Group. I said that the National Women Against Pit Closures should lay aside some money to award some sort of scholarship or help women who wanted to be educated. I think I was in a minority on it. But looking back over it now, one or two women have said to me, 'You know, I wish we'd listened, because now we want to go to college, and there's nobody to help us.'

*RS  Was Lawrence active in the strike?*
IP  Oh yes.
*RS  What did he do?*
IP  Lawrence was at one of the flyers at the strike. Lawrence's main job was picketing. Picketing every pit that needed it. He was at Orgreave, Thorsby, Bevercotes, oh I can't remember them all there's so many. Kiveton, Brookhouse (Lawrence's own pit), Fircroft, I could name more easily the pits he didn't go to, than the pits that he did.
*RS  That was from Day One of the strike?*
IP  Yes. Day One.
*RS  How old is he?*
IP  He's 28. Now the thing was that men with wives and families didn't go on the front lines. It was usually single lads that went on the front. But Lawrence took the spirit. He was an NUM member and he behaved as a trade unionist. He was solid. And he picketed whenever and wherever he was needed.

At Brookhouse, it's a pit of 700 I think, I marched up Pit Lane with my son with approximately 400 people. The media had said that Brookhouse were back, but that wasn't true.

Lawrence was one of the miners who was active in getting Brookhouse shut.
*RS  You mean that he campaigned for it to be shut?*
IP  Yes, well he found that the lodge officials were taking redundancy at 36 years old and leaving a sinking ship. What he said was, 'Mother, it knocked all the stuffing out of us. What was the good of us fighting our own without lodge officials. We've no chance.' All in all Lawrence said it was the best thing that ever happened, Brookhouse shutting. He realises the consequences of a pit shutting, but he also said that he has a wife and family to keep. Had Brookhouse fought, he would've fought alongside them. But when he realised that the Union officials were leaving the ship then he got to look to his future, right?

As far as Lawrence is concerned Shire Oaks is a better pit. It's not so difficult to work. It's a colder pit, but the main thing in a miner's life is that financially he's better off. The morale among the miners and members of the NUM is better. I don't know how you're going to put this Raphael, but they said they don't let the management shit on them, the management respect how far they can go. And if the management overstep the line here at this pit, which I know sounds incredible after all that's happened, they're stamped on and they back off very quickly.
*RS  And this is a pit where quite a lot of people went back before the end of the strike?*
IP  Yes. There was about a hundred out at the end. There is about 850 men and 700 approximately of them returned which left them with 150 who were – I don't like using the word militant, they weren't militant, it gives the world the impression that they were violent, mindless trade unionists, and that's not so.

Lance says that Shire Oaks is like Butlins compared to Brookhouse. The Paddy takes them right to the face.

*RS    The Paddy is the . . .?*

*IP*   Is the train. It takes them right to the face. It's colder than Brookhouse. The Paddy drops them off, where at Brookhouse they usually had to walk. . . . Two miles, one and a half miles, three miles. That's a hell of a lot of mileage a day. This one drops them at the face. The bonus system is not the same bonus system that they had in Yorkshire. Its called 'The Kellingley Option'. I won't go into details but what it basically means is that every man has a fair chance of getting a good bonus. What it's saying is that if the face work come out with a good production then every man in that pit gets the same bonus.

*RS    How much extra then does it mean he's been getting a week?*

*IP*   Well, from nothing to £90 is like going from Butlins to San Tropez, isn't it? It's like travelling first and second class, isn't it?

*RS    So what's his basic wage there then?*

*IP*   His basic wage is a little bit better for some unknown reason. I'm not sure what his basic wage is. It's a hell of a lot better than at Brookhouse. . . . Well he talked about £190.

*RS    That's including the bonus?*

*IP*   Yes. I mean that must be heaven for that lad. It would be heaven for any miner. And he said that the conditions are better. The whole pit is better. It's healthier, if you can say pit life is healthier.

*RS    Tell me about your other son, Tarrance. Was he active in the strike?*

*IP*   Not as active as Lawrence. Nowhere near as active as Lawrence. I mean he supported financially when he was able, which wasn't often. He didn't do the things that Lawrence did.

*RS    He didn't go out on the picket line?*

*IP*   No he didn't. As far as I know. If he did, he went unbeknownst to me. But he didn't actually come picketing with me that's why he's not in the diary. He was very supportive of the miners and he'd never of dreamt of going in, you understand. But Tarrance never liked working with pit, Raphael. Tarrance absolutely hated working with pit. To him it was a hole, this is how he described it. He didn't like it and never did. He took it because it was the only chance of a secure job.

*RS    How long had he been working there?*

*IP*   He started just a little while after Lawrence so they've roughly worked there about the same time. He's 30 now. He went down when he was about 17.

*RS    So it's a long time?*

*IP*   Yes.

*RS    But he hated it all the time?*

*IP*   Yes, he hated every minute, every working day, every working minute. And he was very militant down the pit as well.

*RS   What did he do at the end of the strike?*
*IP*   Tarrance decided that he could no longer stomach pit life. Before the strike the management were playing ducks and drakes, but as he said, 'They didn't give a damn before, and they don't give a shit now.' That's exactly what he said to me.

   He's doing a bit with a friend in a shop. . . . It's a fruit and greengrocery business. . . . In Sheffield. He never misses a second of this, but he hated the pit that much that he was a four day a week man whenever, you know, even when the wages weren't good. There are many men like him in the pit who do it because there's nothing else.
*RS   And so he didn't go back even for a day after the strike?*
*IP*   No.
*RS   Did he take redundancy money?*
*IP*   Well, the manager pulled a stroke on him. He went and asked if he could take redundancy and the manager said 'This pit isn't going to close.' So Tarrance said, 'Well, either way, I couldn't spend another day working with scabs', and the other thing that Tarrance said was that no miner should've gone back without amnesty for the miners who were sacked.

   And I think that a whole year out of the pit (this is only my personal feeling, my son Tarrance has never told me this) but I think that he was maybe, deep inside himself, afraid to go back down. I only feel that as a mother, he's never told me that and I've never discussed it with him because I'm a bit afraid of the answer. So I've never really tackled it, I've been a bit of a coward on that 'cos maybe I wouldn't say I lack courage but I just don't want to hear him say that he's afraid of it, because then I think this fear would transform itself to me and I would be more afraid for Lance. Do you understand what I mean, with having a boy still down the pit?

   When Tarrance came home, I had to give up my dining room. I would really like him to get himself a flat and I'm not pushing him out, it's the last thing I'd do, but we're very much alike in temperament and I've nowhere private, you know, the strike actually has left me with a son who I care for very much but he has no money so he's got to stay with me and so it's taken away the only place that I can sit 'cos he's having to sleep in the dining room.

   I don't know whether the strike, for Tarrance, has been a good thing or a bad thing. He keeps very much to himself his present feelings really. That's not to say that we don't talk and that we don't care but it's left me feeling sometimes that I've no space. To some people this would be a very minor thing, but to me it's very important that I have somewhere to sit quietly and write and keep my mind active because my job doesn't do that for me. So I feel, in a way, that having given everything I have, I'm still giving and the strike's been finished for a year. I'm optimistic for the future because maybe I've an exciting year ahead of me, but I still feel that this strike has put me, like hundreds of women, in a corner.

*RS   How do you mean, put you in a corner?*

*IP*   Well, we've still got strike responsibilities, it's as simple as that. Tarrance would never have been at home but for the strike.

*RS   Because he had his own home before?*

*IP*   Yes, and so consequently, though I love him very much, it tends to fray tempers a little bit, when I desperately want to go and write, or I want to read somewhere quiet, or with guests coming, you know, with everybody up for Sunday, I have to lift the bed up and find somewhere to put it in an already overcrowded bungalow, and so it's probably very minor when you look at what some families are having on top of a whole year of emotional and physical and financial strain and fight, there still are these little legacies that the strike has left us with and regardless of what some people think about Yorkshire families in the lovely green belts, we are a very responsible, caring people and we care about our families, but it just puts that little extra strain on relationships. We certainly wouldn't change things. People probably would say, 'Well that's your fault. You shouldn't have supported the strike.' Well I'll make this quite clear: I'm working class, my children are working class. We're a working-class family and I'm proud of us and I would never deny us. People like my sons are the people that make life easier for the people that never understood the strike. We provide them with the luxuries and comforts and the lights, and the safe way of providing them with luxuries – the lights and hot water. I can remember sliding in the bath one night after being in the picket line. I fell asleep, I woke up and I suddenly thought, 'My God, I'm moaning 'cos I ache after doing a 26-mile run from a picket line on the bike, and I'm moaning and there are 56,000 miners who'd change places with me in this bath, there are 56,000 miners who haven't even got hot water to be able to run a bath.' So, I put myself more or less in my own place which was not to think about 'Oh God, I ache' or 'I haven't got room in my dining room'. But, like a lot of women, I'd like a little space to breathe and a space to be me, me, Iris Preston, not Iris Preston the mother, Iris Preston the worker, Iris Preston the trade unionist, Iris Preston the political animal. I want to be Iris Preston the woman, the writer – not a good writer, but the writer – Iris Preston the reader who can pick up any book she wants in the privacy of wherever it is that she is, that I haven't got, and read it and enjoy it. And I want to be able to shut that door and not answer that phone because I know that somebody on the end of that phone wants Iris Preston to find her this. Do you know how I can get that? And I know I haven't got it because my son's in there and I've got to respect the fact that he's probably changing, you know, he's perhaps going out for a game of pool – 'cos he's quite good at pool – and I've got to wait 'till he's gone and then if I am writing anything, even letters to you, Raphael, I write them in the dining room, but as soon as he walks in I could be in full flow, I've got to stop, he's got to sleep, do you understand? And it grates a little because it's not an easy thing to get a place to live anyway, how the hell is he going to support himself? People say well, okay, he shouldn't have given up his job, but whatever the rights and wrongs of that are, it doesn't alter the fact that it's there and it's got to be dealt with.

I don't know whether I should mention this – it's not something I've ever said when I went for an interview for college – but I know that I couldn't possibly study at home. But to try and explain to a tutor that you've absolutely no room and no space is very difficult, because most of the tutors don't know what you mean by room, they know what you mean by space, but only mentally. I suppose a lot of women have given up a lot more if you think of the women whose husbands are in prison. But then I'm looking at it from my point of view: my kids are not in prison but still I feel as if I am. That's not to say I wouldn't take it all again but I do sometimes feel that I am imprisoned, mostly politically, I feel that the miners have taught me a lot, the youngsters have been wonderful but they've also opened my mind as well as the strike, the youngsters have opened up my mind. I want to learn now and I want to be able to feel that I can do my reading in peace and go on from here because there's got to be a better life for us women than what we've had, there's got to be, and I think the strike shows that there could be. I think one of the things that the strike shows that people really did admire the stand that we took and that they really cared for us as people and that if we want to go forward they'll give us a helping hand. They will give it us if we need it, which is something.

For the women in the mining communities, I really do want a lot for them but they've got to help themselves now as well. I want to see lots more coming in for them, I want them to be able to get a chance of educating. They're a bright lot those mining women, they really are. I want to see them go forward. There's no good going forward for one whole year and then stopping, is there? They did it and some of them couldn't even write anything at all. Yes, you see, on the back pages of my diary it tells you of our writers' weekend at Northern College and of our letter writing, you know, getting together and writing letters, and some of them didn't even know where to start to write letters.

*RS   That was in the middle of the strike?*

*IP*   No, this was more to the end when I realised that some of the women couldn't read, couldn't write while I was at the writers' weekend. . . .

*RS   So the writers' weekend was to teach people to write?*

*IP*   No, the writers' weekend was on the Sheffield Women Against Pit Closures book that we hope eventually to get published, and I took two women, I was asked to write down what these two women were telling me and then it dawned on me halfway through that though they had lively, intelligent minds, they hadn't got the fingers to go with it –

do you understand what I mean? And I thought 'Christ, nineteen eighty bloody four and there's two grown women here who've stood before hundreds of people and given a brilliant speech, have handled hundreds of pounds, organised meals, they've literally been like a little local government and done a bloody better job of it than the government and these two lasses can't write.'

# NAME INDEX

Abercumboi, 164
Aberystwyth, 36
Abrahams, D. 133, 134
Acton Colliery, 151
Afan Valley, 40
Anderson, Rob, 217
Armthorpe: Camden Rally, 224; community, 24, 32; family support, 9; interview, 166-202; pickets, 69-71, 225-6; Welfare, 10
Atkinson, Mr (baker), 131
Atkinson, Mr (NCB), 47, 48

Baddesley, 88
Baghot, 61
Bailey, Alan, 188
Baldwin, Stanley, 2
Barnsley: demonstration, 22, 29; Dodworth dispute, 54; donations, 139; Scargill, 190; seams, 182; shops, 206; style of militancy, 19; transport, 69; women's group, 207
Bartle, Tom, 47, 48
Bates Colliery, 10, 12, 44
Becket, Don, 130
Bell, J., 130
Belmont, Arthur, 55
Bentinck Colliery, 20, 72-85, 232
Bentley, 227
Betteshanger, 1, 152
Betts, L., 130
Bevercotes, 69-70, 71, 242, 245
Beynon, Huw, 43
Blackhall, 43, 44, 45, 46, 49
Blaengwnfi, 233
Bloomfield, Barbara, 9, 20, 23, 72, 154
Blyth, 12, 33
Boanas, Guy, 202
Boldon, 45

Bottomore, Colin, 72-7, 80
Bradford, 134
Briggs, Mr, 137
Bristow (leader of Doncaster panel), 190
Britannia Colliery, 60-1
Broadway, 129, 131, 229
Brode, 227
Brodsworth, 128, 227
Brogden, Mike, 10, 166
Bromage, Jean, 155, 159-60
Bromage, Verdun 'Nobby', 159-60
Brookes, Joey, 130, 134
Brookhouse, 25, 100, 117, 241-5
Brown, Harry, 132, 136
Bullcliff, 95
Burn, Mr (NCB), 50, 51
Burrell, Ann, 171
Butcher, Ian, 219

Callan, Tom, 46, 49
Cambrian Combine, 1
Campbell, Beatrix, 162
Chambers, Barry, 45
Chambers, Gwenllian, 160
Chambers, Lyndon 'Chick', 160
Charlton, Bob, 143, 145, 153
Chedle, 91
Childs, Len, 130
Chipchase, Mark and Liz, 67
Christian, Sheila, 187
Ciebow, Steve, 199
Clark, Audrey, 202
Clark, Todd, 72, 75, 77-82, 232
Cleethorpes, 133
Clegg, Tony, 70
Cliff, Dave, 25, 86
Clydach Vale, 55
Coalville, 33

Colgan, Jimmy, 217
Cook, A.J., 19, 164
Cortonwood: closure, 24, 53-4, 67-8, 93-4; loss at, 93, 96; pickets, 5; return to work, 237; strike flashpoint, 14, 20, 67-9; women, 242, 243
Coventry, 128, 172
Cox, Ann, 126
Cudworth, 109, 114
Curran, Peter, 128, 131
Currie, Agnes, 185
Cwm Colliery, 55, 58

Dangerfield, George, 1
Dartfield Main, 68
Davis, Brian, 164
Dawdon, 43
Deeming, Mr, 228, 229
Denby Grange, 95
Derbyshire, 65, 69, 84
Dickens, Charles, 3
Dinnington, 242
Dodworth, 54, 96, 226
Doncaster: after the strike, 237-8; closure threat, 24, 93-4; Panel, 51-4, 224-31; pickets, 71, 188-90; solidarity, 25; style of militancy, 19
Douglass, Dave, 7-8, 14, 24, 51, 69, 92, 224, 231, 236
Dowling, Felicity, 187
Durham, 19, 43, 52, 58, 239

Easington, 43, 44, 47, 48, 49
Eaton, Michael, 5
Eden, 45
Edlington, 227, 232, 237
Edwardes, Michael, 13
Eland, Kevin, 209
Elmsall, North, 122
Elmsall, South, 142-53
Elscar Colliery, 68, 69, 94
Evans, Glynis, 159
Evans, Ivor, 55
Evans, John 'Chuch', 159
Evans, Roy, 217
Ezra, Derek, 63

Ferndale, 157
Ferrymoor Ridings, 23, 95

Fields, Terry, 216
Fircroft, 245
Fisher, Mark, 216
Florence Colliery, 86-92
Flowers, John, 132, 136
Foster, B., 130
Fox, Jill, 119
Francis, Hywel, 163
Freeman, Tommy, 131
Fretwell, Irene, 174
Frickley, 32, 139-53, 224
Fryston, 96
Fullerton, D., 130

Gilbert, Audrey, 107, 108, 110
Gilfach Goch, 1
Girvan, Bobby, 16, 118
Glyn, Andrew, 36
Glyncorrwg, 37, 40, 233, 235
Goldthorpe, 194, 225, 228
Gormley, Joe, 63
Grant, C., 130
Gray, Derek, 50
Greatorix, Neil, 72, 80
Grimethorpe, 1, 12, 108, 119-21, 202-15
Grimsby, 133
Grunwick, 188

Hallows, Carol, 242
Hancock, Gail, 202, 212, 214
Hancock, Harold, 12, 119
Hancock, Ken, 202, 212, 213, 214
Hancock, Kevin, 210
Harper, Lennie, 72, 82-5
Hatfield Main: after the strike, 238, 239; 'Arrest Officer', 10; Camden Rally, 224; Dave Douglass, 51, 92; pickets, 69-70, 189, 226; return to work, 225-6; seam, 182; strike outbreak, 15, 24; surveillance, 229; welfare organisation, 128-38
Haworth, 69, 71, 172, 189, 199
Head, Rose, 131-2
Heath, Edward, 2
Hem Heath, 25, 86-92
Hetton, East, 5
Hetton, South, 45
Hickleton, 228
Holditch, 86, 87

Horden Colliery, 43-51
Horner, Arthur, 19
Houghton, 45, 96
Hudson, Janet, 243
Hudson, Ray, 43
Hume, Bob, 128
Hume, Dot, 130

Ireland, 110

Jackson, Bob, 168
Jacques, John, 176
Jarrow, 38
John, Dr Angela V., 233
Jones, Brian, 128, 130
Jones, Donna, 232, 233, 234
Jones, P., 130

Keneally, Margaret, 202, 211
Kent, 24, 52, 152, 224, 226, 237
Kenyon, Lord Chief Justice, 3-4
Killeen, P., 130
Kinnock, Neil, 85, 113, 197
Kiveton, 25, 108, 243, 245
Knight, Clifford, 123, 126
Knight, Iris, 122, 126

Lanarkshire, 1
Lancashire, 38
Lancaster, 12
Langley, Stan, 48
Larkin, Jim, 3
Lea Hall, 88
Leamington Spa, 33
Lee, Gary, 204
Leicester, 238
Leicestershire, 69
Lewis Merthyr, 14, 54, 63-4
Lindley, Lord Justice, 3
Littleton, 88
Liverpool, 59, 187-8
London, 88, 125, 131, 174, 186, 216
Lowe, Allan, 32, 139-53
Lowe, Stephen, 217, 218
Lynk, Roy, 77, 84

McAdam, Malcolm, 197
McGahey, Mick, 3
McGee, Tom, 49, 51
MacGregor, Ian: account of strike, 7;

appointment, 14, 64; axeman, 14,
    20, 56, 63, 65; children's view, 201;
    Doncaster coalfield, 93; Scargill, 55
McGuinness, J., 137
Macadoo, Ann, 126
Macready, General, 1
Maerdy: closure threat, 57;
    community, 9, 23, 26; joining
    underground, 64; Oxford, 11, 18;
    women's support group, 154-65
Mahoney, Christine, 177
Mahony, John, 170
Maid, Sharon, 133
Main, Jack, 130, 134, 138
Mansfield, 16, 88, 118-19, 217
Manvers, 96
Martin, Bill, 219
Merthyr Vale, 11, 18
Miller, Jim, 133
Mills, Tim, 145, 146
Moorends, 129
Morris, Ray, 244
Moses, Ken, 21
Myrion, Wilfred, 63

Nock, Mary, 126
Nottingham, 88
Nottinghamshire: ballot in 1983, 14;
    failure of strike, 7, 20, 69, 72-85,
    86-7; picketing in, 71; wages, 52

Ollerton, 70, 104, 128
Orgreave: battle of, 4-5, 6, 16, 20, 228;
    newspaper sellers, 212; picketing,
    4-5, 245; posters, 139
Oxford, 11, 18

Page, Maureen, 119
Patton, Ray, 216
Plummer, B., 130
Porthcawl, 14, 55, 58, 60
Prendergast, David, 84
Preston, 3
Preston, Iris, 21, 29, 100, 240
Preston, Lance, 101, 106-7, 116, 240,
    242, 245-6
Preston, Tarrance, 101, 246-8
Proctor, Gordon, 46-7, 48, 50
Proverbs, Keith, 139-53

Redbrooke, 96
Rhondda: adoption of villages, 33; Clark's factory, 59; Lewis Merthyr, 14, 155; Maerdy, 26, 154-5; results of closures, 39; strike in 1910, 1
Richards, Mike, 163
Riggott, Andy, 129
Risley, 219
Robe, Elaine, 132
Robens, Lord, 43
Roberts, Joy, 109, 110
Robinson, Barbara, 126
Rossington: anniversary strike, 238; community, 183, 194; management, 227; pickets, 70, 189; priority system, 231; seam, 182
Rotherham, 16, 243
Rymer, Edward, 6

Sadd, C., 131
Sadler, Dave, 43
St John's Colliery, 40, 234, 235
Saltley, 6
Scarborough, 137-8
Scargill: caricature, 3; charisma, 16-17, 19-20; on closures, 13, 58, 61, 65; experience, 190; failure, 73-5; government view, 12; MacGregor, 55, 56; miners' attitudes to, 26, 75-6, 77, 190, 239; photograph, 4; speeches, 15, 23-4, 30, 125, 192
Selby, 38, 61, 190, 238
Sheffield, 19, 22, 24, 88, 187, 242
Shirebrook, 216
Shire Oaks, 245-6
Shotton, 24
Silverdale, 86, 87
Silverwood, 68, 237
Skinner, Dennis, 157
Slack, Bert, 3
Smith, Herbert, 19
Smith, Tim, 85
Snowdown Colliery, 139
Staffordshire, North, 86-92
Stainforth, 92, 129, 131, 229
Stancliffe, Dorothy, 123, 124, 126
Stancliffe, Terrence, 123, 126
Standish, J., 130, 132
Stoke, 216, 218-21
Suddaby, J., 132

Taylor, Harry, 177
Taylor, Jack, 23, 71, 190
Team Valley, 45
Thatcher, Margaret: account of strike, 2-5; miners' attitude to, 20, 55, 76, 161, 201; values, 7, 37, 115
Thomas, Peter, 16
Thompson, Inky, 225, 228
Thompson, Sammy, 224
Thoresby, 101, 241, 245
Thorne, 129
Thornett, Alan, 2
Ti Mawr, 63-4
Tower Colliery, 15
Tremanheere, 1
Trentham Workshops, 88
Tudor-Hart, Julian, 37

Upton, 122-6

Vanstone, P., 130

Wakefield, N., 130
Wales, South, 14, 21, 40, 59, 64, 80, 163
Walker, Allison, 126
Walker, Elsie, 205
Walters, Barbara, 40, 42, 233
Walters, Roy, 15, 63
Wandsworth, 32, 139-53
Ward, Colin, 122, 123, 126
Ward, Lyn, 122, 123, 124, 126
Warsop Main Colliery, 82
Webster, Glan 'Corker', 160
Webster, Megan, 155, 160
Welbeck, 25
Whelan, Albert, 21
Wilkinson, Arthur, 128, 130
Williams, Barbara, 159
Williams, Doris, 161
Williams, Gwen, 157
Willis, Norman, 113
Wilson, Harold, 85
Windhill, 171
Wirte, Phillip, 233
Wolstanton, 86, 87
Womersley family, 124
Wood, Sue and Carol, 130
Woolley, 171

Yarmouth, 84
Yeardley, L., 130
Yorkshire, 20-4, 188-90, 224-5, 236-7

Yorkshire, North, 190
Yorkshire, South, 14, 22, 25, 171

# SUBJECT INDEX

'adopting', 33, 131, 199
arrests, 129, 130, 179
army, 1, 2, 3

babies, *see* children
badges, 25, 31, 123, 143, 144, 148
ballot: earlier, 13, 63, 98;
  Nottinghamshire, 72-3, 82, 86-7,
  189; strategic arguments, 15, 17, 20,
  61, 65-6
banks, 25, 167, 168, 194-6, 197, 241
bonus schemes, 52, 56, 60, 61, 63, 65,
  89, 246
British Leyland, 2, 13
British Steel Corporation, 44, 45
building societies, 25, 197, *see also*
  mortgages

cameras (NCB), 114-15, 121, 228-9
children: babies, 107, 122-4; clothes,
  107, 109, 178, 181, 186, 192, 214;
  food, 123; hardship, 178, 180, 181-3,
  201; holidays, 138, 167, 172; toys,
  133; treats, 30, 167, 185, 193, *see
  also* Christmas parties
Christmas: appeal, 18, 33, 132;
  donations, 11, 133, *see also*
  donations; parties, 12, 134, 136, 175,
  201; presents, 125, 133-6, 179, 193,
  194, 201; trees, 134
cigarettes, 129, 184, 201, 202
closures, *see* pit closures
clothes, 122, 136, 202
clothing depots
coal: imports, 58; industry, 35-9;
  market, 38, 44, 55, 83; picking, 21,
  120-1, 124, 140, 235; prices, 36;
  production, 236, 237; stocks, 7, 58,
60, 79, 93, 128, 188; *see also*
  geology, pit closures, stockpiling,
  technology (new)
coke, 44, 45, 55-6
collections: CND meeting, 110,
  door-to-door, 33-4, 208; dustmen's, 144
  factory, 190-1; GCHQ rally, 112-13;
  London, 174; neighbours, 192;
  shops, 187; street, 199; work-place,
  169-70, 190-1
Colliery Review Procedure, 94
Communist Party, 154, 158, 163-4
community: creation of, 123-4, 170,
  175-6, 191; restoration of, 9-10, 167,
  187, 194; *see also* banks, building
  societies, councils, food distribution,
  food kitchens, miners' welfare
  centres, pit lodges, publicans, pubs,
  schools, shopkeepers, social clubs
conferences, 65
Conservative Party, 3-5, 76, 85, 197
COSA, 89, 206, 226
councillors, parish, 108, 187
councils, 172, 177, 184
councils, parish, 132

debts: clearing up, 240, 241, 244; loan
  sharks, 183; recklessness, 29; relief,
  180; size of, 6-7; types of, 164-5,
  170, 186, 200; union help; *see also*
  banks, HP, mortgages
demonstrations, 76, 88, 139, *see also*
  marches
Department of Health and Social
  Security, 8, 27, *see also* Social
  Security
deputies, 7, 19, 156, 203, *see also*
  NACODS

dole, 61-2, 67, 99, *see also* Social Security

**domestic economy**, *see* cigarettes, clothes, coal picking, debts, drink, food supplies, fuel, health, hire purchase, mortgages, rent, savings, Social Security

donations, 114, 124, 125, 142, 146, 172

drink: beer brewing, 173; club prices, 191, 198; friends buy, 172; giving up, 6; Maerdy Hall, 156-7, 164; scrumpy, 202

electricity board: arranging payment, 169, 200; cutting off supply, 168, 184; size of bills, 214, 240; weekly payment, 167, 168, 192, 200

Employment Protection Act, 94

entertainment: buffet-disco, 136-8; concerts, 172; sport, 12, 131, 133

family: at Christmas, 136, 186, 194; help from children, 177, 178; help from grandparents and parents, 9, 25, 161, 175, 185, 192-3, 194, 196, 248; help from sisters, 136, 177, 185-6; Maerdy, 157

feminism, *see* women's movement

film crews, 118, 130, 133, 137

food distribution, 124, 143, 182, 208

food kitchens: description, 11; 'false pride', 7; fund-raising for, 139, 174; old men, 191; organisation, 129-36, 174-5, 177; shopkeepers' donations, 25, *see also* shopkeepers; starting, 21, 174; women's action groups, 28, 177; *see also* soup kitchens

food parcels: cost of, 132-3, 134, 136; distribution, 124, 130, 133, 135, 169, 191; fund-raising for, 105; single lads, 27, 185; women's action group, 109

food supplies: bread, 109; bulk-buying, 188; funds for, 130, 131, 184; meat, 109, 129, 130; stolen, 202; vegetables, 129-30, 202; *see also* shopkeepers

fuel: canisters, 107; coal, 119-20, 136, 172, 174, 176, 181; distribution, 27;

open cast coal, 183; wood, 11, 81, 136

fund raising, 124, 127, 178, 242

Gala, Wakefield Miners', 130

gas board, 240

geology, 45

government, 6, 12-13, 63, 128, 152

Greenham Common, 157, 158

health: injuries, 183, *see also* violence; miners' lungs, 40, 57, 59-60, 156, 185; strike diet, 182; supporters', 105

hire purchase, 182, 186, 200

ILP Leeds District, 131

kinship, 9, *see also* family

Labour Party: effect of strike on, 32-3, 125, 126, 188, 197; election, 233; helping at Hatfield, 137-8; Maerdy, 157, 158; miners' attitudes to, 76, 85, 126, 197; 'solidarity' with miners, 33, 198; 'twinning', 18; women, 122, 211-12

leadership, 16-20, 88

letters, 114, 124, 139-53, 199, 216-23

lock-outs, 13

magistrates, 1

managers, *see* pit managers

marches, 112-13, 125, 143, 146

**media**, 116, 142, *see also* film crews, newspapers, radio, television

Militant, 218

Miners' National Christmas Appeal, 18, *see also* Christmas

miners' support groups, 33, *see also* support groups

miners' welfare centres: Armthorpe, 168, 180, 182, 184-7, 192, 196-8, 201; Hatfield, 129-36; role, 10-11; South Elmsall, 122

Mines and Quarries Act, 227

Monopolies and Mergers Commission, 35

mortgages: clearing back-payments, 241; effect on strike, 13, 24-5; not

paying, 167, 168-9, 186, 192, 197;
paying, 173

NACODS, 7, 19, 119, 156, 227, 230
National Women Against Pit Closures,
243, 244, *see also* women
**NCB (National Coal Board)**: after the
strike, 182, 214; case, 35; coaches,
88; conciliator, 5; Cortonwood, 67-8;
fuel allowances, 9; headquarters, 88;
Horden Colliery, 43-51; joining pits,
64; NACODS, 230; negotiations, 7,
18; pit closures, 24, 36-9, 64-5; press
officers, 15; strategy, 13, 14, 21,
36-9; super-pits, 24; surveillance
equipment, 114-15, 121, 228-9;
turning clock back, 23; relationship
with NUM, 13, 14, 22, 152; *see also*
deputies, MacGregor, pit managers,
redundancy, sackings
newsletter, 90
newspapers: 34, 64; *Barnsley
Chronicle*, 206; *Daily Express*, 64,
152; *Daily Mail*, 64, 146; *Daily
Mirror*, 17, 64, 167; *Daily Telegraph*,
6; *Evening Standard*, 146; *Militant*,
212; *Newsline*, 212; *Sentinel*, 86;
*Socialist Worker*, 212; *Sun*, 3, 64,
142, 146; *Times*, 4; *Yorkshire Miner*,
139
**NUM (National Union of Mineworkers)**:
after the strike, 236-9; Armthorpe,
166, 176, 188-90, 197; bonus
schemes, 63; conduct of strike, 35-6;
constitution, 22; defeat, 6; funds, 18,
23, 128, 209; Grimethorpe, 120, 209,
212, 213-14; Hatfield, 92-9, 128;
lodges, 21, 27, 158; loyalty to, 7, 23,
25-6; Maerdy, 158, 164; NCB, 13,
14, 22, 152; negotiations, 19; North
Staffs, 86-92; Nottinghamshire,
72-87, 101, 232; panels, 51-4; pit
closures, 13; press officer, 15; return
to work, 116, 163, 224-30; Rhondda,
154; role, 5; Scargill, 16-17; strike
outbreak, 12; women's support
groups, 28, 212

Oxfam, 122
overmen, 7

overtime ban, 7, 54, 73, 89, 236

panels, 51-4
pay, *see* wages
pensioners, 7, 9, 30, 129, 172
pickets: after the strike, 237;
Armthorpe, 69-71, 166, 169, 172,
180-1, 189-90, 225-6; 'Arthur's
fliers', 8, 106; Bentinck, 72-3, 84;
Cortonwood, 69; in earlier disputes,
52, 53; end of, 35; flying, 8-9, 12, 84,
245; food for, 128-9, 180, 185;
Frickley, 141, 145, 147, 148;
Hatfield, 69-70, 128-9, 225-6, 236;
Hem Heath, 87, 88, 90; legislation,
58; Maerdy, 154; miners' welfare
centre, 10-11; North Staffs, 86-8, 90;
return to work, 148, 224-6; violence,
34, *see also* violence; women, 106-7,
*see also* women; young miners, 8-9
pit closures: Cortonwood, 67-8, 93-4;
economic arguments, 35-9; Horden,
45-6, 49; Houghton Main, 96; NCB
announcement, 13-15, 128; NUM
responsibility, 60-1; South Wales,
56-7; strike ballots, 63, 65, 98
pit delegates, 7-8, 51, 92, 213
pit deputies, *see* deputies
pit lodges, 21, 27
pit managers, 1, 13, 21, 59, 89, 176
pit villages, 37, 39, 173-4
*Plan for Coal*, 27, 35, 44
**police**: activists and, 185; attitudes to,
22, 160-1, 196, 201, 211;
Grimethorpe, 209-11; horses, 118;
Mansfield, 118-19; Mets, 143;
protect working miners, 128, 142;
riot squad, 120-1, 132-3, 179, 209-10,
219; role, 1-2; rumours, 182; shops
serving, 167, 174, 180, 196; specials,
1, 182; strategy, 16; surveillance
equipment, 114-15, 121, 228-9;
truncheons, 113; violence, 103-8,
118-21, 132-3, 209-10, 219; *see also*
arrests, pickets, road blocks,
violence
**political parties**, *see* Conservative, ILP,
Labour, Militant, SDP, SWP
prison, 151, 198, 216-23, 237
publicans, 29

public meetings, 187
pubs, 76
pumping stations, 45

radio, 146
raffles, 124, 178, 187
redundancy, 44, 94, 240, 245, 247
redundancy payments, 6, 8, 13, 56-7,
    64, 152
Redundancy Payments Act (1967), 8,
    94
rent, 184, 214
return to work: Bentinck, 80;
    Brookhouse, 115-17, 243; Frickley,
    148; Grimethorpe, 214-15; Hatfield,
    138, 224-30; Maerdy, 163-4;
    Yorkshire, 224-30, 236-7
Richmond and Twickenham
    Unemployed Worker and TU
    Centre, 125
Ridley Report, 199
riots, 118-21, 167, see also violence
road blocks, 12, 16, 102, 104
Ruskin College, Oxford, 7, 16, 67, 158

sackings, 138, 148-9, 151-2, 215, 237,
    240
savings, 6-7, 177, 180
'scabs': after the strike, 148-9, 238,
    239; children's view, 181; contempt
    for, 27; Cortonwood, 69; definition,
    152-3; Frickley, 142, 148-9; Hatfield,
    131; intimidation, 183; issue, 36;
    management treatment, 174; phone
    calls from, 185; suspected, 18, 199;
    verbal violence against, 8, 127
schools, 114, 175, 178, 181-3, 199, 215
SDP, 197
Sheffield Women Against Pit Closures
    (SWAPC), 242, 243, 244, 249
shopkeepers: bakers, 131, 167, 170,
    204; butchers, 109, 129, 130, 204,
    206; cash and carry, 130, 136, 137;
    cigarettes, 129, 201; clothes shop,
    186; Co-op, 204-6; donations, 25, 29;
    dress shop, 179-80; electrical, 204;
    Gateway, 137; newsagent, 129, 177,
    204; offer of shop, 122; Ollerton,
    102-3; serving police, 167, 174, 180,
    196; sweets, 204; television rental,

170; vegetables, 130, 204, 206;
    video, 168, 196, 203
social clubs, 156, 157
Social Security, 124, 128, 173, 180
solidarity, 15, 25, 27, 33, 116, see also
    community, family, trade union
soup kitchens, 129, 143, 170, 171, see
    also food
South Yorkshire Liaison Group, 243-4
stockpiling, 58, 60
strike: breaking, 5, 102, see also scabs;
    leadership, 16-20; outbreak, 12-15,
    20, 67, 69, 70, 128; pay, 6, 97, 119,
    180; see also ballot, pickets, return
    to work
strikes (earlier): (1875), 155; (1910), 1;
    (1926), 2, 6, 13, 19, 26, 27, 180, 234;
    (1943), 1; (1947), 1; (1972), 6, 15,
    27, 63, 128, 163, 172, 177, 192;
    (1974), 2, 84, 128, 163, 172, 192,
    197, 204; (1978), 190; (1981), 15
Supplementary Benefit, 124
support groups, 32-3, 122-6, 137, 145,
    244, see also 'adopting', collections,
    demonstrations, raffles, trades
    councils, trade union support,
    'twinning', women
support, international, 134, 136
Swan Hunter's, 13
SWP (Socialist Workers Party), 142,
    163, 211

technology (new), 21, 34, 165, 184, 203
television, 21, 34, 118, 165, 184, 203
Television History Workshop, 14, 20,
    55
theft, 174, 202
trades councils, 33, 144, 145
trade unions: ASLEF/NUR, 129,
    132-3, 136; ASTMS, 224; CPSA,
    115; GMBATU, 140; Liverpool
    Tobacco Union, 134; London
    Tobacco Workers' Union, 134;
    NGA, 130; NUJ, 224; NUPE, 131-2,
    134; see also COSA, NACODS,
    NUM, TUC
trade union support: Christmas
    presents, 134, 136; funds from, 129,
    131, 169-70; lack of, 33, 115, 151;
    late appeal, 15; support groups,

32-3; 'twinning', 18; visits, 130, 131, 132-3, 134-6
transport, 69, 90, 131, 172
TUC (Trade Union Congress), 15, 139
'twinning', 18, 21, 144

union, breakaway, 77, 78-9, 82, 84-5
Union of Democratic Mineworkers, 72, 78, *see also* union, breakaway

violence, 72-3, 76, 79-80, 103, 180-1, 200, *see also* police, riots

wages, 52-3, 61, 214, 241-2, 246, *see also* bonus schemes
Welfare Centres, *see* miners' welfare centres
wives: attitude to strike, 79, 81, 168, 173, 188; diet, 182; leaving home, 77, 79, 169, 170; marriage tensions, 77, 79, 82, 169, 170, 179, 198; new roles, 29, 81, 168, 188; working miners', 76; *see also* women's support groups
Women Against Pit Closures, 124, 126,

243, 244, *see also* Sheffield Women Against Pit Closures
women on picket line: Armthorpe, 185; Bevercotes, 71; change of attitude, 178, 192; childminding prevents, 175, 193; miners' attitude to, 106-7, 163, 168; shops, 207-8; *see also* wives
women's action groups, 108, 116, 166, 171, 187, 198
women's movement, 28, 157, 158, 162-3, 192
**women's support groups**: after the strike, 233, 242, 243, 244; Armthorpe, 166-7, 172, 174-5, 187; effect on women, 29, 175-6, 192; formation, 21; Frickley, 143, 151; Grimethorpe, 108, 206-9, 211-12, 215; Hatfield, 128-30, 226; independence, 22; Maerdy, 154-65; role, 27-8, 112; Rotherham, 243; *see also* Sheffield Women Against Pit Closures, wives, Women Against Pit Closures, women's movement
work: conditions of, 41, 53, 62, 91, 229-32; hours of, 53; *see also* health